History of the American Negro in the Great World War

by

W. Allison Sweeney

Printed on acid free ANSI archival quality paper.

978-1-78139-254-6
© 2012 Benediction Classics, Oxford.

History of the American Negro in the Great World War

His Splendid Record in the Battle Zones of Europe

Including a resume of his past services to his country in the wars of the revolution, of 1812, the war of the rebellion, the Indian wars on the frontier, the Spanish-American war, and the late imbroglio with Mexico.

By

W. Allison Sweeney

Contributing Editor of the Chicago Defender

1919

This History of The American Negro in the Great World War is reinforced by the official records of the War Department including tributes from French and American commanders.

W. Allison Sweeney

SPOKEN AND WRITTEN WORDS BY J.E. MORELAND INTERNATIONAL SECRETARY Y.M.C.A.

ROBERT SENGSTACKE ABBOTT EDITOR CHICAGO DEFENDER

RALPH TYLER EX-THIRD AUDITOR THE NAVY

JULIUS ROSENWALD PHILANTHROPIST

COLONEL CHARLES YOUNG UNITED STATES ARMY

WILLIS O. TYLER MEMBER LOS ANGELES BAR

CAPT. R.P. ROOTS VETERAN SPANISH-AMERICAN WAR

*****

WITH A COMPLETE SUMMARY OF THE ACTIVITIES OF THE 370th "OLD EIGHTH" IN THE WORLD WAR FROM THE COUNTRY'S CALL TO THE DAY OF ITS MUSTERING OUT

BY CAPT. JOHN H. PATTON, ADJUTANT

FOREWORD[1]

He was a red headed messenger boy and he handed me a letter in a NILE GREEN ENVELOPE, and this is what I read:

Dear Mr. Sweeney:

When on the 25th of March the last instalment of the MSS of the "History of the American Negro in the Great World War" was returned to us from your hands, bearing the stamp of your approval as to its historic accuracy; the wisdom and fairness of the reflections and recommendations of the corps of compilers placed at your service, giving you full authority to review the result of their labors, your obligation to the publishers ceased.

The transaction between us, a purely business one, had in every particular upon your part been complied with. From thenceforward, as far as you were obligated to the publishers, this History; what it is; what it stands for; how it will be rated by the reading masses—should be, and concretely, by your own people you so worthily represent and are today their most fearless and eloquent champion, is, as far as any obligation you may have been under to us, not required of you to say.

Nevertheless, regardless of past business relations now at an end, have you not an opinion directly of the finished work? A word to say; the growth of which you have marked from its first instalment to its last?

-The Publishers-

* * * * *

HAVE I—

A word to say? And of this fine book?

---

[1] The original formatting of the Foreword has been kept completely unchanged.

W. Allison Sweeney

The best history of the American negro in the great world war, that as yet has been written or will be for years to come?

*****

DOES—

The rose in bud respond to the wooing breath of the mornings of June?

IS—

The whistle of robin red breast clearer and more exultant, as its watchful gaze, bearing in its inscrutable depths the mystery of all the centuries; the Omniscience of DIVINITY, discovers a cherry tree bending to—

"The green grass"

from the weight of its blood red fruit?

*****

DOES—

The nightingale respond to its mate; caroling its amatory challenge from afar; across brake and dale and glen; beyond a

"Dim old forest" the earth bathed in the silver light of the harvest moon!

*****

EVEN SO—

And for the same reason which the wisest of us cannot explain, that the rose, the robin and nightingale respond to the lure that invites, the zephyrs that caress, I find myself moved to say not only a word—a few, but many, of praise and commendation of this book; the finished work, so graciously and so quickly submitted for my inspection by the publishers.

THERE ARE—

Books and books; histories and histories, treatise after treatise; covering every realm of speculative investigation; every field of fact and fancy; of inspiration and deed, past and present, that in this 20th century of haste and bustle, of miraculous mechanical equipment, are born daily and die as quickly. But there are also books, that like some men marked before their birth for a place amongst the "Seats of the MIGHTY"; an association with the IMMORTALS, that

"Were not born to die."

This book seems of that glorious company.

History of the American Negro in the Great World War

* * * * *

IN THE—

Spiritualized humanity that broadened the vision and inspired the pens of the devoted corps of writers, responding to my suggestions and oversight in its preparation; the getting together of data and facts, is reflected the incoming of a NEW AND BROADER CHARITY—a stranger in our midst—of glimpse and measurement of the Negro. Beyond the written word of the text, the reader is gripped with a certain FELT but unprinted power of suggestion, a sense of the nation's crime against him; the Negro, stretching back through the centuries; the shame and humiliation that is at last overtaking it, that has not been born of the "Print Shops" since the sainted LINCOLN went his way, leaving behind him a trail of glory, shining like the sun; in the path of which, freed through the mandate of his great soul, MARCHED FOUR MILLION NEGROES, now swollen to twelve, their story, the saddest epic of the ages, of whom and in behalf of whom their children; the generation now and those to come, this History was collated and arranged. It is an EVANGEL proclaiming to the world, their unsullied patriotism; their rapid fire loyalty, that through all the years of the nation's life, has never flickered—

```
"Has burned and burned
Forever the same",
```

from Lexington to the cactus groves of Mexico; in the slaughter hells of Europe; over fields and upon spots where, in the centuries gone, the legions of Caesar, of Hannibal and Attila, of Charlemagne and Napoleon had fought and bled, and perished! Striding "Breast forward" beneath the Stars and Stripes as this History crowds them on your gaze, through the dust of empires and kingdoms that; before the CHRIST walked the earth; before Christianity had its birth, wielded the sceptres of power when civilization was young, but which are now but vanishing traditions.

You are thrilled! History nor story affords no picture more inspiring.

MAKING DUE ALLOWANCE—

For its nearness to the living and dead, whose heroic and transcendant achievements on the battle spots of the great war secured for them a distinction and fame that will endure until—

"The records of valor decay",

it is a most notable publication, quite worthy to be draped in the robes that distinguishes History from narrative; from "a tale that is told"; a story for the entertainment of the moment.

W. Allison Sweeney

AS INTERPOLATED—

By the writers of its text; read between the lines of their written words; it is a History; not alone of the American Negro on the "tented field"; the bloody trenches of France and Belgium, it is also a History and an arraignment, a warning and a prophecy, looking backwards and forward, the Negro being the objective focus, of many things.

IT PRESENTS—

For the readers retrospection, as vividly as painted on a canvas, a phantasmagoric procession of past events, and of those to come in the travail of the Negro; commencing with the sailing of the first "Slaver's Ship" for the shores of the "New World", jammed fore and aft, from deck to hold, with its cargo of human beings, to the conclusion of the great war in which, individually and in units he wrote his name in imperishable characters, and high on the scroll on which are inscribed the story of those, who, in their lives wrought for RIGHT and, passing, died for MEN! For a flag; beneath and within its folds his welcome has been measured and parsimonious;—a country; the construing and application of its laws and remedies as applied to him, has inflicted intolerable INJUSTICE: Has persecuted more often than blessed. And so and thus, its perusal finished, its pages closed and laid aside, you are shaken and swayed in your feelings, even as a tree, bent and riven before the march and sweep of a mighty hurricane.

*****

LOOKING BACKWARDS—

The spell of the book strong upon you, you see in your mind's eye, thousands of plantations covering a fourth of a continent of a new and virgin land. The toilers "Black Folk"; men, women and children—SLAVES!

*****

YOU HEAR—

The crack of the "driver's" lash; the sullen bay of pursuing hounds.

*****

JUST OVER YONDER—

Is the "Auction Block". You hear the moans and screams of mothers torn from their offspring. You see them driven away, herded like cattle, chained like convicts, sold to "master's" in the "low lands", to toil—

"Midst the cotton and the cane."

YOU LISTEN—

Sounding far off, faint at first, growing louder each second, you hear the beat of drums; the bugle's blast, sounding to arms; You see great armies, moving hitherward and thitherward. Over one flies the Stars and Stripes, over the other the Stars and Bars; a nation in arms! Brother against brother!

* * * * *

YOU LOOK—

And lo, swinging past are many Black men; garbed in "Blue", keeping step to the music of the Union. You see them fall and die, at Fort Pillow, Fort Wagner, Petersburg, the Wilderness, Honey Hill—SLAUGHTERED! Above the din; the boom of cannon, the rattle of small arms, the groans of the wounded and dying, you hear the shout of one, as shattered and maimed he is being borne from the field; "BOYS, THE OLD FLAG NEVER TOUCHED THE GROUND!"

* * * * *

THE SCENE SHIFTS—

Fifty years have passed. You hear the clamor, the murmur and shouts of gathering mobs. You see Black men and women hanging by their necks to lamp posts, from the limbs of trees; in lonely spots—DEAD! You see smoke curling upwards from BURNING HOMES! There are piles of cinders and—DEAD MENS BONES!

* * * * *

NEARING ITS END—

The procession sweeps on. Staring you in the face; hailing from East, West, North and South are banners; held aloft by unseen hands, bearing on them—the quintessence of AMERICA'S INGRATITUDE,—these devices:

W. Allison Sweeney

"For American Negroes:

JIM CROW steam and trolley cars;

JIM CROW resident districts;

JIM CROW amen corners;

JIM CROW seats in theatres;

JIM CROW corners in cemeteries."

* * * * *

HEREIN—

Lies the strength and worth of this unusual book, well and deservingly named: A History of the American Negro in the Great World War. Beyond merely recounting that story; than which there has been nothing finer or more inspiring since the long away centuries when the chivalry of the Middle Ages, in nodding plume and lance in rest, battled for the Holy Sepulchre, it brings to the Negro of America a message of cheer and reassurance. A sign, couched in flaming characters for all men to see, appealing to the spiritualized divination of the age, proclaiming that God is NOT DEAD! That a NEW day is dawning; HAS dawned for the Negro in America. A NEW liberty; broader and BETTER. A NEW Justice, unshaded by the spectre of: "Previous condition!" That the unpaid toil of thirty decades of African slavery in America is at last to be liquidated. That the dead of our people, upon behalf of this land that it might have a BIRTH, and having it might not PERISH FROM THE EARTH, did not die in vain. That, in their passage from earth, heroes—MARTYRS—in a superlative sense they were seen and marked of the Father; were accorded a place of record in the pages of the great WHITE BOOK with golden seals, in the up worlds; above the stars and beyond the flaming suns.

IT IS A HISTORY—

That will be read with instruction and benefit by thousands of whites, but, and mark well this suggestion, it is one that should be OWNED AND READ BY EVERY NEGRO IN THE LAND.

* * * * *

TYPOGRAPHICALLY—

Mechanically; that is to say, in those features that reflect the finished artistic achievement of the Print, Picture and Binding art; as seen in the bold clear type of its text, its striking and beautiful illustrations, its illuminating title heads of division and chapter; indicating at a glance the information to follow; the whole appealing to the aesthetic; the sticklers for the rare and beautiful; not overlooking its superb binding, it is most pleasing to the sight, and worthy of the title it bears.

W. Allison Sweeney.

Contents

CHAPTER I   Spiritual Emancipation of Nations   15
CHAPTER II   Handwriting on the Wall   23
CHAPTER III   Militarism and Autocracy Doomed   37
CHAPTER IV   Awakening of America   45
CHAPTER V   Huns Sweeping Westward   61
CHAPTER VI   The Hour And The Man   67
CHAPTER VII   Negroes Respond to the Call   75
CHAPTER VIII   Recrudescence Of South's Intolerance   82
CHAPTER IX   Previous Wars In Which The Negro Figured   86
CHAPTER X   From Lexington To Carrizal   93
CHAPTER XI   Hour Of His Nation's Peril   103
CHAPTER XII   Negro Slackers And Pacifists Unknown   111
CHAPTER XIII   Roster Of Negro Officers   126
CHAPTER XIV   Across Dividing Seas   157
CHAPTER XV   Over There   174
CHAPTER XVI   Through Hell and Suffering   181
CHAPTER XVII   Narrative of an Officer.   191
CHAPTER XVIII   Blood of the Black and White in One Rivulet of Departing Life   208
CHAPTER XIX   Comrades on The March. Brothers in the Sleep of Death   215
CHAPTER XX   Mid Shot and Shell   231
CHAPTER XXI   The Long, Long Trail   238
CHAPTER XXII   Glory That Wont Come Off   250
CHAPTER XXIII   Nor Storied Urn, Nor Mounting Shaft   257
CHAPTER XXIV   Those Who Never Will Return   274
CHAPTER XXV   Quiet Heroes Of The Brawny Arm   280
CHAPTER XXVI   Unselfish Workers In The Vineyard   292
CHAPTER XXVII   Negro In Army Personnel   299
CHAPTER XXVIII   The Knockout Blow   302
CHAPTER XXIX   Homecoming Heroes   311
CHAPTER XXX   Reconstruction And The Negro   322
CHAPTER XXXI   The Other Fellow's Burden   327
CHAPTER XXXII   An Interpolation   334
CHAPTER XXXIII   The New Negro And The New America   344
The Peace Treaty   350

W. Allison Sweeney

CHAPTER I

Spiritual Emancipation of Nations

The March of Civilization—World Shocks to Stir the World Heart—False Doctrines of the Hun—The Iron Hand Concealed—The World Begins to Awaken—German Designs Revealed—Rumblings in Advance ofThe Storm—Tragedy That Hastened the Day—Tolstoy's Prophecy—Vindication of Negro Faith in Promises of the Lord—Dawn of Freedom for all Races

The march of civilization is attended by strange influences. Providence which directs the advancement of mankind, moves in such mysterious ways that none can sense its design or reason out its import. Frequently the forces of evil are turned to account in defeating their own objects. Great tragedies, cruel wars, cataclysms of woe, have acted as enlightening and refining agents. Out of the famines of the past came experiences which inculcated the thrift and fore-handedness of today.

Out of man's sufferings have come knowledge and fortitude. Out of pain and tribulation, the attribute of sympathy—the first spiritual manifestation instrumental in elevating the human above the beast. Things worth while are never obtained without payment of some kind.

Individual shocks stir the individual heart and conscience. Great world shocks are necessary to stir the world conscience and heart; to start those movements to right the wrongs in the world. So long as peace reigned commerce was uninterrupted, and the acquisition of wealth was not obstructed, men cared little for the intrigues and ambitions of royalty. If they sensed them at all, they lulled themselves into a feeling of security through the belief that progress had attained too far, civilization had secured too strong a hold, and democracy was too firmly rooted for any ordinary menace to be considered.

So insidious and far reaching had become the inculcation of false philosophies summed up in the general term Kultur, that the subjects of the autocratic-ridden empires believed they were being guided by benign influences. Many enlightened men; at least it seems they must have been enlightened, in Germany and Austria—men who possessed liberated intellects and were not in the pay of the Kulturists—professed to believe that despotism in the modern world could not be other than benevolent.

The satanic hand was concealed in the soft glove; the cloven hoof artistically fitted into the military boot; the tail carefully tucked inside the uniform or dress suit; fiendish eyes were taught to smile and gleam in sympathy and humor, or were masked behind the heavy lenses of professorial dignity; the serpent's hiss was trained to song, or drowned in crashing chords and given to the world as a sublime harmony.

Suddenly the world awoke! The wooing harmony had changed to a blast of war; the conductor's baton had become a bayonet; the soft wind instrument barked the rifle's tone; its notes were bullets that hissed and screamed; tinkling cymbals sounded the wild blare of carnage, and sweet-throated horns of silver and brass bellowed the cannon's deadly roar.

Civilization was so shocked that for long the exact sequence of events was not comprehended. It required time and reflection to clear away the brain benumbing vapors of the dream; to reach a realization that liberty actually was tottering on her throne. German propagandists had been so well organized, and so effectively did they spread their poison; especially in the western world that great men; national leaders were deceived, while men in general were slow to get the true perspective; much later than those at the seat of government.

A few far-seeing men had been alive to the German menace. Some English statesmen felt it in a vague way, while in France where the experience of 1870-71, had produced a wariness of all things German, a limited number of men with penetrating, broadened vision, had beheld the fair exterior of Kaiserism, even while they recognized in the background, the slimy abode of the serpent. For years they had sounded the warning until at last their feeble voices attracted attention.

France, with her traditions of Napoleon, Moreau, Ney, Berthier and others, with rare skill set about the work of perfecting an army under the tutelage and direction of Joffre and Foch. The defense maintained by its army in the earlier part of the struggle provided the breathing space required by the other allies. All through the struggle the staying power of the French provided example and created the necessary morale for the co-operating Allied forces, until our own gallant soldiers could be mustered and sent abroad for the knockout blow.

As is usual where conspiracies to perform dark deeds are hatched a clew or record is left behind. In spite of Germany's protestations of innocence, her loud cries that the war was forced upon her, there is ample evidence that for years she had been planning it; that she wanted it and only awaited the opportune time to launch it. It was a gradual unearthing and examination of this evidence that at length revealed to the world the astounding plot.

It is not necessary to touch more than briefly the evidence of Germany's designs, and the intrigues through which she sought world domination and the throttling of human liberty. The facts are now too well established to need further confirmation. The ruthless manner in which the Kaiser's forces prosecuted the war, abandoning all pretense of civilization and relapsing into the most utter barbarism, is enough to convince anyone of her definite and well prepared program, which she was determined to execute by every foul means under the sun.

She had skillfully been laying her lines and building her military machine for more than forty years. As the time approached for the blow she intended to strike, she found it difficult to conceal her purposes. Noises from the armed camp—bayings of the dogs of war—occasionally stirred the sleeping world; an awakening almost occurred over what is known as the Morocco incident.

On account of the weakness of the Moroccan government, intervention by foreign powers had been frequent. Because of the heavy investment of French capital and because the prevailing anarchy in Morocco threatened her interests in Algeria, France came to be regarded as having special interests in Morocco. In 1904 she gained the assent of Britain and the cooperation of Spain in her policy. Germany made no protest; in fact, the German Chancellor, von Bulow, declared that Germany was not specially concerned with Moroccan affairs. But in 1905 Germany demanded a reconsideration of the entire question.

France was forced against the will of her minister of foreign affairs, Delcasse, to attend a conference at Algeciras. That conference discussed placing Morocco under international control, but because France was the only power capable of dealing with the anarchy in the country, she was left in charge, subject to certain Spanish rights, and allowed to continue her work. The Germans again declared that they had no political interests in Morocco.

In 1909, Germany openly recognized the political interests of France in Morocco. In 1911 France was compelled by disorders in the country to penetrate farther into the interior. Germany under the pretext that her merchants were not getting fair treatment in Morocco, reopened the entire question and sent her gunboat Panther, to Agadir on the west coast of Africa, as if to establish a port there, although she had no interests in that part of the country. France protested vigorously and Britain supported her.

Matters came very close to war. But Germany was not yet ready to force the issue. Her action had been simply a pretext to find out the extent to which England and France were ready to make common cause. She recalled her gunboat and as a concession to obtain peace, was permitted to acquire some territory in the French Congo country. But German newspapers and German political utterances showed much bitterness. Growling and snarling grew apace in Germany, and to those who made a close study of the situation it became evident that Germany sooner or later intended to launch a war.

One of the characteristic German utterances of the time, came from Albrect Wirth, a German political writer of standing, in close touch with the thought and aims of his nation. The utterance about to be quoted may, in the light of later events, appear indiscreet, as Germany wished to avoid an appearance of responsibility for the world war; but the minds of the German people had to be prepared and this could not be accomplished without some of the writers and public men letting the cat out of the bag. Wirth said:

"Morocco is easily worth a big war, or several. At best—and even prudent Germany is getting to be convinced of this—war is only postponed and not abandoned. Is such a postponement to our advantage? They say we must wait for a better moment. Wait for the deepening of the Kiel canal, for our navy laws to take full effect. It is not exactly diplomatic to announce publicly to one's adversaries, 'To go to war now does not tempt us, but three years hence we shall let loose a world war'— No; if a war is really planned, not a word of it must be spoken; one's designs must be enveloped in profound mystery; then brusquely, all of a sudden, jump on the enemy like a robber in the darkness." The heavy footed German had difficulty in moving with the stealth of a robber, but the policy here recommended was followed.

In 1914, the three years indicated by Wirth had expired. There began to occur dark comings and goings; mysterious meetings and conferences on the continent of Europe. The German emperor, accompanied by the princes and leaders of the German states, began to cruise the border and northern seas of the Fatherland, where they would be safe from listening ears, prying eyes, newspapers, telephones and telegraphs. It became known that the Kaiser was cultivating the weak-minded Russian czar in an attempt to win his country from its alliance with England and France. There were no open rumblings of war, but the air was charged with electricity like that preceeding a storm.

An unaccountable business depression affected pretty much the entire world. Money, that most sensitive of all things, began to show nervousness and a tendency to go into hiding. The bulk of the world was still asleep to the real meaning of events, but it had begun to stir in its dreams, as if some prescience, some premonition had begun to reach it even in its slumbers.

Finally the first big event occurred—the tragedy that was not intended to accomplish as much, but which hastened the dawn of the day in which began the Spiritual Emancipation of the governments of earth. The Archduke Francis Ferdinand, nephew of the emperor of Austria, heir to the throne of Austria-Hungary and commander in chief of its army, and his wife the duchess of Hohenburg, were assassinated June 28, 1914, by a Serbian student, Gavrio Prinzip. The assassination occurred at Sarajevo in Bosnia, a dependency, or rather, a Slavic state that had been seized by Austria. It was the lightning flash that preceeded the thunder's mighty crash.

Much has been written of the causes which led to the tragedy. Prinzip may have been a fanatic, but he was undoubtedly aided in his act by a number of others. The natural inference immediately formed was that the murder was the outcome of years of ill feeling between Serbia and Austria-Hungary, due to the belief of the people in the smaller state, that their aspirations as a nation were hampered and blocked by the German element in the Austrian empire. The countries had been on the verge of war several years before over the seizure of Bosnia and Herzegovina by Austria, and later over the disposition of Scutari and certain Albanian territory conquered in the Balkan-Turkish struggle.

Events are coming to light which may place a new construction on the causes leading to the assassination at Sarajevo. It was undoubtedly the pretext sought by Germany for starting the great war. Whether it may not have been carefully planned to serve that object and the Serbian Prinzip, employed as a tool to bring it about, is not so certain.

Several years prior to the war, the celebrated Russian, Tolstoy, gave utterance to a remarkable prophecy. Tolstoy was a mystic, and it was not unusual for him to go into a semi-trance state in which he professed to peer far into the future and obtain visions of things beyond the ken of average men. The Russian czar was superstitious and it is said that the German emperor had a strong leaning towards the mystic and psychic. In fact, it has been stated that the Kaiser's claim to a partnership with The Almighty was the result of delusions formed in his consultations with mediums—the modern descendants of the soothsayers of olden times.

Tolstoy stated that both the Czar and the Kaiser desired to consult with him and test his powers of divination. The three had a memorable sitting. Some time afterwards the results were given to the world. Tolstoy predicted the great war, and he stated his belief that the torch which would start the conflagration would be lighted in the Balkans about 1913.

Tolstoy was not a friend of either Russian or German autocracy, hence his seance may have been but a clever ruse to discover what was in the minds of the two rulers. Germany probably was not ready to start the war in 1913, but there is abundant warrant for the belief that she was trimming the torch at that time, and, who knows, the deluded Prinzip may have been the torch.

The old dotard Francis Joseph who occupied the throne of Austria-Hungary, was completely under the domination of the Germans. He could be relied upon to further any designs which the Kaiser and the German war lords might have.

The younger man, Francis Ferdinand, was not so easy to handle as his aged uncle. Accounts agree that he was arrogant, ambitious and had a will of his own. He was unpopular in his country and probably unpopular with the Germans. Being of the disposition he was, it is very likely that the Kaiser found it difficult to bend him completely to his will. Being a stumbling block in the way of German aims, is it not reasonably probable that Germany desired to get rid of him, thus leaving Austria-Hungary completely in the power of its tool and puppet, Francis Joseph, and in the event of his death, in the power of the young and supplicant Karl; another instrument easily bent to the German will?

The wife of the archduke, assassinated with him, was a Bohemian, her maiden name being Sophie Chotek. She was not of noble blood as Bohemia had no nobles. They had been driven out of the country centuries before and their titles and estates conferred on indigent Spanish and Austrian adventurers. Not being of noble birth, she was but the morgantic wife of the Austrian heir. Titles were afterwards conferred upon her. She was made a countess and then a duchess. Some say she had been an actress; not unlikely, for actresses possessed an especial appeal to Austrian royalty. The cruel Hapsburgs rendered dull witted and inefficient by generations of inbreeding, were fascinated by the bright and handsome women of the stage. At any rate, Sophie Chotek belonged to that virile, practical race Bohemians, (also called Czechs) that gave to the world John Huss, who lighted the fires of religious and civil liberty in Central Europe, giving advent later to the work of Martin Luther.

Bohemians had always been liberty-loving. They had been anxious for three centuries to throw off the yoke of Austria. There is no record that Sophie Chotek sympathized with the aims of her countrymen or that she was not in complete accord with the views of her husband and the political interests of the empire. But the experiences of the Germans and Austrians had taught them that a Bohemian was likely to remain always a Bohemian and that his freedom-loving people would not countenance plans having in view the enslavement of other nations. The Germans may have looked with suspicion upon the Bohemian wife of the archduke and thought it advisable to remove her also.

Prinzip was thrown into prison and kept there until he died. No statement he may have made ever had a chance to reach the world. No one knows whether he was a German or a Serbian tool. He does not seem to have been an anarchist; neither does he seem to have been of the type that would commit such a crime voluntarily, knowing full well the consequences. It is not hard to believe that he was under pay and promised full protection.

Probably no Bohemian considers Sophie Chotek a martyr; indeed, the evidence is strong that she was not. Her heart and soul probably were with her royal spouse. But an interesting outcome is, that her assassination, a contributing cause to the war, finally led to the downfall of Germany, the wreck of Austria, the freedom of her native country, and that Spiritual Emancipation of nations and races, then so gloriously under way.

Also, to the thoughtful and philosophic observer of maturing symptoms transpiring continuously in the affairs of mankind; the fate of those nations of earth that in their strength and arrogance mock the Master, furnish a striking corroborative vindication of the Negro's faith in the promises of the Lord; the glory and power of His coming. From the date, reckoning from moment and second, that Gavrio Prinzip done to death the heir to the throne of Austria-Hungary and his duchess, there commenced not alone a new day, a new hope and Emancipation of the whites of earth; empire kingdom, principality and tribe, but of the blacks; the Negro as well, so mysteriously; bewilderingly, moves God His wonders to perform.

It was that subliminated faith in the ubiquity and omniscience of God; the unchangeableness of His word; than which the world has witnessed; known nothing finer; the story of the concurrent causes that projected the Negro into the World War, from whence he emerged covered with glory, followed by the plaudits of mankind, that became the inspiration of this work—his story of devotion, valor and patriotism; of unmurmuring sacrifice; worthy the pens of the mighty, but which the historian, as best he may will tell: "**NOTHING** extenuate, nor set down **AUGHT** in malice."

CHAPTER II

Handwriting on the Wall

Likened to Belshazzar—The Kaiser's Feasts—In his Heart Barbaric Pride of the Potentates of Old—German Madness for War—Insolent Demands—Forty-eight Hours to Prevent a World War—Comment of Statesmen and Leaders—The War Starts—Italy Breaks Her Alliance—Germanic Powers Weighed and Found Wanting—Spirit Wins Over Materialism—Civilization's Lamp Dimmed but not Darkened

Belshazzar of Babylon sat at a feast. Very much after the fashion of modern kings they were good at feasting in those olden days. The farthest limits of the kingdom had been searched for every delight and delicacy. Honeyed wines, flamingo's tongues, game from the hills, fruits from vine and tree, spices from grove and forest, vegetables from field and garden, fish from stream and sea; every resource of Mother Earth that could contribute to appetite or sensual pleasure was brought to the king's table. Singers, minstrels, dancers, magicians, entertainers of every description were summoned to the palace that they might contribute to the vanity of the monarch, and impress the onlooking nations about him.

He desired to be known and feared as the greatest monarch on earth; ruling as he did over the world's greatest city. His triumphs had been many. He had come to believe that his power proceeded directly from the god Bel, and that he was the chosen and anointed of that deity.

This was the period of his prime; of Babylon's greatest glory; his kingdom seemed so firmly established he had no thought it could be shaken. But misleading are the dreams of kings; his kingdom was suddenly menaced from without, by Cyrus of Persia, another great monarch. There were also dangers from within, but courtiers and flatterers kept this knowledge from him. Priests of rival gods had set themselves up within the empire; spies from without and conspirators within were secretly undermining the power of the intrenched despot.

Such was Belshazzar in his pride; such his kingdom and empire. And, so it was, this was to be an orgy that would set a record for all time to come.

Artists and artisans of the highest skill had been summoned to the work of beautifying the enormous palace; its gardens and grounds, innumerable slaves furnishing the labor. The gold and silver of the nation was gathered and beaten into ornaments and woven into beautiful designs to grace the occasion. There was a profusion of the most gorgeous plumage and richest fabrics, while over all were sprinkled in unheard of prodigality, the rarest gems and jewels. It was indeed to be a fitting celebration of the glory of Bel, and the power and magnificence of his earthly representative; heathen opulence, heathen pride and sensuality were to outdo themselves.

The revel started at a tremendous pace. No such wines and viands ever before had been served. No such music ever had been heard and no such dancers and entertainers ever before had appeared, but, fool that he was, he had reckoned without his host; had made a covenant with Death and Hell and had known it not, and the hour of atonement was upon him; the handwriting on the wall of the true and outraged God, conveyed the information; short and crisp, that he had been weighed; he and his kingdom in the balance and found wanting; the hour—his hour, had struck; the time of restitution and atonement long on the way, had come; Babylon was to fall—FELL!—and for twenty-five centuries its glory and its power has been a story that is told; its magnificence but heaps of sand in the desert where night birds shriek and wild beasts find their lair.

In the Kaiser's heart was the same barbaric pride, the same ambition, the same worship of a false god and the same belief that he was the especial agent of that deity.

His extravagances of vision and ambition were no less demoralizing to humanity and civilization, than those that brought decay and ruin to the potentates of old. He graced them with all the luxury and exuberance that modern civilization, without arousing rebellious complaint among his subjects, would permit. His gatherings appeared to be arranged for the bringing together of the bright minds of the empire, that there might be an exchange of thought and sentiment that would work to the good of his country and the happiness of the world. Frequently ministers, princes and statesmen from other countries were present, that they might become acquainted with the German idea—its kultur—working for the good of humanity.

Here was The Beast mentioned in Revelations, in a different guise; wearing the face of benevolence and clothed in the raiment of Heaven. There were feasts of which the German people knew nothing, and to which foreign ambassadors were not invited. At these feasts the wines were furnished by Belial. They were occasions for the glorification of the German god of war; of greed and conquest; ambition and vanity; without pity, sympathy or honor.

Ruthless, vain, arrogant minds met the same qualities in their leader. Some knew and welcomed the fact that the devil was their guest of honor; perhaps others did not know it. Deluded as they all were and blinded by pride and self-seeking, the same handwriting that told Belshazzar of disaster was on the wall, but they could not or would not see it. There was no Daniel to interpret for them.

German madness for war asserted itself in the ultimatum sent by Austria to Serbia after the assassination at Sarajevo. Sufficient time had hardly elapsed for an investigation of the crime and the fixing of the responsibility, before Austria made a most insolent demand upon Serbia.

The smaller nation avowed her innocence of any participation in the murder; offered to make amends, and if it were discovered that the conspiracy had been hatched on Serbian soil, to assist in bringing to justice any confederates in the crime the assassin may have had.

Negro soldiers on the rifle range at Camp Grant, Illinois. Being taught marksmanship. An ideal location resembling battle areas in France.

Medical Detachment 365th Infantry. A Representative Group of Medical Officers and Their Field Assistants. This Branch of the 92nd Division Rendered Most Valorous Service.

Bayonet exercises in the training camp.

Sports and physical exercise in the training camp.

Negro troops drilling. Scene at Camp Meade, MD., where a portion of the 93rd Division and other efficient units were trained.

An equine barber shop near the camp. One of the duties incident to the training camp.

Troopers of 10th cavalry going into Mexico. These heroic negro soldiers were ambushed near Carrizal and suffered a loss of half their number in one of the

bravest fights on record.

Tenth cavalry survivors of Carrizal. Despoiled of their uniforms by the Mexicans they arrive at El Paso in overalls. Lem Spillsbury, white scout in center. Each soldier has a bouquet of flowers.

America's war time president. This photograph of Woodrow Wilson was especially posed

during the war. In his study at the White House.

Dr. J.E. Moorland, senior secretary of colored men's dept., international Y.M.C.A. the man largely responsible for success of his race in "Y" work.

A typical group of "Y" workers, secretary Snyder and staff. Y.M.C.A. no.7, camp Grant,Illinois.

President Woodrow Wilson (at head of table) and his war cabinet. Left—W.G. Mcadoo Secretary of the Treasury; Thomas W. Gregory, Atty. Genl.; Josephus Daniels, Sec. of Navy; D.F. Houston, Sec. of Agriculture; William B. Wilson, Sec. of Labor. Right— Robert Lansing, Sec. of State; Newton D. Baker, Sec. of War; A.S. Burleson, Postmaster-General; Franklin K. Lane, Sec. of Interior; William C. Redfield, Sec. of Commerce.

With a war likely to involve the greater part of Europe hanging on the issue, it was a time for cool judgment, sober statesmanship and careful action on all sides. Months should have been devoted to an investigation.

But Germany and Austria did not want a sober investigation. They were afraid that while it was proceeding the pretext for war might vanish. As surmised above, they also may have feared that the responsibility for the act would be placed in quarters that would be embarrassing to them.

On July 23, 1914, just twenty-five days after the murder, Austria delivered her demands upon Serbia and placed a time limit of forty-eight hours for their acceptance. With the fate of a nation and the probable embroiling of all Europe hanging on the outcome, forty-eight hours was a time too brief for proper consideration. Serbia could hardly summon her statesmen in that time. Nevertheless the little country, realizing the awful peril that impended, and that she alone would not be the sufferer, bravely put aside all selfish considerations and practically all considerations of national pride and honor.

The records show that every demand which Austria made on Serbia was granted except one, which was only conditionally refused. Although this demand involved the very sovereignty of Serbia—her existence as a nation—the government offered to submit the matter to mediation or arbitration. But Austria, cats-pawing for Germany, did not want her demands accepted. The one clause was inserted purposely, because they knew it could not be accepted. With Serbia meeting the situation honestly and going over ninety percent of the way towards an amicable adjustment, the diplomacy that could not obtain peace out of such a situation, must have been imbecile or corrupt to the last degree.

An American historian discussing causes in the early stages of the war, said:

> *"The German Imperial Chancellor pays no high compliment to the intelligence of the American people when he asks them to believe that 'the war is a life-and-death struggle between Germany and the Muscovite races of Russia', and was due to the royal murders at Sarajevo.*
>
> *"To say that all Europe had to be plunged into the most devastating war of human history because an Austrian subject murdered the heir to the Austrian throne on Austrian soil in a conspiracy in which Serbians were implicated, is too absurd to be treated seriously. Great wars do not follow from such causes, although any pretext, however trivial, may be regarded as sufficient when war is deliberately sought.*

> "Nor is the Imperial Chancellor's declaration that 'the war is a life-and-death struggle between Germany and the Muscovite races of Russia' convincing in the slightest degree. So far as the Russian menace to Germany is concerned, the Staats-Zeitung is much nearer the truth when its editor, Mr. Ridder, boasts that 'no Russian army ever waged a successful war against a first-class power.'
>
> "The life-and-death struggle between Germany and the Muscovite races of Russia is a diplomatic fiction invented after German Autocracy, taking advantage of the Serbian incident, set forth to destroy France. It was through no fear of Russia that Germany violated her solemn treaty obligations by invading the neutrality of Belgium and Luxemburg. It was through no fear of Russia that Germany had massed most of her army near the frontiers of France, leaving only six army corps to hold Russia in check. Germany's policy as it stands revealed by her military operations was to crush France and then make terms with Russia. The policy has failed because of the unexpected resistance of the Belgians and the refusal of Great Britain to buy peace at the expense of her honor."

A nearer and equally clear view is expressed for the French by M. Clemenceau, who early in the war said:

> "For twenty-five years William II has made Europe live under the weight of a horrible nightmare. He has found sheer delight in keeping it in a state of perpetual anxiety over his boastful utterances of power and the sharpened sword.
>
> "Five threats of war have been launched against us since 1875. At the sixth he finds himself caught in the toils he had laid for us. He threatened the very springs of England's power, though she was more than pacific in her attitude toward him.
>
> "For many years, thanks to him, the Continent has had to join in a giddy race of armaments, drying up the sources of economic development and exposing our finances to a crisis which we shrank from discussing. We must have done with this crowned comedian, poet, musician, sailor, warrior, pastor; this commentator absorbed in reconciling Hammurabi with the Bible, giving his opinion on every problem of philosophy, speaking of everything, saying nothing." M. Clemenceau summed up the Kaiser as "another Nero; but Rome in flames is not sufficient for him—he demands the destruction of the universe."

The Socialist, Upton Sinclair, speaking at the time, blamed Russia as well as Germany and Austria. He also inclined to the view that the assassination at Sarajevo was instigated by Austria. He said:

"I assert that never before in human history has there been a war with less pretense of justification. It is the supreme crime of the ages; a blow at the very throat of civilization. The three nations which began it, Austria, Russia and Germany, are governed, the first by a doddering imbecile, the second by a weak-minded melancholic, and the third by an epileptic degenerate, drunk upon the vision of himself as the war lord of Europe. Behind each of These men is a little clique of blood-thirsty aristocrats. They fall into a quarrel among themselves. The pretext is that Serbia instigated the murder of the heir apparent to the Austrian throne. There is good reason far believing that as a matter of fact this murder was instigated by the war party in Austria, because the heir apparent had democratic and anti-military tendencies. First they murder him and then they use his death as a pretext for plunging the whole of civilization into a murderous strife."

Herman Ridder, editor of the Staats-Zeitung of New York contributed a German-American view. Mr. Ridder saw the handwriting on the wall and he very soundly deprecated war and pictured its horrors. But he could not forget that he was appealing to a large class that held the German viewpoint. He therefore found it necessary to soften his phrase with some hyphenated sophistry. He dared not say that Germany was the culprit and would be the principal sufferer. His article was:

"Sooner or later the nations engaged in war will find themselves spent and weary. There will be victory for some, defeat for others, and profit for none. There can hardly be any lasting laurels for any of the contending parties. To change the map of Europe is not worth the price of a single human life. Patriotism should never rise above humanity.

"The history of war is merely a succession of blunders. Each treaty of peace sows the seed of future strife.

"War offends our intelligence and outrages our sympathies. We can but stand aside and murmur 'The pity of it all. The pity of it all.'

"War breeds socialism. At night the opposing hosts rest on their arms, searching the heavens for the riddle of life and death, and wondering what their tomorrow will bring forth. Around a thousand camp fires the steady conviction is being driven home that this sacrifice of life might all be avoided. It seems difficult to realize that millions of men, skilled by years of constant application, have left the factory, the mill, or the desk to waste not only their time but their very lives and possibly the lives of those dependent on them to wage war, brother against brother.

"The more reasonable it appears that peace must quickly come, the more hopeless does it seem. I am convinced that an overwhelming majority of the

populations of Germany, England and France are opposed to this war. The Governments of these states do not want war.

"War deals in human life as recklessly as the gambler in money.

"Imagine the point of view of a commanding general who is confronted with the task of taking a fortress; 'That position will cost me five thousand lives; it will be cheap at the price, for it must be taken.'

"He discounts five thousand human lives as easily as the manufacturer marks off five thousand dollars for depreciation. And so five thousand homes are saddened that another flag may fly over a few feet of fortified masonry. What a grim joke for Europe to play upon humanity."

There were not wanting those to point out to Mr. Ridder that the sacrifice of life could have been avoided had Germany and its tool Austria, played fair with Serbia and the balance of Europe. Also, his statement that the government of Germany did not want the war has been successfully challenged from a hundred different sources.

H.G. Wells, the eminent English author, contributed a prophecy which translated very plainly the handwriting on the wall. He said:

"This war is not going to end in diplomacy; it is going to end diplomacy.

"It is quite a different sort of war from any that have gone before. At the end there will be no conference of Europe on the old lines, but a conference of the world. It will make a peace that will put an end to Krupp, and the spirit of Krupp and Kruppism and the private armament firms behind Krupp for evermore."

Austria formally declared war against Serbia, July 28, 1914. During the few days intervening between the dispatch of the ultimatum to Serbia and the formal declaration of war, Serbia and Russia, seeing the inevitable, had commenced to mobilize their armies. On the last day of July, Germany as Austria's ally, issued an ultimatum with a twelve hour limit demanding that Russia cease mobilization. They were fond of short term ultimatums. They did not permit more than enough time for the dispatch to be transmitted and received, much less considered, before the terms of it had expired. Russia demanded assurances from Austria that war was not forthcoming and it continued to mobilize. On August 1, Germany declared war. France then began to mobilize.

Germany invaded the duchy of Luxemburg and demanded free passage for its troops across Belgium to attack France at that country's most vulnerable point. King Albert of Belgium refused his consent on the ground that the neutrality of his country had been guaranteed by the powers of Europe, including Germany itself, and appealed for diplomatic help from Great Britain. That country, which had sought through its foreign secretary, Sir Edward Grey, to preserve the peace of Europe, was now aroused. August 4, it sent an ultimatum to Germany demanding that the neutrality of Belgium be respected. As the demand was not complied with, Britain formally declared war against Germany.

Italy at that time was joined with Germany and Austria in what was known as the Triple Alliance. But Italy recognized the fact that the war was one of aggression and held that it was not bound by its compact to assist its allies. The sympathies of its people were with the French and British. Afterwards Italy repudiated entirely its alliance and all obligations to Germany and Austria and entered the war on the side of the allies. Thus the country of Mazzini, of Garibaldi and Victor Emmanuel, ranged itself on the side of emancipation and human rights.

The refusal of Italy to enter a war of conquest was the first event to set the balance of the world seriously thinking of the meaning of the war. If Italy refused to join its old allies, it meant that Italy was too honorable to assist their purposes; Italy knew the character of its associates. When it finally repudiated them altogether and joined the war on the other side, it was a terrific indictment of the Germanic powers, for Italy had much more to gain in a material way from its old alliance. It simply showed the world that spirit was above materialism; that emancipation was in the air and that the lamp of civilization might be dimmed but could not be darkened by the forces of evil.

CHAPTER III

Militarism and Autocracy Doomed

Germany's Machine—Her Scientific Endeavor to Mold Soldiers—Influence on Thought and Lives of the People—Militarism in the Home—The Status of Woman—False Theories and False Gods—The System Ordained to Perish—War's Shocks—America Inclines to Neutrality—German and French Treatment of Neutrals Contrasted—Experiences of Americans Abroad and Enroute Home—Statue of Liberty Takes on New Beauty—Blood of Negro and White to Flow

Those who had followed the Kaiser's attitudes and their reflections preceeding the war in the German military party, were struck by a strange blending of martial glory and Christian compunction. No one prays more loudly than the hypocrite and none so smug as the devil when a saint he would be.

During long years the military machine had been under construction. Human ingenuity had been reduced to a remarkable state of organization and efficiency. One of the principal phases of Kultur was the inauguration of a sort of scientific discipline which made the German people not only soldiers in the field, but soldiers in the workshop, in the laboratory and at the desk. The system extended to the schools and universities and permeated the thought of the nation. It particularly was reflected in the home; the domestic arrangements and customs of the people. The German husband was the commander-in-chief of his household. It was not that benevolent lordship which the man of the house assumes toward his wife and family in other nations. The stern note of command was always evident; that attitude of "attention!" "eyes front!" and unquestioning obedience.

German women always were subordinate to their husbands and the male members of their families. It was not because the man made the living and supported the woman. Frequently the German woman contributed as much towards the support of the family as the males; it was because the German male by the system which had been inculcated into him, regarded himself as a superior being and his women as inferiors, made for drudgery, for child-bearing, and for contributors to his comforts and pleasures. His attitude was pretty much like that of the American Indian towards his squaw.

Germany was the only nation on earth pretending to civilization in which women took the place of beasts of burden. They not only worked in the fields, but frequently pulled the plow and other implements of agriculture. It was not an uncommon sight in Germany to see a woman and a large dog harnessed together drawing a milk cart. When it became necessary to deliver the milk the woman slipped her part of the harness, served the customer, resumed her harness and went on to the next stop. In Belgium, in Holland and in France, women delivered the milk also, but the cart always was drawn by one or two large dogs or other animals and the woman was the driver. In Austria it was a strange sight to foreigners, but occasioned no remark among the people, to see women drawing carts and wagons in which were seated their lords and masters. Not infrequently the boss wielded a whip.

The pride of the German nation was in its efficient workmen. Friends of the country and its system have pointed to the fact of universal labor as its great virtue; because to work is good. Really, they were compelled to work. Long hours and the last degree of efficiency were necessary in order to meet the requirements of life and the tremendous burdens of taxation caused by the army, the navy, the fortifications and the military machine in general; to say nothing of the expense of maintaining the autocratic pomp of the Kaiser, his sons and satellites. Every member of the German family had his or her task, even to the little three-year-old toddler whose business it was to look after the brooms, dust rags and other household utensils. There was nothing of cheerfulness or even of the dignity of labor about this. It was hard, unceasing, grinding toil which crushed the spirits of the people. It was part of the system to cause them to welcome war as a diversion.

To the German mind everything had an aspect of seriousness. The people took their pleasures seriously. On their holidays, mostly occasions on which they celebrated an event in history or the birthday of a monarch or military hero, or during the hours which they could devote to relaxation, they gathered with serious, stolid faces in beer gardens. If they danced it was mostly a cumbersome performance. Generally they preferred to sit and blink behind great foaming tankards and listen to intel-intellectual music. No other nation had such music. It was so intellectual in itself that it relieved the listeners of the necessity of thinking. There was not much of melody in it; little of the dance movement and very little of the lighter and gayer manifestations of life. It has been described as a sort of harmonious discord, typifying mysterious, tragic and awe-inspiring things. The people sat and ate their heavy food and drank their beer, their ears engaged with the strains of the orchestra, their eyes by the movements of the conductor, while their tired brains rested and digestion proceeded.

To the average German family a picnic or a day's outing was a serious affair. The labor of preparation was considerable and then they covered as much of the distance as possible by walking in order to save carfare. In the parade was the tired, careworn wife usually carrying one, sometimes two infants in her arms. The other children lugged the lunch baskets, hammocks, umbrellas and other paraphernalia. At the head of the procession majestically marched the lord of the outfit, smoking his cigar or pipe; a suggestion of the goose-step in his stride, carrying nothing, except his dignity and military deportment. With this kind of start the reader can imagine the good time they all had.

MILITARISM AND AUTOCRACY DOOMED Joy to the German mind in mass was an unknown quantity. The literature on which they fed was heavier and more somber than their music. When the average German tried to be gay and playful he reminded one of an elephant trying to caper. Their humor in the main, manifested itself in coarse and vulgar jests.

For athletics they had their turn vereins in which men went through hard, laborious exercises which made them muscle-bound. Their favorite sports were hunting and fencing—the desire to kill or wound. They rowed some but they knew nothing of baseball, boxing, tennis, golf or the usual sports so popular with young men in England, France and America. Aside from fencing, they had not a sport calculated to produce agility or nimbleness of foot and brain.

Their emotions expanded and their sentiments thrilled at the spectacle of war. Uniforms, helmets and gold lace delighted their eyes. The parade, the guard mount, the review were the finest things they knew. To a people trained in such a school and purposely given great burdens that they might attain fortitude, war was second nature. They welcomed it as a sort of pastime.

In the system on which Kultur was based, it was necessary to strike deeply the religious note; no difference if it was a false note. The German ear was so accustomed to discord it could not recognize the true from the false. The Kaiser was heralded to his people as a deeply religious man. In his public utterances he never failed to call upon God to grant him aid and bless his works.

One of the old traditions of the Fatherland was that the king, being specially appointed by God, could do no wrong. To the thinking portion of the nation this could have been nothing less than absurd fallacy, but where the majority do not think; if a thing is asserted strongly and often enough, they come to accept it. It becomes a belief. The people had become so impressed with the devoutness of the Kaiser and his assumption of Divine guidance, that the great majority of them believed the kaiser was always right; that he could do no wrong. When the great blow of war finally was struck the Kaiser asked his God to look down and bless the sword that he had drawn; a prayer altogether consistent coming from his lips, for the god he worshipped loved war, was a god of famine, rapine and blood. From the moment of that appeal, military autocracy and absolute monarchy were doomed. It took time, it took lives, it took more treasure than a thousand men could count in a lifetime. But the assault had been against civilization, on the very foundation of all that humanity had gained through countless centuries. The forces of light were too strong for it; would not permit it to triumph.

The President of the United States, from the bedside of his dying wife, appealed to the nations for some means of reaching peace for Europe. The last thoughts of his dying helpmate, were of the great responsibility resting upon her husband incident to the awful crisis in the lives of the nations of earth, that was becoming more pronounced with each second of time.

The Pope was stricken to death by the great calamity to civilization. A few minutes before the end came he said that the Almighty in His infinite mercy was removing him from the world to spare him the anguish of the awful war.

The first inclination of America was to be neutral. She was far removed from the scenes of strife and knew little of the hidden springs and causes of the war. Excepting in the case of a few of her public men; her editors, professors and scholars, European politics were as a sealed book.

The president of the United States declared for neutrality; that individual and nation should avoid the inflaming touch of the war passion. We kept that attitude as long as was consistent with national patience and the larger claims of **HUMANITY** and universal **JUSTICE.**

As an evidence of our lack of knowledge of the impending conflict, a party of Christian men were on the sea with the humanitarian object in view of attending a world's peace conference in Constance, Germany—Germany of all places, then engaged in trying to burn up the world. Arriving in Paris, the party received its first news that a great European war was about to begin. Steamship offices were being stormed by crowds of frantic American tourists. Martial law was declared. The streets were alive with soldiers and weeping women. Shops were closed, the clerks having been drafted into the army. The city hummed with militarism.

Underneath the excitement was the stern, stoic attitude of the French in preparing to meet their old enemy, combined with their calmness in refraining from outbreaks against German residents of Paris. One of the party alluding to the incongruous position in which the peace delegates found themselves, said:

> *"It might be interesting to observe the unique and almost humorous situation into which these peace delegates were thrown. Starting out a week before with the largest hope and most enthusiastic anticipation of effecting a closer tie between nations, and swinging the churches of Christendom into a clearer alignment against international martial attitudes, we were instantly 'disarmed,' bound, and cast into chains of utter helplessness, not even feeling free to express the feeblest sentiment against the high rising tide of military activity. We were lost on a tempestuous sea; the dove of peace had been beaten, broken winged to shore, and the olive branch lost in its general fury."*

Describing conditions in Paris on August 12, he says:

> *"We are in a state of tense expectation, so acute that it dulls the senses; Paris is relapsing into the condition of an audience assisting at a thrilling drama with intolerably long entr'acts, during which it tries to think of its own personal affairs.*
>
> *"We know that pages of history are being rapidly engraved in steel, written in blood, illuminated in the margin with glory on a background of heroism and suffering, not more than a few score miles away.*
>
> *"The shrieking camelots (peddlers) gallop through the streets waving their news sheets, but it is almost always news of twenty-four hours ago. The*

iron hand of the censor reduces the press to a monotonous repetition of the same formula. Only headlines give scope for originality. Of local news there is none. There is nothing doing in Paris but steady preparation for meeting contingencies by organizing ambulances and relief for the poor."

From the thousands of tales brought back by American tourists caught in Germany at the outbreak of the war, there is more than enough evidence that they were not treated with that courtesy manifested towards them by the French. They were arrested as spies, subjected to all sorts of embarrassments and indignities; their persons searched, their baggage and letters examined, and frequently were detained for long periods without any explanation being offered. When finally taken to the frontier, they were not merely put across—frequently they were in a sense thrown across.

Nor were the subjects of other nations, particularly those with which Germany was at war, treated with that fine restraint which characterized the French. Here is an account by a traveller of the treatment of Russian subjects:

"We left Berlin on the day Germany declared war against Russia. Within seventy-five miles of the frontier, 1,000 Russians in the train by which they were travelling were turned out of the carriage and compelled to spend eighteen hours without food in an open field surrounded by soldiers with fixed bayonets.

"Then they were placed in dirty cattle wagons, about sixty men, women and children to a wagon, and for twenty-eight hours were carried about Prussia without food, drink or privacy. In Stettin they were lodged in pig pens, and next morning were sent off by steamer to Rugen, whence they made their way to Denmark and Sweden without money or luggage. Sweden provided them with food and free passage to the Russian frontier. Five of our fellow-passengers went mad."

The steamship Philadelphia—note the name, signifying brotherly love, so completely lost sight of in the conflict—was the first passenger liner to reach America after the beginning of the European war. A more remarkable crowd never arrived in New York City by steamship or train. There were men of millions and persons of modest means who had slept side by side on the journey over; voyagers with balances of tens of thousands of dollars in banks and not a cent in their pocketbooks; men able and eager to pay any price for the best accommodations to be had, yet satisfied and happy sharing bunks in the steerage.

There were women who had lost all baggage and had come alone, their friends and relatives being unable to get accommodations on the vessel. There were children who had come on board with their mothers, with neither money nor reservations, who were happy because they had received the very best treatment from all the steamship's officers and crew and because they had enjoyed the most comfortable quarters to be had, surrendered by men who were content to sleep in most humble surroundings, or, if necessary, as happened in a few cases, to sleep on the decks when the weather permitted.

Wealthy, but without funds, many of the passengers gave jewelry to the stewards and other employees of the steamship as the tips which they assumed were expected even in times of stress. The crew took them apologetically, some said they were content to take only the thanks of the passengers. One woman of wealth and social position, without money, and having lost her check book with her baggage, as had many others of the passengers, gave a pair of valuable bracelets to her steward with the request that he give them to his wife. She gave a hat—the only one she managed to take with her on her flight from Switzerland—to her stewardess.

The statue of Liberty never looked so beautiful to a party of Americans before. The strains of the Star Spangled Banner, as they echoed over the waters of the bay, were never sweeter nor more inspiring. As the Philadelphia approached quarrantine, the notes of the American anthem swelled until, as she slowed down to await the coming of the physicians and customs officials, it rose to a great crescendo which fell upon the ears of all within many hundred yards and brought an answering chorus from the throngs who waited to extend their hands to relatives and friends.

There was prophecy in the minds of men and women aboard that ship. Some of them had been brought into actual contact with the war; others very near it. In the minds of all was the vision that liberty, enlightenment and all the fruits of progress were threatened; that if they were to be saved, somehow, this land typified the spirit of succor; somehow the aid was to proceed from here.

Liberty never had a more cherished meaning to men of this Republic. In the minds of many the conviction had taken root, that if autocracy and absolute monarchy were to be overthrown; that "government of the people, by the people, for the people" should "not perish from the earth," it would eventually require from America that supreme sacrifice in devotion and blood that at periods in the growth and development of nations, is their last resort against the menace of external attack, and, regardless of the reflections of theorists and philosophers, the best and surest guarantee of their longevity; that the principles upon which they were builded were something more than mere words, hollow platitudes, meaning nothing, worthy of nothing, inspiring nothing. It was the dawning of a day; new and strange in its requirements of America whose isolation and policy, as bequeathed by the fathers, had kept it aloof from the bickerings and quarrels of the nations that composed the "Armed Camp" of Europe, during which, as subsequent events proved, the blood of the Caucasian and the Negro would upon many a hard fought pass; many a smoking trench in the battle zone of Europe, run together in one rivulet of departing life, for the guarantee of liberty throughout all the earth, and the establishment of justice at its uttermost bounds and ends.

CHAPTER IV

Awakening of America

President Clings to Neutrality—Monroe Doctrine andWashington's Warning—German Crimes andGerman Victories—Cardinal Mercier's Letter—Military Operations—First Submarine Activities—The Lusitania Outrage—Exchange of Notes—United States Aroused—Role of Passive Onlooker Becomes Irksome—First Modification of Principles of Washington andMonroe—Our Destiny Looms

August 4, 1914, President Wilson proclaimed the neutrality of the United States. A more consistent attempt to maintain that attitude was never made by a nation. In an appeal addressed to the American people on August 18th, the president implored the citizens to refrain from "taking sides." Part of his utterance on that occasion was:

> *"We must be impartial in thought as well as in action, must put a curb upon our sentiments as well as upon every transaction that might be construed as a preference of one party to the struggle before another.*
>
> *"My thought is of America. I am speaking, I feel sure, the earnest wish and purpose of every thoughtful American that this great country of ours, which is, of course, the first in our thoughts and in our hearts, should show herself in this time of peculiar trial a nation fit beyond others to exhibit the fine poise of undisturbed judgment, the dignity of self-control, the efficiency of dispassionate action; a nation that neither sits in judgment upon others, nor is disturbed in her own counsels, and which keeps herself fit and free to do what is honest and disinterested and truly serviceable for the peace of the world.*

American poise had been somewhat disturbed over the treatment of American tourists caught in Germany at the outbreak of the war. American sentiment was openly agitated by the invasion of Belgium and the insolent repudiation by Germany of her treaty obligations. The German chancellor had referred to the treaty with Belgium as "a scrap of paper." These things had created a suspicion in American minds, having to do with what seemed Germany's real and ulterior object, but in the main the people of this county accepted the president's appeal in the spirit in which it was intended and tried to live up to it, which attitude was kept to the very limit of human forbearance.

A few editors and public men, mostly opposed to the president politically, thought we were carrying the principle of neutrality too far; that the violation of Belgium was a crime against humanity in general and that if we did not at least protest against it, we would be guilty of national stultification if not downright cowardice. Against this view was invoked the time-honored principles of the Monroe Doctrine and its great corollary, Washington's advice against becoming entangled in European affairs. Our first president, in his farewell address, established a precept of national conduct that up to the time we were drawn into the European war, had become almost a principle of religion with us. He said:

> *"Against the insidious wiles of foreign influence (I conjure you to believe me, fellow citizens) the jealousy of a free people ought to constantly awake, since history and experience prove that foreign influence is one of the most baneful foes of republican government—Europe has a set of primary interests which to us have none or a very remote relation. Hence she must be engaged in frequent controversies, the causes of which are essentially foreign to our concern. Hence, therefore, it must be unwise in us to implicate ourselves by artificial ties in the ordinary vicissitudes of her politics or the ordinary combinations and collisions of her friendships or enmities."*

The Monroe Doctrine was a statement of principles made by President Monroe in his famous message of December 2, 1823. The occasion of the utterance was the threat by the so-called Holy Alliance to interfere forcibly in South America with a view to reseating Spain in control of her former colonies there. President Monroe, pointing to the fact that it was a principle of American policy not to intermeddle in European affairs, gave warning that any attempt by the monarchies of Europe "to extend their system to any portion of this hemisphere" would be considered by the United States "as dangerous to our peace and safety." This warning fell in line with British policy at the time and so proved efficacious.

Official Red Cross photographs negro soldiers and red cross workers in front of canteen, Hamlet, N.C.

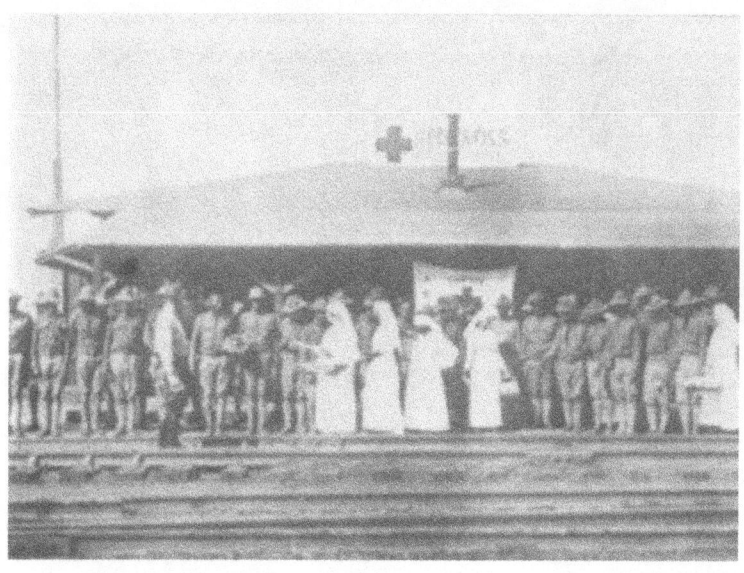

Photo from Underwood & Underwood, n.y. colored Red Cross workers from the canteen at Atlanta, GA., feeding soldiers at railway station.

Official Red Cross photographs colored women in hospital garments class of branch no. 6. New Orleans chapter, American Red Cross. Louise J. Ross, director.

Photo from Underwood & Underwood, N.Y. Red Cross workers. Prominent colored women of Atlanta, GA., who organized canteen for relief of negro soldiers going to and returning from war.

The game is on. A baseball match between negro and white troops in one of the training areas in France.

Official photographs, U.S. Army Col. William Hayward of 369th Infantry playing baseball with his negro soldiers at St. Nazaire, France.

Jazz and Southern melodies hasten cure. Negro sailor entertaining disabled navy men in hospital for convalescents.

Enjoying a bit of cake baked at the American Red Cross canteen at is-Sur-Tille, France.

Corporal Fred. Mcintyre of 369th Infantry, with picture of the Kaiser which he captured from a German officer.

Lieut. Robert l. Campbell, negro officer of the 368th Infantry who won fame and the D.S.C. in Argonne Forest. He devised a clever piece of strategy and displayed great heroism in the execution of it.

Emmett J. Scott, appointed by Secretary Baker, as special assistant during the World War. He was formerly confidential secretary to the late Booker T. Washington.

(Top)—General Diaz, Commander-in-Chief Italian armies. Marshal Foch, Commander-in-Chief Allied Forces.

(center)—General Pershing, Commander-in-Chief American armies. Admiral Sims, in charge of American naval operations overseas.

(bottom)—King Albert, Commander-in-Chief Belgian army. Field Marshal Haig, head of British armies.

In a later section of the same message the proposition was also advanced that the American continent was no longer subject to colonization. This clause of the doctrine was the work of Monroe's secretary of state, John Quincy Adams, and its occasion was furnished by the fear that Russia was planning to set up a colony at San Francisco, then the property of Spain, whose natural heir on the North American continent, Adams held, was the United States. It is this clause of the document that has furnished much of the basis for its subsequent development.

In 1902 Germany united with Great Britain and Italy to collect by force certain claims against Venezuela. President Roosevelt demanded and finally, after threatening to dispatch Admiral Dewey to the scene of action, obtained a statement that she would not permanently occupy Venezuelan territory. Of this statement one of the most experienced and trusted American editors, avowedly friendly to Germany, remarked at the time, that while he believed "it was and will remain true for some time to come, I cannot, in view of the spirit now evidently dominant in the mind of the emperor and among many who stand near him, express any belief that such assurances will remain trustworthy for any great length of time after Germany shall have developed a fleet larger than that of the United States." He accordingly cautioned the United States "to bear in mind probabilities and possibilities as to the future conduct of Germany, and therefore increase gradually our naval strength." Bismarck pronounced the Monroe Doctrine "an international impertinence," and this has been the German view all along.

Dr. Zorn, one of the most conservative of German authorities on international affairs, concluded an article in Die Woche of September 13, 1913, with these words: "Considered in all its phases, the Monroe Doctrine is in the end seen to be a question of might only and not of right."

The German government's efforts to check American influence in the Latin American states had of late years been frequent and direct. They comprised the encouragement of German emigration to certain regions, the sending of agents to maintain close contact, presentation of German flags in behalf of the Kaiser, the placing of the German Evangelical churches in certain South American countries under the Prussian State Church, annual grants for educational purposes from the imperial treasury at Berlin, and the like.

The "Lodge resolution," adopted by the senate in 1912, had in view the activities of certain German corporations in Latin America, as well as the episode that immediately occasioned it; nor can there be much doubt that it was the secret interference by Germany at Copenhagen that thwarted the sale of the Danish West Indies to the United States in 1903.

In view of a report that a Japanese corporation, closely connected with the Japanese government, was negotiating with the Mexican government for a territorial concession off Magdalena Bay, in lower California, the senate in 1912 adopted the following resolution, which was offered by Senator Lodge of Massachusetts:

> *"That when any harbor or other place in the American continent is so situated that the occupation thereof for naval or military purposes might threaten the communications or the safety of the United States, the government of the United States could not see without grave concern, the possession of such harbor or other place by any corporation or association which has such a relation to another government, not American, as to give that government practical power of control for naval or military purposes."*

All of the above documents, arguments and events were of the greatest importance in connection with the great European struggle. America was rapidly awakening, and the role of a passive onlooker became increasingly irksome. It was pointed out that Washington's message said we must not implicate ourselves in the "ordinary vicissitudes" of European politics. This case rapidly was assuming something decidedly beyond the "ordinary." As the carnage increased and outrages piled up, the finest sensibilities of mankind were shocked and we began to ask ourselves if we were not criminally negligent in our attitude; if it was not our duty to put forth a staying hand and use the extreme weight of our influence to stop the holocaust.

From August 4 to 26, Germany overran Belgium. Liege was occupied August 9; Brussels, August 20, and Namur, August 24. The stories of atrocities committed on the civil population of that country have since been well authenticated. At the time it was hard to believe them, so barbaric and utterly wanton were they. Civilized people could not understand how a nation which pretended to be not only civilized, but wished to impose its culture on the remainder of the world, could be so ruthless to a small adversary which had committed no crime and desired only to preserve its nationality, integrity and treaty rights.

Germany did not occupy Antwerp until October 9, owing to the stiff resistance of the Belgians and engagements with the French and British elsewhere. But German arms were uniformly victorious. August 21-23 occurred the battle of Mons-Charleroi, a serious defeat for the French and British, which resulted in a dogged retreat eventually to a line along the Seine, Marne and Meuse rivers.

The destruction of Louvain occurred August 26, and was one of the events which inflamed anti-German sentiment throughout the world. The beautiful cathedral, the historic cloth market, the library and other architectural monuments for which the city was famed, were put to the torch. The Belgian priesthood was in woe over these and other atrocities. Cardinal Mercier called upon the Christian world to note and protest against these crimes. In his pastoral letter of Christmas, 1914, he thus pictures Belgium's woe and her Christian fortitude:

> *"And there where lives were not taken, and there where the stones of buildings were not thrown down, what anguish unrevealed! Families hitherto living at ease, now in bitter want; all commerce at an end, all careers ruined; industry at a standstill; thousands upon thousands of workingmen without employment; working women; shop girls, humble servant girls without the means of earning their bread, and poor souls forlorn on the bed of sickness and fever crying: 'O Lord, how long, how long?'—God will save Belgium, my brethren; you can not doubt it. Nay, rather, He is saving her—Which of us would have the heart to cancel this page of our national history? Which of us does not exult in the brightness of the glory of this shattered nation? When in her throes she brings forth heroes, our mother country gives her own energy to the blood of those sons of hers. Let us acknowledge that we needed a lesson in patriotism—For down within us all is something deeper than personal interests, than personal kinships, than party feeling, and this is the need and the will to devote ourselves to that most general interest which Rome termed the public thing, Res publica. And this profound will within us is patriotism."*

Meanwhile there was a slight offset to the German successes. Russia had overrun Galicia and the Allies had conquered the Germany colony of Togoland in Africa. But on August 26 the Russians were severely defeated in the battle of Tannenburg in East Prussia. This was offset by a British naval victory in Helgoland Bight. (August 28.) So great had become the pressure of the German armies that on September 3 the French government removed from Paris to Bordeaux. The seriousness of the situation was made manifest when two days later Great Britain, France and Russia signed a treaty not to make peace separately. Then it became evident to the nations of the earth that the struggle was not only to be a long one, but in all probability the most gigantic in history.

The Germans reached the extreme point of their advance, culminating in the Battle of the Marne, September 6-10. Here the generalship of Joffre and the strategy of Foch overcame great odds. The Germans were driven back from the Marne to the River Aisne. The battle line then remained practically stationary for three years on a front of three hundred miles.

The Russians under General Rennenkampf were driven from East Prussia September 16. Three British armored cruisers were sunk by a submarine September 22. By September 27 General Botha had gained some successes for the Allies, and had under way an invasion of German Southwest Africa. By October 13 Belgium was so completely occupied by the Germans that the government withdrew entirely from the country and established itself at Le Havre in France. By the end of the year had occurred the Battle of Yser in Belgium (October 16-28); the first Battle of Ypres (decisive day October 31), in which the British, French and Belgians saved the French channel ports; De Wet's rebellion against the British in South Africa (October 28); German naval victory in the Pacific off the coast of Chile (November 1); fall of Tsingtau, German possession in China, to the Japanese (November 7); Austrian invasion of Serbia (Belgrade taken December 2, recaptured by the Serbians December 14); German commerce raider Emden caught and destroyed at Cocos Island (November 10); British naval victory off the Falkland Islands (December 8); South African rebellion collapsed (December 8); French government returned to Paris (December 9); German warships bombarded West Hartlepool, Scarborough and Whitby on the coast of England (December 16). On December 24 the Germans showed their Christian spirit in an inauguration of the birthday of Christ by the first air raid over England. The latter part of the year 1914 saw no important action by the United States excepting a proclamation by the president of the neutrality of the Panama canal zone.

The events of 1915 and succeeding years became of great importance to the United States and it is with a record of those having the greatest bearing on our country that this account principally will deal.

On January 20 Secretary of State Bryan found it necessary to explain and defend our policy of neutrality. January 28 the American merchantman William P. Frye was sunk by the German cruiser Prinz Eitel Friedrich. On February 10 the United States dispatched a note to the German government holding it to a "strict accountability if any merchant vessel of the United States is destroyed or any American citizens lose their lives." Germany replied February 16 stating that her "war zone" act was an act of self-defense against illegal methods employed by Great Britain in preventing commerce between Germany and neutral countries. Two days later the German official blockade of Great Britain commenced and the German submarines began their campaign of piracy and pillage.

The United States on February 20 sent an identic note to Germany and Great Britain suggesting an agreement between them respecting the conduct of naval warfare. The British steamship Falaba was sunk by a submarine March 28, with a loss of 111 lives, one of which was an American. April 8 the steamer Harpalyce, in the service of the American commission for the aid of Belgium, was torpedoed with a loss of 15 lives. On April 22 the German embassy in America sent out a warning against embarkation on vessels belonging to Great Britain. The American vessel Cushing was attacked by a German aeroplane April 28. On May 1 the American steamship Gullflight was sunk by a German submarine and two Americans were lost. That day the warning of the German embassy was published in the daily papers. The Lusitania sailed at 12:20 noon.

Five days later occurred the crime which almost brought America into the second year of the war. The Cunard line steamship Lusitania was sunk by a German submarine with a loss of 1,154 lives, of which 114 were Americans. After the policy of frightfulness put into effect by the Germans in Belgium and other invaded territories, the massacres of civilians, the violation of women and killing of children; burning, looting and pillage; the destruction of whole towns, acts for which no military necessity could be pleaded, civilization should have been prepared for the Lusitania crime. But it seems it was not. The burst of indignation throughout the United States was terrible. Here was where the terms German and Hun became synonomous, having in mind the methods and ravages of the barbaric scourge Attilla, king of the Huns, who in the fifth century sacked a considerable portion of Europe and introduced some refinements in cruelty which have never been excelled.

The Lusitania went down twenty-one minutes after the attack. The Berlin government pleaded in extenuation of the sinking that the ship was armed, and German agents in New York procured testimony which was subsequently proven in court to have been perjured, to bolster up the falsehood. In further justification, the German government adduced the fact that the ship was carrying ammunition which it said was "destined for the destruction of brave German soldiers." This contention our government rightly brushed aside as irrelevant.

The essence of the case was stated by our government in its note of June 9 as follows:

> *"Whatever be the other facts regarding the Lusitania, the principal fact is that a great steamer, primarily and chiefly a conveyance for passengers, and carrying more than a thousand souls who had no part or lot in the conduct of the war, was sunk without so much as a challenge or a warning, and that men, women and children were sent to their death in circumstances unparalleled in modern warfare."*

Three notes were written to Germany regarding the Lusitania sinking. The first dated May 13 advanced the idea that it was impossible to conduct submarine warfare conformably with international law. In the second dated June 9 occurs the statement that "the government of the United States is contending for something much greater than mere rights of property or privileges of commerce. It is contending for nothing less high and sacred than the rights of humanity." In the third note dated July 21, it is asserted that "the events of the past two months have clearly indicated that it is possible and practicable to conduct submarine operations within the so-called war zone in substantial accord with the accepted practices of regulated warfare." The temper of the American people and the president's notes had succeeded in securing a modification of the submarine campaign.

It required cool statesmanship to prevent a rushing into war over the Lusitania incident and events which had preceded it. There was a well developed movement in favor of it, but the people were not unanimous on the point. It would have lacked that cooperation necessary for effectiveness; besides our country was but poorly prepared for engaging in hostilities. It was our state of unpreparedness continuing for a long time afterwards, which contributed, no doubt, to German arrogance. They thought we would not fight.

But the United States had become thoroughly awakened and the authorities must have felt that if the conflict was to be unduly prolonged, we must eventually be drawn into it. This is reflected in the modified construction which the president and others began to place on the Monroe Doctrine. The great underlying idea of the doctrine remained vital, but in a message to congress delivered December 7, 1915, the president said:

"In the day in whose light we now stand there is no claim of guardianship, but a full and honorable association as of partners between ourselves and our neighbors in the interests of America." Speaking before the League to Enforce Peace at Washington, May 27, 1916, he said: "What affects mankind is inevitably our affair, as well as the affair of the nations of Europe and of Asia." In his address to the senate of January

22, 1917, he said: "I am proposing, as it were, that the nations should with one accord adopt the doctrine of President Monroe as the doctrine of the world—that no nation should seek to extend its policy over any other nation or people, but that every people should be left free to determine its own policy, its own way of development, unhindered, unthreatened, unafraid, the little along with the great and powerful." This was a modifying and enlarging of the doctrine, as well as a departure from Washington's warning against becoming entangled with the affairs of Europe.

CHAPTER V

Huns Sweeping Westward

Toward Shores of Atlantic—Spread Ruin and Devastation—Capitals of Civilization Alarmed—Activities of Spies—Apologies and Lies—German Arms Winning—Gain Time to Forge New Weapons—Few Victories for Allies—Roumania Crushed—Incident of U-53

The powerful thrusts of the German armies toward the English channel and the Atlantic ocean, the pitiless submarine policy, and the fact that Germany and Austria had allied with them Bulgaria and Turkey, began to spread alarm in the non-belligerent nations of the world.

That Germany was playing a Machiavellian policy against the United States soon became evident. After each submarine outrage would come an apology, frequently a promise of reparation and an agreement not to repeat the offense, with no intention, however, of keeping faith in any respect. As a mask for their duplicity, the Germans even sent a message of sympathy for the loss of American lives through the sinking of the Lusitania; which but intensified the state of mind in this country.

Less than three weeks after the Lusitania outrage the American steamship Nebraskan was attacked (May 25) by a submarine. The American steamship Leelanaw was sunk by submarines July 25. The White Star liner Arabic was sunk by a submarine August 19; sixteen victims, two American.

Our government received August 24 a note from the German ambassador regarding the sinking of the Arabic. It stated that the loss of American lives was contrary to the intention of the German government and was deeply regretted. On September 1 Ambassador von Bernstorff supplemented the note with a letter to Secretary Lansing giving assurance that German submarines would sink no more liners.

The Allan liner Hesperian was sunk September 4 by a German submarine; 26 lives lost, one American.

On October 5 the German government sent a communication regretting again and disavowing the sinking of the Arabic, and stating its willingness to pay indemnities.

Meanwhile depression existed among the Allies and alarm among nations outside the war over the German conquest of Russian Poland. They captured Lublin, July 31; Warsaw, August 4; Ivangorod, August 5; Kovno, August 17; Novogeorgievsk, August 19; Brest-Litovsk, August 25, and Vilna, September 18.

Activities of spies and plottings within the United States began to divide attention with the war in Europe and the submarine situation. Dr. Constantin Dumba, who was Austro-Hungarian ambassador to the United States, in a letter to the Austrian minister of foreign affairs, dated August 20, recommended "most warmly" to the favorable consideration of the foreign office "proposals with respect to the preparation of disturbances in the Bethlehem steel and munitions factory, as well as in the middle west."

He felt that "we could, if not entirely prevent the production of war material in Bethlehem and in the middle west, at any rate strongly disorganize it and hold it up for months."

The letter was intrusted to an American newspaper correspondent named Archibald, who was just setting out for Europe under the protection of an American passport. Archibald's vessel was held up at Falmouth, England, his papers seized and their contents cabled to the United States. On September 8 Secretary Lansing instructed our ambassador at Vienna to demand Dr. Dumba's recall and the demand was soon acceded to by his government.

On December 4 Captain Karl Boy-Ed, naval attache of the German embassy in Washington, was dismissed by our government for "improper activity in naval affairs." At the same time Captain Franz von Papen, military attache of the embassy, was dismissed for "improper activity in military matters." In an intercepted letter to a friend in Germany he referred to our people as "those idiotic Yankees."

As a fitting wind-up of the year and as showing what the German promise to protect liners amounted to, the British passenger steamer Persia was sunk in the Mediterranean by a submarine December 30, 1915.

The opening of 1916 found the president struggling with the grave perplexities of the submarine problem, exchanging notes with the German government, taking fresh hope after each disappointment and endeavoring by every means to avert the impending strife and find a basis for the preservation of an honorable peace.

It was now evident to most thinking people that the apparent concessions of the Germans were granted merely to provide them time to complete a larger program of submarine construction. This must have been evident to the president; but he appears to have possessed an optimism that rose above his convictions.

Our government, January 18, put forth a declaration of principles regarding submarine attacks and inquired whether the governments of the allies would subscribe to such an agreement. This was one of the president's "forlorn hope" movements to try and bring about an agreement among the belligerents which would bring the submarine campaign within the restrictions of international law. Could such an agreement have been effected, it would have been of vast relief to this country and might have kept us out of the war. The Allies were willing to subscribe to any reasonable agreement provided there was assurance that it would be maintained. They pointed out, however, the futility of treating on the basis of promises alone with a nation which not only had shown a contempt for its ordinary promises, but had repudiated its sacred obligations.

A ray of hope gleamed across our national horizon when Germany, on February 16, sent a note acknowledging her liability in the Lusitania affair. But the whole matter was soon complicated again by the "armed ship" issue. Germany had sent a note to the neutral powers that an armed merchant ship would be treated as a warship and would be sunk on sight. Secretary Lansing made the statement for this government that by international law commercial ships have a right to arm themselves for self-defense. It was an additional emphasis on the position that the submarine campaign as conducted by Germany was simply piracy and had no standing in international law. President Wilson, in a letter to Senator Stone February 24, said that American citizens had a right to travel on armed merchant ships, and he refused to advise them against exercising the right.

March 24 the French steamer Sussex, engaged in passenger traffic across the English channel, was torpedoed and sunk without warning. About eighty passengers, including American citizens, were killed or wounded.

Several notes passed between our government and Germany on the sinking of the Sussex and other vessels. Our ambassador at Berlin was instructed to take energetic action and to insist upon adequate attention to our demands. April 18 our government delivered what was considered an ultimatum to the effect that unless Germany abandoned her methods of submarine warfare, the United States would sever diplomatic relations. The president addressed congress on the matter the following day.

Germany had not yet completed her program of submarine building and thought it wise to temporize with the American government for a while longer. May 4 she replied to the ultimatum of April 18, acknowledged the sinking of the Sussex and in the main acceded to all the demands of the United States. There were certain phases which indicated that Germany wished to use this country as a medium for securing certain agreements from the Allies. The president accepted the German conditions generally, but made it clear in his reply that the conditions could not depend upon any negotiations between this country and other belligerents. The intimation was plain enough that the United States would not be a catspaw for German aims.

Up to this time in the year 1916 the advantage in arms had been greatly on the side of Germany and her allies. In January the British had evacuated the entire Gallipoli peninsula and the campaign in Turkey soon came to grief. Cettinje, the capital of Montenegro, had also fallen to the Teutonic allies, and that country practically was put out of the war.

The British had made important gains in the German colonies in Africa and had conquered most of the Kamerun section there. Between February and July the Germans had been battling at the important French position of Verdun, with great losses and small results. Practically all the ground lost was slowly regained by the French in the autumn. The Russians had entered Persia in February, and April 17 had captured the important city of Trebizond in Armenia from the Turks. But on April 29 General Townshend surrendered his entire British force to the Turks at Kut el Amara, after being besieged for 143 days and finally starved into submission.

Throughout the balance of the year the advantage was greatly on the side of the Germans, for the latter part of the year saw the beginning of the crushing of Roumania, which had entered the war August 27 on the side of the Allies. Bucharest, the capital, fell to the Germans December 6; Dobrudja, January 2, and Focsani, January 8 of the ensuing year, 1917. The crushing of Roumania was accomplished almost entirely by treachery. The Germans knew the plans of all the principal fortifications; the strength and plans of the Roumanian forces, and every detail calculated to be of benefit. The country had been honeycombed with their spies prior to and during the war, very much as Russia had been. It is quite evident that men high in the councils of the Roumanian government and in full possession of the military secrets of the country were simply disguised German agents.

Between July and November had occurred the great battles of the Somme during which the Allies had failed to break the German lines. The Austrians in June had launched a great attack and made much progress against the Italians in the Trentino. The principal offsets to the German gains during the last seven months of the year 1916 were the Russian offensive in Volhynia and Bukovina, and the counter drive of the Italians against the Austrians. The Russians captured Czernovitz June 17, and by the end of the month had overrun the whole of Bukovina. The Italians drove out the Austrians between August 6 and September 1, winning August 9 the important city and fortress of Gorizia.

Submarine incidents important to this government were not lacking during the latter half of the year. The German submarine U-53 suddenly appeared October 8 in the harbor at Newport, R.I. The commander delivered letters for the German ambassador and immediately put to sea to begin ravages on British shipping off the Nantucket coast. Among the five or six vessels sunk was the steamer Stephano, which carried American passengers. The passengers and crews of all the vessels were picked up by American destroyers and no lives were lost. The episode, which was an eight-day wonder, and resulted in a temporary tie-up of shipping in eastern ports, started numerous rumors and several legal questions, none of which, however, turned out finally to have been of much importance, as U-53 vanished as suddenly as it had appeared, and its visit was not succeeded by any like craft. It is not improbable that the purpose of the German government in sending the boat to our shores was to convey a hint of what we might expect if we should become involved with Germany. October 28 the British steamer Marina was torpedoed with a loss of six American lives.

The straining of President Washington's advice and the Monroe Doctrine were again evident throughout the year. President Wilson in an address before the League to Enforce Peace, May 27, had said that the United States was ready to join any practical league for preserving peace and guaranteeing the political and territorial integrity of nations. November 29 our government sent a protest to Germany against the deportation of Belgians.

Almost immediately upon the invasion of Belgium the German authorities, in pursuance of their system of terrorization, shipped to Germany considerable groups of the population. On October 12, 1915, a general order was issued by the German military government in Belgium providing that persons who should "refuse work suitable to their occupation and in the execution of which the military administration is interested," should be subject to one year's imprisonment or to deportation to Germany. Numerous sentences, both of men and women, were imposed under that order.

The wholesale deportation of Belgian workmen to Germany, which began October 3, 1916, proceeded on different grounds, for, having stripped large sections of the country of machinery and raw materials, the military authorities now came forward with the plea that it was necessary to send the labor after it. The number of workmen deported is variously estimated at between one and three hundred thousand.

"The rage, the terror, the despair" excited by this measure all over Belgium, our minister, Brand Whitlock, reported, "were beyond anything we had witnessed since the day the Germans poured into Brussels. I am constantly in receipt of reports from all over Belgium that bear out the stories of brutality and cruelty.

"In tearing away from nearly every humble home in the land a husband and a father or a son and brother, the Germans have lighted a fire of hatred that will never go out. It is one of those deeds that make one despair of the future of the human race, a deed coldly planned, studiously matured, and deliberately and systematically executed, a deed so cruel that German soldiers are said to have wept in its execution, and so monstrous that even German officers are now said to be ashamed." Poland and the occupied parts of France experienced similar treatment.

CHAPTER VI

The Hour and the Man

A Beacon Among the Years—Trying Period for President Wilson—Germany Continues Dilatory Tactics—Peace Efforts Fail—All Honorable Means Exhausted—Patience Ceases to be a Virtue—Enemy Abandons All Subterfuge—Unrestricted Submarine Warfare—German Intrigues With Mexico—The Zimmermann Note—America Seizes the Sword—War is Declared—Pershing Goes Abroad—First Troops Sail—War Measures—War Operations

An enormous beacon light in history will attach to the year 1917. The outstanding feature of course was the entry of the United States into the great war—the deciding factor in the struggle. It marked the departure of America from the traditional policy of political isolation from Europe. History will record that it was not a voluntary, but a forced, departure, due to the utter disregard by Germany of our rights on the seas, at home and elsewhere.

The first thirty days of the year found the man at the head of our government still hoping against hope, still struggling with all the odds against him, still courageously engaged in efforts for peace. It was a particularly trying time for President Wilson, as a large portion of his own party and most of the nation was arrayed against him. The people in general felt that the time for writing notes, for parleying had passed.

On December 12, 1916, Germany, in a formal note, had offered to enter into peace negotiations, but did not specify any terms. The note referred in boastful language to the victorious German armies. It was rejected by the Allies as empty and insincere. The president on December 18, 1916, had addressed all the beligerents asking them to indicate precisely the terms on which, they would make peace. Germany's reply to this note was no more satisfactory than before. The Allies replied demanding restorations, reparation and indemnities.

On the 22nd of January the president appeared before the senate in his famous "peace without victory" address, in which he advocated a world league for peace. His views were received sympathetically, though the Allies pointed out that no peace based on the condition of things before the war could be durable, and that as matters stood it would be a virtual victory for Germany. It was the president's last effort to bring peace to the world without resorting to armed force.

The most biased historian is bound to affirm that Woodrow Wilson exhausted every effort not only to keep the United States honorably at peace, but to bring about a pacific attitude and understanding among the belligerents. When finally he saw that no argument save that of the sword would avail, when finally the hour struck, he became the man of the hour courageously and nobly.

After President Wilson's failure to bring about even a pacific attitude among the warring nations, no peace appeal from any quarter calculated to receive respectful attention was made, excepting that issued by Pope Benedict August 15, four months after the United States had declared war. The President summarized the Pope's proposals as follows:

> *"His Holiness in substance proposes that we return to the status existing before the war, and that then there be a general condonation, disarmament, and a concert of nations based upon an acceptance of the principle of arbitration; that by a similar concert freedom of the seas be established; and that the territorial claims of France and Italy, the perplexing problems of the Balkan States and the restitution of Poland be left to such conciliatory adjustments as may be possible in the new temper of such a peace, due regard being paid to the aspirations of the peoples whose political fortunes and affiliations will be involved."*

The president's reply to the Pope forcibly stated the aim of the United States to free the world from the menace of Prussian militarism controlled by an arrogant and faithless autocracy. Distinguishing between the German rulers and the people, President Wilson asserted that the United States would willingly negotiate with a government subject to the popular will. The note disavowed any intention to dismember countries or to impose unfair economic conditions. In part the President's language was:

> *"Responsible statesmen must now everywhere see, if they never saw before, that no peace can rest securely upon political or economic restrictions meant to benefit some nations and cripple or embarrass others, upon vindictive action of any sort, or any kind of revenge or deliberate injury. The American people have suffered intolerable wrongs at the hands of the Imperial German Government, but they desire no reprisal upon the German people,*

who have themselves suffered all things in this war, which they did not choose. They believe that peace should rest upon the rights of peoples, not the rights of governments—the rights of peoples great or small, weak or powerful—their equal right to freedom and security and self government and to a participation upon fair terms in the economic opportunities of the world, the German people, of course, included, if they will accept equality and not seek domination."

About five weeks prior to the Pope's proposition, the Germans had again put forth a peace feeler. On July 19, the German reichstag adopted resolutions in favor of peace on the basis of mutual understanding and lasting reconciliation among the nations. The resolutions sounded well but they were accompanied by expressions to the effect that Germany in the war was the victim of aggression and that it approved the acts of its government. They referred to the "men who are defending the Fatherland," to the necessity of assuring the freedom of the seas, and to the impossibility of conquering a united German nation. There was no doubt in the mind of any neutral or any belligerent opposing Germany that the German government was the real aggressor and that the freedom of the seas had never been restricted except by Germany herself, hence there was no tendency to accept this as a serious bid for peace. The resolutions figured largely in German internal politics but were without effect elsewhere.

Stockholm, Sweden was the scene of a number of peace conferences but as they were engineered by socialists of an extreme type and others holding views usually classed as anarchistic, no serious attention was paid to them. The "pacifists" in the Allied and neutral countries were more or less active, but received little encouragement. Their arguments did not appeal to patriotism.

Going back to the beginning of the year, within a week after the President's "peace without victory" speech before the senate, Germany replied to it by announcing that beginning February 1, it would begin unrestricted submarine warfare in certain extensive zones around the British Isles, France and Italy. It would, however, out of the kindness of its heart, permit the United States to use a narrow track across the sea with a landing at Falmouth, one ship a week, provided the American ships were painted red and white and carried various kinds of distinguishing marks.

This of course was a direct repudiation by Germany of all the promises she had made to the United States. The President saw the sword being forced into his hands but he was not yet ready to seize it with all his might. He preferred first to exhaust the expediency of an armed neutrality. On February 3, he went before a joint session of the house and senate and announced that Ambassador von Bernstorff had been given his passports and all diplomatic relations with the Teuton empire severed. On February 12, an attempt at negotiation came through the Swiss minister who had been placed in charge of German diplomatic interests in this country. The President promptly and emphatically replied that no negotiations could be even considered until the submarine order had been withdrawn.

On February 26, the lower house of congress voted formal permission for the arming of American merchant ships as a protection against submarine attacks, and appropriated one hundred million dollars for the arming and insuring of the ships. A similar measure in the senate was defeated by Senator Robert M. LaFollette of Wisconsin, acting under a loose rule of the senate which permitted filibustering and unlimited debate. The session of congress expired March 4, and the President immediately called an extra session of the senate which amended its rules so that the measure was passed.

Senator LaFollette's opposition to the war and some of his public utterances outside the senate led to a demand for his expulsion from that body. A committee of investigation was appointed which proceeded perfunctorilly for about a year. The senator was never expelled but any influence he may have had and any power to hamper the activities of the government, were effectually killed for the duration of the war. The suppression of the senator did not proceed so much from congress or the White House, as from the press of the country. Without regard to views or party, the newspapers of the nation voluntarily and patriotically entered what has been termed a "conspiracy of silence" regarding the activities of the Wisconsin senator. By refusing to print his name or give him any sort of publicity he was effectively sidetracked and in a short time the majority of the people of the country forgot his existence. It was a striking demonstration that propaganda depends for its effectiveness upon publicity, and has given rise to an order of thought which contends that the newspapers should censor their own columns and suppress movements that are detrimental or of evil tendency, by ignoring them. Opposed to this is the view that the more publicity a movement gets, and the fuller and franker the discussion it evokes, the more quickly will its merits or demerits become apparent.

If any evidence was lacking of German duplicity, violation of promises and general double-dealing, it came to light in the famous document known as the "Zimmermann Note" which came into the hands of the American state department and was revealed February 28. It was a confidential communication from Dr. Alfred Zimmermann, German Foreign Minister, addressed to the German Minister in Mexico and proposed an alliance of Germany, Mexico and Japan against the United States. Its text follows:

> *"On the 1st of February we intend to begin submarine warfare unrestricted. In spite of this it is our intention to endeavor to keep neutral the United States of America. If this attempt is not successful, we propose an alliance on the following basis with Mexico: That we shall make war together and together make peace. We shall give general financial support, and it is understood that Mexico is to reconquer the lost territory in New Mexico, Texas and Arizona. The details are left to you for settlement. You are instructed to inform the president of Mexico of the above in the greatest confidence as soon as it is certain there will be an outbreak of war with the United States, and suggest that the president of Mexico on his own initiative, should communicate with Japan suggesting adherence at once to this plan; at the same time offer to mediate between Germany and Japan. Please call to the attention of the President of Mexico that the employment of ruthless submarine warfare now promises to compel England to make peace in a few months."*

The American steamers City of Memphis, Vigilancia and Illinois had been sunk and fifteen lives lost in pursuance of the German submarine policy to torpedo without warning and without any regard to the safety of crews or passengers, all ships found within the barred zones. The President could no longer postpone drawing the sword. Being convinced that the inevitable hour had struck, he proved himself the man of the hour and acted with energy. A special session of congress was called for April 2. The day is bound to stand out in history for in the afternoon the President delivered his famous message asking that war be declared against Germany. He said that armed neutrality had been found wanting and in the end would only draw the country into war without its having the status of a belligerent. One of the striking paragraphs of the message follows:

> *"With a profound sense of the solemn and even tragical character of the step I am taking, and of the grave responsibility which it involves, but in unhesitating obedience to what I deem my constitutional duty, I advise that the congress declare the recent course of the imperial German government to be in fact nothing less than war against the government and people of the United States; that it formally accept the status of belligerent which has*

thus been thrust upon it and that it take immediate steps not only to put the country in a more thorough state of defence, but also to exert all its power and employ all its resources to bring the government of the German empire to terms and end the war."

Congress voted a declaration of war April 6. Only six senators out of a total of 96, and fifty representatives out of a total of 435, voted against it. Congress also, at the request of the President, voted for the creation of a national army and the raising to war strength of the National Guard, the Marine corps and the Navy. Laws were passed dealing with espionage, trading with the enemy and the unlawful manufacture and use of explosives. Provision was made for the *insurance of soldiers and sailors*, for priority of shipments, for the seizure and use of enemy ships in American harbors, for conserving and controlling the food and fuel supply of the country, for stimulating agriculture, for enlarging the aviation branch of the service, for extending credit to foreign governments, for issuing bonds and for providing additional revenues by increasing old and creating new taxes.

The extra session of congress lasted a few days over six months. In that time it passed all the above measures and others of less importance. It authorized the expenditure of over nineteen billions of dollars ($19,321,225,208). Including the amount appropriated at the second session of the preceeding congress, the amount reached the unheard of total of over twenty-one billions of dollars ($21,390,730,940).

German intrigues and German ruthlessness created an additional stench in the nostrils of civilization when on September 8, the United States made public the celebrated "Spurlos Versenkt" telegram which had come into its possession. It is a German phrase meaning "sunk without leaving a trace" and was contained in a telegram from Luxburg, the German minister at Buenos Aires. The telegram (of May 19, 1917) advised that Argentine steamers "be spared if possible or else sunk without a trace being left." The advice was repeated July 9. The Swedish minister at Buenos Aires sent these messages in code as though they were his own private dispatches.

On August 26, the British Admiralty had communicated to the International Conference of Merchant Seaman, a statement of the facts in twelve cases of sinkings during the previous seven months in which it was shown how "spurlos versenkt" was applied. It was shown that in these cases the submarine commanders had deliberately opened fire on the crews of the vessels after they had taken to their small boats or had attempted to dispose of them in some other way.

Within six weeks after the declaration of war our government was preparing to send troops to France. An expeditionary force comprising about one division of Regulars was announced May 14. General Pershing who was to command arrived in England June 8, and in France June 13. The first body of our troops reached France June 27 and the second a little later. The safe passage of these troops was remarkable, as their departure had been made known to Germany through her spies, and submarines laid in wait for the transports. The vigilance of our convoying agencies continued throughout the war and was one of the high spots of excellence reached in our part of the struggle. Of a total of over 2,000,000 soldiers transported to France and many thousands returned on account of sickness and furloughs, only 661 were lost as a direct result of German submarine operations.

On December 7, the United States declared war against Austria-Hungary. This was largely on the insistence of Italy and was valuable and gratifying to that ally.

President Wilson on December 26, issued a proclamation taking over the railroads of the country, W.G. McAdoo was appointed director general. The proclamation went into effect two days later and the entire rail transportation system, for the first time in the history of the nation, passed under the control and management of the government.

Excepting the revolution in Russia which led to the abdication of Czar Nicholas II (March 11-15) and so disorganized the country that it never figured effectively in the war afterwards, the year was one of distinct advantage to the Allies.

Kut el Amara was retaken by the British February 24. Bagdad fell to the same forces March 11. From March 17th to 19th the Germans retired to the "Hindenburg Line" evacuating a strip of territory in France 100 miles long and averaging 13 miles in width, from Arras to Soissons. Between April 9 and May 14, the British had important successes in the Battle of Arras, capturing Vimy Ridge April 9. Between April 16 and May 6 the French made gains in the Battle of the Aisne, between Soissons and Reims. Between May 15 and September 15 occurred an Italian offensive in which General Cadorna inflicted severe defeats on the Austrians on the Carso and Bainsizza plateaus.

The British blew up Messines Ridge, south of Ypres, June 7 and captured 7,500 German prisoners. June 12 King Constantine of Greece was forced to abdicate and on June 29, Greece entered the war on the side of the Allies. A mutiny in the German fleet at Wilhelmshaven and Kiel occurred July 30 and a second mutiny September 2.

August 20-24 the French recaptured high ground at Verdun, lost in 1916. October 23-26 a French drive north of the Aisne won important positions including Malmaison fort. The Germans retreated from the Chemin de Dames, north of the Aisne, November 2. Between November 22 and December 13 occurred the Battle of Cambrai in which the British employed "tanks" to break down the wire entanglements instead of the usual artillery preparations. Bourlon Wood dominating Cambrai was taken November 26. A surprise counterattack by the Germans December 2, compelled the British to give up one-fourth of the ground gained. Jerusalem was captured by the British December 9.

The British national labor conference on December 29, approved a continuation of the war for aims similar to those defined by President Wilson.

Aside from the collapse of Russia, culminating in an armistice between Germany and the Bolsheviki government of Russia at Brest-Litovsk, December 15, the most important Teutonic success was in the big German-Austrian counterdrive in Italy, October 24 to December 1. The Italians suffered a loss of territory gained during the summer and their line was shifted to the Piave river, Asiago plateau and Brenta river.

Brazil declared war on Germany October 26.

CHAPTER VII

Negroes Respond to the Call

Swift and Unhalting Array—Few Permitted to Volunteer—Only National Guard Accepted—No New Units Formed—Selective Draft their Opportunity—Partial Division of Guardsmen—Complete Division of Selectives—Many in Training—Enter Many Branches of Service—Negro Nurses Authorized—Negro Y.M.C.A. Workers—Negro War Correspondent—Negro Assistant to Secretary of War—Training Camp for Negro Officers—First Time in Artillery—Complete Racial Segregation

When the call to war was sounded by President Wilson, no response was more swift and unhalting than that of the Negro in America. Before our country was embroiled the black men of Africa had already contributed their share in pushing back the Hun. When civilization was tottering and all but overthrown, France and England were glad to avail themselves of the aid of their Senegalese, Algerian, Soudanese and other troops from the tribes of Africa. The story of their valor is written on the battlefields of France in imperishable glory.

Considering the splendid service of the—in many cases—half wild blacks from the region of the equator, it seems strange that our government did not hasten sooner and without demur to enlist the loyal Blacks of this country with their glowing record in former wars, their unquestioned mental attainments, their industry, stamina and self reliance. Yet at the beginning of America's participation in the war, it was plain that the old feeling of intolerance; the disposition to treat the Negro unfairly, was yet abroad in the land.

He was willing; anxious to volunteer and offered himself in large numbers at every recruiting station, without avail. True, he was accepted in numerous instances, but the condition precedent, that of filling up and rounding out the few Negro Regular and National Guard organizations below war strength, was chafing and humiliating. Had the response to the call for volunteers been as ardent among all classes of our people; especially the foreign born, as it was from the American Negro, it is fair to say that the selective draft would not necessarily have been so extensive.

It was not until the selective draft was authorized and the organization of the National Army began, that the Negro was given his full opportunity. His willingness and eagerness to serve were again demonstrated. Some figures dealing with the matter, taken from the official report of the Provost Marshall General (General E.H. Crowder) will be cited later on.

Of the four colored regiments in the Regular Army, the 24th infantry had been on the Mexican border since 1916; the 25th infantry in Hawaii all the years of the war; the Ninth cavalry in the Philippines since 1916, and the 10th cavalry had been doing patrol and garrison duty on the Mexican border and elsewhere in the west since early in 1917. These four regiments were all sterling organizations dating their foundation back to the days immediately following the Civil war. Their record was and is an enviable one. It is no reflection on them that they were not chosen for overseas duty. The country needed a dependable force on the Mexican border, in Hawaii, the Philippines, and in different garrisons at home.

A number of good white Regular Army regiments were kept on this side for the same reasons; not however, overlooking or minimizing the fact not to the honor of the nation in its final resolve, that there has always been fostered a spirit in the counsels and orders of the Department of War, as in all the other great government departments, to restrain rather than to encourage the patriotic and civic zeal of their faithful and qualified Negro aids and servants. That is to say, to draw before them a certain imaginary line; beyond and over which the personal ambitions of members of the race; smarting for honorable renown and promotion; predicated on service and achievement, they were not permitted to go. A virtual "Dead Line"; its parent and wet nurse being that strange thing known as American Prejudice, unknown of anywhere else on earth, which was at once a crime against its marked and selected victims, and a burden of shame which still clings to it; upon the otherwise great nation, that it has condoned and still remains silent in its presence.

Negro National Guard organizations had grown since the Spanish-American war, but they still were far from being numerous in 1917. The ones accepted by the war department were the Eighth Illinois Infantry, a regiment manned and officered entirely by Negroes, the 15th New York Infantry all Negroes with five Negro officers, all the senior officers being white; the Ninth Ohio, a battalion manned and officered by Negroes; the

1st Separate Battalion of the District of Columbia, an infantry organization manned and officered by Negroes; and Negro companies from the states of Connecticut, Maryland, Massachusetts and Tennessee. Massachusetts also had a company known as the 101st Headquarters company and Military Police. The Eighth Illinois became the 370th Infantry in the United States army; the 15th New York became the 369th Infantry; the Ninth Ohio battalion and the companies from Connecticut, Maryland, Massachusetts and Tennessee, as well as the District of Columbia battalion, were all consolidated into the 372nd Infantry.

When the above organizations had been recruited up to war strength there were between 12,000 and 14,000 colored men representing the National Guard of the country. With a population of 12,000,000 Negroes to draw from; the majority of those suitable for military service anxious to enlist, it readily can be seen what a force could have been added to this branch of the service had there been any encouragement of it. There was not lacking a great number of the race, many of them college graduates, competent to act as officers of National Guard units. Many of those commissioned during the Spanish-American war had the experience and age to fit them for senior regimental commands. The 8th Illinois was commanded by Colonel Franklin A. Denison, a prominent colored attorney of Chicago and a seasoned military man. He was the only colored man of the rank of Colonel who was permitted to go to France in the combatant or any other branch of the service. After a brief period in the earlier campaigns he was invalided home very much against his will.

The 15th New York was commanded by Colonel William Hayward, a white man. He was devoted to his black soldiers and they were very fond of him. Officers immediately subordinate to him were white men. The District of Columbia battalion might have retained its colored commander, Major James E. Walker, as he was a fine soldierly figure and possessed of the requisite ability, but he was removed by death while his unit was still training near Washington. Some of the Negro officers of National Guard organizations retained their commands, but the majority were superseded or transferred before sailing or soon after arrival in France.

The 369th, the 370th and the 372nd infantry regiments in the United States army, mentioned as having been formed from the colored National Guard units, became a part of the 93rd division. Another regiment, the 371st, formed from the draft forces was also part of the same division. This division was brigaded with the French from the start and saw service through the war alongside the French poilus with whom they became great friends. There grew up a spirit of which, side by side, they faced and smashed the savage Hun, never wavered or changed. Besides the soldiers from Illinois, New York, Ohio, District of Columbia, Connecticut, Maryland and Tennessee, there were Negro contingents from Mississippi and South Carolina in the 93rd division. One of the regiments of this division, the 369th (15th New York) was of the first of the American forces to reach France, following mutual admiration between these two widely different representatives of the human family, that during the period in the expeditionary force of Regulars which reached France June 13, 1917; being among the first 100,000 that went abroad. However, the 93rd division, exclusively Negro, had not been fully formed then and the regiment did not see much real fighting until the spring and summer of 1918.

Negro nurses carrying banner of famous negro regiment. Marching down fifth avenue, New York. In great parade which opened Red Cross drive.

The 92nd division was another exclusively Negro division. There were many more Negro troops in training in France and large numbers at training camps in this country, but the 92nd and 93rd, being the earlier formed and trained divisions, saw practically all the fighting. Units belonging to one or both divisions fought with special distinction in the Forest of Argonne, near Chateau Thierry, Belleau Wood, St. Mihiel district, Champagne sector, at Metz and in the Vosges mountains.

In the 92nd division was the 325th Field Signal battalion, the only Negro signal unit in the American army. The division also contained the 349th, 350th and 351st Artillery regiments, each containing a machine gun battalion; the 317th Trench Mortar battery; the balance being made up of Negro engineers, hospital units, etc., and the 365th, 366th, 367th and 368th Infantry regiments.

Enlisted, drafted and assigned to active service, upwards of 400,000 Negroes participated in the war. The number serving abroad amounted to about 200,000. They were inducted into the cavalry, infantry, field and coast artillery, radio (wireless telegraphy, etc.), medical corps, ambulance and hospital corps, sanitary and ammunition trains, stevedore regiments, labor battalions, depot brigades and engineers. They also served as regimental clerks, surveyors and draftsmen.

Sixty served as chaplains and over 350 as Y.M.C.A. secretaries, there being a special and highly efficient Negro branch of the Y.M.C.A. Numerous others were attached to the War Camp Community Service in cities adjacent to the army camps.

Negro nurses were authorized by the war department for service in base hospitals at six army camps—Funston, Sherman, Grant, Dix, Taylor and Dodge. Race women also served as canteen workers in France and in charge of hostess houses in this country.

One Negro, Ralph W. Tyler, served as an accredited war correspondent, attached to the staff of General Pershing, Dr. R. R. Moton, who succeeded the late Booker T. Washington as head of the Tuskegee Institute, was sent on a special mission to France by President Wilson and Secretary Baker.

A race woman, Mrs. Alice Dunbar Nelson of Wilmington, Delaware, was named as a field worker to mobilize the Negro women of the country for war work. Her activities were conducted in connection with the Women's Committee of the Council of National Defense.

The most conspicuous honor paid to a Negro by the administration and the war department, was in the appointment, October 1, 1917, of Emmett J. Scott as special assistant to the Secretary of War. This was done that the administration might not be accused of failing to grant full protection to the Negroes, and that a thorough examination might be made into all matters affecting their relation to the war and its many agencies.

Having been for 18 years confidential secretary to Booker T. Washington, and being at the time of his appointment secretary of the Tuskegee Normal and Industrial Institute for Negroes, Mr. Scott was peculiarly fitted to render necessary advice to the war department with respect to the Negroes of the various states, to look after all matters affecting the interests of Negro selectives and enlisted men, and to inquire into the treatment accorded them by the various officials connected with the war department. In the position occupied by him, he was thus enabled to obtain a proper perspective both of the attitude of selective service officials to the Negro, and of the Negro to the war, especially to the draft. In a memorandum on the subject addressed to the Provost Marshall General, December 12, 1918, he wrote:

> *"The attitude of the Negro was one of complete acceptance of the draft, in fact of an eagerness to accept its terms. There was a deep resentment in many quarters that he was not permitted to volunteer, as white men by the thousands were permitted to do in connection with National Guard units and other branches of military service which were closed to colored men. One of the brightest chapters in the whole history of the war is the Negro's eager acceptance of the draft and his splendid willingness to fight. His only resentment was due to the limited extent to which he was allowed to join and participate in combatant or 'fighting' units. The number of colored draftees accepted for military duty, and the comparatively small number of them claiming exemptions, as compared with the total number of white and colored men called and drafted, presents an interesting study and reflects much credit upon this racial group."*

Over 1,200 Negro officers, many of them college graduates, were commissioned during the war. The only training camp exclusively for Negro officers was at Fort Des Moines, Iowa. This camp ran from June 15, 1917, to October 15, 1917. A total of 638 officers was graduated and commissioned from the camp. Negro Regulars and Negro National Army men who had passed the tests for admission to officers training camps were sent mainly to the training schools for machine gun officers at Camp Hancock, Augusta, Georgia; the infantry officers training school at Camp Pike, Little Rock, Arkansas, and the artillery officers training school at Camp Taylor, Louisville, Kentucky. They were trained along with the white officers. The graduates from these camps along with a few National Guardsmen who had taken the officers' examinations, and others trained in France, made up the balance of the 1,200 commissioned.

In connection with the artillery training an interesting fact developed. It had been charged that Negroes could not develop into artilleryman. A strong prejudice against inducting them into that branch of the service had always existed in the army. It was especially affirmed that the Negro did not possess the mathematical ability necessary to qualify as an expert artillery officer. Nevertheless, out of a number of Negro aspirants, very small in comparison with the white men in training for officers' commissions at the camp, five of the Negroes stood alongside their white brothers at the head of the class. The remainder were sprinkled down the line about in the same proportion and occupying the same relative positions as the whites. The prejudice against the Negro as an artilleryman was further and effectually dispelled in the record made by the 349th, 350th and 351st artillery regiments and their machine gun battalions in the 92nd division.

With the exception of the training camp for officers at Des Moines, Iowa, no important attempt was made to establish separate Negro training camps. In the draft quotas from each state were whites and blacks and all with few exceptions, were sent to the most convenient camp. Arrangements existed, however, at the different camps for the separate housing and training of the Negro troops. This was in line with the military policy of the Government, as well as in deference to the judgment of both white and black officers. It undoubtedly was necessary to separate the two races. Furthermore, as the military policy called for regiments, battalions and, divisions made up entirely of Negroes, it was proper to commence the organization at the training camps. Companies formed in this manner thus became homogeneous, accustomed to one another individually and to their officers.

The situation was different from the Spanish-American war, where Negro units, at least in one case, served in white regiments. Racial strife and rivalry were eliminated. The only rivalry that existed was the good-natured and healthy one of emulation between members of the same race. On the field of battle there was rivalry and emulation between the whites and blacks, but it was the rivalry of organizations and not of races. The whole was tempered by that splendid admiration and fellow-feeling which comes to men of all races when engaged as partners in danger or near death; in the defense and promotion of a great cause; the eternal verities of Justice and Humanity.

CHAPTER VIII

Recrudescence of South's Intolerance

Confronted by Racial Prejudice— Splendid Attitude of Negro Shamed It—Kept Out of Navy—Only One Per Cent of Navy Personnel Negroes—Modified Marines Contemplated—Few Have Petty Officers' Grades—Separate Ships Proposed—Negro Efficiency in Navy—Material for "Black Ships"—Navy Opens Door to Negro Mechanics

Old feelings of race prejudice and intolerance, appearing mainly in the South, confronted the Negro at the beginning of the war. The splendid attitude of the Negro shamed and overcame this feeling in other sections of the country, and was beginning to have its effect even in the South. It is true that men of the race were not accepted for voluntary enlistment in numbers of consequence in any section, but had the voluntary system continued in vogue, the willingness and desire of the race to serve, coupled with the very necessities of the case, would have altered the condition.

No new Negro volunteer units were authorized, but the demand for men would soon have made it imperative. It would have been combatted by a certain element in the South, but the friends of the few volunteer units which did exist in that section were firm in their championship and were winning adherents to their view that the number should be increased. The selective draft with its firm dictum that all men within certain ages should be called and the fit ones chosen, put an end to all contention. The act was not passed without bitter opposition which developed in its greatest intensity among the Southern senators and representatives; feelings that were inspired entirely by opposition to the Negro.

It would have been a bad thing for the country and would have prolonged the war, and possibly might have lost it, if the selective draft had been delayed. But it would have been interesting to see how far the country, especially the South, would have progressed in the matter of raising a volunteer army without accepting Negroes. Undoubtedly they soon would have been glad to recruit them, even in the South.

Unfortunately for the Negro, the draft was not able to prevent their being kept out of the Navy. It is a very desirable branch of the service vitiated and clouded, however, with many disgusting and aristocratic traditions. When the Navy was young and the service more arduous; when its vessels were merely armed merchantmen, many of them simply tubs and death traps and not the floating castles of today, the services of Negroes were not disdained; but times and national ideals had changed, and, the shame of it, not to the credit of a Commonwealth, for whose birth a Negro had shed the first blood, and a Washington had faced the rigors of a Valley Forge, a Lincoln the bullet of an assassin.

The annual report of the Chief of the Bureau of Navigation, rendered to the Secretary of the Navy and covering the fiscal year ending June 30, 1918, showed that in the United States Navy, the United States Naval Reserve Force and the National Naval Volunteers, there was a total of 435,398 men. Of that great number only 5,328 were Negroes, a trifle over one percent. Between June and November 1918, the Navy was recruited to a total force somewhat in excess of 500,000 men. Carrying out the same percentage, it is apparent that the aggregate number of Negroes serving, in the Navy at the close of the war, could not have been much in excess of 6,000.

Some extra enlistments of Negroes were contemplated, as the Navy had in process of establishment just prior to the armistice, a new service for Negro recruits. It was to be somewhat similar to the Pioneer units of the army, partaking in some degree of the character of Marines, just as the Pioneers partake of the character of infantry, but in general respects resembling more the engineer and stevedore units. About 600 men had been selected for this service when the project was abandoned on account of the ending of the war.

With the exception of a very limited number who have been permitted to attain the rank of petty officer, Negroes in the Navy were confined to menial occupations. They were attached to the firing forces as coal passers, while others served as cooks assistants, mess attendants and in similar duties. Quite a number were full rated cooks. A few were water tenders, electricians and gunners' mates, each of which occupations entitled them to the aforesaid rank of petty officer. Among the petty officers some had by sheer merit attained the rank of chief petty officer, which is about equal to the rank of sergeant in the army.

The idea of separate ships for the Negro might to some degree ameliorate the sting incident to race prohibition in that arm of government service. The query is advanced that if we can have black colonels, majors, captains and lieutenants in the army, why cannot we have black commanders, lieutenants, ensigns and such in the Navy?

Negroes have often and in divers ways displayed their intelligence and efficiency in the Navy. Take, for instance, the case of John Jordan, a Negro of Virginia, who was chief gunner's mate on Admiral Dewey's flagship the "Olympia" during the Spanish-American war, and was the man who fired the first shot at the enemy at Manila Bay. A Negro chief electrician, Salisbury Brooks, was the originator of inventions which were adopted without reservation by the Navy designers and changed the construction of modern battle ships.

One of the principal instructors on the U.S.S. Essex, the government training ship at Norfolk, is Matthew Anderson, a Negro. He has trained thousands of men, many of them now officers, in the art and duties of seamanship. Scores of Negroes; men of the type of these in the Navy, would furnish the nucleus for officers and crews of separate Negro ships.

In a recent issue of "Our Navy" a magazine devoted entirely to naval affairs, especially as regards the enlisted man, a writer reflects the opinion of these men in the following article:

"Whether you like the black man or not, whether you believe in a square deal for him or not, you can't point an accusing finger at his patriotism, his Americanism or his fighting ability. It is fair to neither the white man nor the black man to have the black man compete with the white man in the Navy. True, we have black petty officers here and there in the Navy, and in some cases black chief petty officers. It stands to reason that they must have been mighty good men to advance. They surely must know their business—every inch of it—to advance to these ratings. Yet they are not wanted in these ratings because they involve the black man having charge of white men under him. Outside of the messman branch you will find comparatively few Negroes in the Navy today.

> *"There should be 'black ships' assigned to be manned by American Negroes. These are days of democracy, equality and freedom," continues the writer. "If a man is good enough to go over the top and die for these principles, he is good enough to promote in the Navy. Why not try it? Put the black men on their own ships. Promote them, rate them, just the same as the white man. But above all keep them on their own ships. It is fair to*

them and fair to the white men. The Brazilian and Argentine navies have 'black ships.'"

Recruiting officers of the Navy have recently opened the doors to discharged Negro soldiers, and some civilians. If physically fit they are permitted to enlist as machinists and electricians. The Navy has opened a school for machinists at Charleston, S.C., and a school for electricians at Hampton Roads, Va.

Men for the machinists' school are enlisted as firemen 3rd class. While in training they are paid $30 a month. They also receive their clothing allotment, their food, dry comfortable quarters in which to live, and all text books and practical working tools. In return for this chance to become proficient in a very necessary trade, all that is required of those enlisting is a knowledge of common fractions, ambition to learn the trade, energy and a strict attention to the instruction given them.

Subjects taught in the course are arithmetic, note book sketching, practical engineering, theoretical engineering, clipping and filing, drilling, pipe fitting, repair work, rebabbiting, brazing, tin smithing, lathes, shapers, milling machines and grinders. It will be seen that they get a vast amount of mechanical knowledge and practically two trades, machinists and engineering.

In the electrical school the course is equally thorough. The men get a high grade of instruction, regardless of cost of material and tools. The best text books that can be had are available for their use.

This liberality in order to get machinists and electricians in the Navy, argues that some change of attitude towards the Negro is contemplated.

It may evolve into the establishment of "black ships." The Negro sailor has been pleading for years that his color has been a bar to him. With a ship of his own, would come his chance. He would strive; do all within his power to make it a success and would succeed.

CHAPTER IX

Previous Wars in Which the Negro Figured

Shot Heard Around the World—Crispus Attucks—Slave Leads Sons of Freedom—The Boston Massacre—Anniversary Kept for Years—William Nell, Historian—3,000 Negroes in Washington's Forces—A Stirring History—Negro Woman Soldier—Border Indian Wars—Negro Heroes

Our American school histories teach us that the "shot which was heard around the world",—the opening gun of the Revolutionary war, was fired at Lexington in 1775. The phrase embodies a precious sentiment; time has molded many leaders, the inspiration for almost a century and a half of the patriotic youth of our land. This is as it should be. All honor and all praise to the deathless heroes of that time and occasion.

But why has not history been more just; at least, more explicit? Why not say that the shot which started the Revolution—that first great movement for human liberty and the emancipation of nations—was fired five years earlier; was fired not by, but at, a Negro, Crispus Attucks? The leader of the citizens in that event of March 5, 1770, known as the Boston Massacre, he was the first man upon whom the British soldiers fired and the first to fall; the pioneer martyr for American independence.

It is perhaps fitting; a manifestation of the inscrutable ways of Providence, that the first life given in behalf of a nation about to throw off a yoke of bondage, was that of a representative of a race; despised, oppressed and enslaved.

Botta the historian, in speaking of the scenes of the 5th of March says:

> *"The people were greatly exasperated. The multitude ran towards King street, crying, 'Let us drive out these ribalds; they have no business here.' The rioters rushed furiously towards the Custom House; they approached the sentinel, crying 'Kill him, kill him!' They assaulted him with snowballs, pieces of ice, and whatever they could lay their hands upon.*

> *"The guard were then called, and in marching to the Custom House, they encountered a band of the populace, led by a mulatto named Attucks, who brandished their clubs and pelted them with snowballs. The maledictions, the imprecations, the execrations of the multitude, were horrible. In the midst of a torrent of invective from every quarter, the military were challenged to fire. The populace advanced to the points of their bayonets.*
>
> *"The soldiers appeared like statues; the cries, the howlings, the menaces, the violent din of bells still sounding the alarm, increased the confusion and the horrors of these moments; at length the mulatto Attucks and twelve of his companions, pressing forward, environed the soldiers and striking their muskets with their clubs, cried to the multitude: 'Be not afraid, they dare not fire; why do you hesitate, why do you not kill them, why not crush them at once?'*
>
> *"The mulatto lifted his arms against Captain Preston, and having turned one of the muskets, he seized the bayonet with his left hand, as if he intended to execute his threat At this moment, confused cries were heard: 'The wretches dare not fire!' Firing succeeds. Attucks is slain. Other discharges follow. Three were killed, five severely wounded and several others slightly."*

Attucks was killed by Montgomery, one of Captain Preston's soldiers. He had been foremost in resisting and was first slain. As proof of a front engagement, he received two balls, one in each breast. The white men killed with Attucks were Samuel Maverick, Samuel Gray and Jonas Caldwell.

John Adams, afterwards President of the United States, was counsel for the soldiers in the investigation which followed. He admitted that Attucks appeared to have been the hero of the occasion and the leader of the people. Attucks and Caldwell, not being residents of Boston, were buried from Faneuil Hall, the cradle of liberty. The citizens generally participated in the solemnities.

If the outrages against the American colonists had not been so flagrant, and so well imbedded as indisputable records of our history; if the action of the military authorities had not been so arbitrary, the uprising of Attucks and his followers might be looked upon as a common, reprehensible riot and the participants as a band of misguided incendiaries. Subsequent reverence for the occasion, disproves any such view. Judge Dawes, a prominent jurist of the time, as well as a brilliant exponent of the people, alluding in 1775 to the event, said:

"The provocation of that night must be numbered among the master-springs which gave the first motion to a vast machinery—a noble and comprehensive system of national independence."

Ramsey's History of the American Revolution, says:

> *"The anniversary of the 5th of March was observed with great solemnity; eloquent orators were successively employed to preserve the remembrance of it fresh in the mind. On these occasions the blessings of liberty, the horrors of slavery, and the danger of a standing army, were presented to the public view. These annual orations administered fuel to the fire of liberty and kept it burning with an irresistible flame."*

The 5th of March continued to be celebrated for the above reasons until the anniversary of the Declaration of American Independence was substituted in its place; and its orators were expected to honor the feelings and principles of the former as having given birth to the latter. On the 5th of March 1776, Washington repaired to the intrenchments. "Remember" said he, "It is the 5th of March, and avenge the death of your brethren."

In the introduction to a book entitled "The Colored Patriots of the American Revolution" by William C. Nell, a Negro historian, Harriet Beecher Stowe said in 1855:

"The colored race have been generally considered by their enemies, and sometimes even by their friends, as deficient in energy and courage. Their virtues have been supposed to be principally negative ones." Speaking of the incidents in Mr. Nell's collection she says: "They will redeem the character of the race from this misconception and show how much injustice there may often be in a generally accepted idea". Continuing, she says:

> *"In considering the services of the colored patriots of the Revolution, we are to reflect upon them as far more magnanimous, because rendered to a nation which did not acknowledge them as citizens and equals, and in whose interests and prosperity they had less at stake. It was not for their own land they fought, not even for a land which had adopted them, but for a land which had enslaved them, and whose laws, even in freedom, oftener oppressed than protected. Bravery, under such circumstances, has a peculiar beauty and merit.*
>
> *"And their white brothers—may remember that generosity, disinterested courage and bravery, are of no particular race and complexion, and that the image of the Heavenly Father may be reflected alike by all. Each rec-*

ord of worth in this oppressed and despised people should be pondered, for it is by many such that the cruel and unjust public sentiment, which has so long proscribed them, may be reversed, and full opportunities given them to take rank among the nations of the earth."

Estimates from competent sources state that not less than 3,000 Negro soldiers did service in the American army during the Revolution. Rhode Island first made her slaves free men and then called on them to fight. A black regiment was raised there, of which Colonel Christopher Green was made commander. Connecticut furnished a black battalion under command of Colonel David Humphrey.

Prior to the Revolution, two Virginia Negroes, Israel Titus and Samuel Jenkins, had fought under Braddock and Washington in the French and Indian war.

It has been said that one of the men killed when Major Pitcairn commanding the British advance on Concord and Lexington, April 19, 1775, ordered his troops to fire on the Americans, was a Negro bearing arms. Peter Salem a Negro did service during the Revolution, and is said to have killed this same Major Pitcairn, at the battle of Bunker Hill. In some old engravings of the battle, Salem is pictured as occupying a prominent position. These pictures were carried on some of the currency of the Monumental bank of Charlestown, Massachusetts and the Freeman's bank of Boston. Other black men fought at Bunker Hill, of whom we have the names of Salem Poor, Titus Coburn, Alexander Ames, Barzillai Lew and Gato Howe. After the war these men were pensioned.

Prince, a Negro soldier, was Colonel Barton's chief assistant in capturing the British officer, Major General Prescott at Newport, R.I. Primus Babcock received an honorable discharge from the army signed by General Washington. Lambo Latham and Jordan Freeman fell with Ledyard at the storming of Fort Griswold. Freeman is said to have killed Major Montgomery, a British officer who was leading an attack on Americans in a previous fight. History does not record whether or not this was the same or a related Montgomery to the one who killed Crispus Attucks at Boston.

Hamet, one of General Washington's Negroes, was drawing a pension as a revolutionary soldier as late as 1839, Oliver Cromwell served six years and nine months in Col. Israel Shreve's regiment of New Jersey troops under Washington's immediate command. Charles Bowles became an American soldier at the age of sixteen years and served to the end of the Revolution. Seymour Burr and Jeremy Jonah were Negro soldiers in a Connecticut regiment.

A Negro whose name is not known obtained the countersign by which Mad Anthony Wayne was enabled to take Stony Point, and guided and helped him to do so.

Jack Grove was a Negro steward on board an American vessel which the British captured. He figured out that the vessel could be retaken if sufficient courage were shown. He insisted and at length prevailed upon his captain to make the attempt, which was successful.

There was in Massachusetts during those Revolutionary days one company of Negro men bearing a special designation, "The Bucks." It was a notable body of men. At the close of the war its fame and services were recognized by John Hancock presenting to it a beautiful banner.

The European struggle recently ended furnished a remarkable example of female heroism and devotion to country in the case of the Russian woman who enlisted as a common soldier in the army of the Czar, served with distinction and finally organized an effective unit of female soldiers known as the "Battalion of Death." More resourceful and no less remarkable and heroic, is the case of Deborah Gannet, a Negro woman soldier of the Revolution, which may be summed up in the following resolution passed by the General Court of Massachusetts during the session of 1791:—

> *"XXIII—Whereas, it appears to this court that the said Deborah Gannett enlisted, under the name of Robert Shurtliff, in Capt Webb's company, in the Fourth Massachusetts regiment, on May 20, 1782, and did actually perform the duties of a soldier, in the late army of the United States to the 23rd day of October, 1783, for which she has received no compensation; and, whereas, it further appears that the said Deborah exhibited an extraordinary instance of female heroism by discharging the duties of a faithful, gallant soldier, and at the same time preserving the virtue and chastity of her sex unsuspected and unblemished, and was discharged from the service with a fair and honorable character, therefore,*
>
> *"Resolved, that the Treasurer of this Commonwealth be, and he hereby is, directed to issue his note to the said Deborah for the sum of thirty-four pounds, bearing interest from October 23, 1783."*

There is not lacking evidence that Negroes distinguished themselves in the struggles of the pioneer settlers against the Indians. This was particularly true of the early history of Kentucky. The following incidents are recorded in Thompson's "Young People's History of Kentucky:"

> "Ben Stockton was a slave in the family of Major George Stockton of Fleming county. He was a regular Negro, and though a slave, was devoted to his master. He hated an Indian and loved to moralize over a dead one; getting into a towering rage and swearing magnificently when a horse was stolen; handled his rifle well, though somewhat foppishly, and hopped, danced and showed his teeth when a prospect offered to chase 'the yaller varmints'. His master had confidence in his resolution and prudence, while he was a great favorite with all the hunters, and added much to their fun on dull expeditions. On one occasion, when a party of white men in pursuit of Indians who had stolen their horses called at Stockton's station for reinforcements, Ben, among others, volunteered. They overtook the savages at Kirk's Springs in Lewis county, and dismounted to fight; but as they advanced, they could see only eight or ten, who disappeared over the mountain. Pressing on, they discovered on descending the mountain such indications as convinced them that the few they had seen were but decoys to lead them into an ambuscade at the base, and a retreat was ordered. Ben was told of it by a man near him; but he was so intent on getting a shot that he did not hear, and the order was repeated in a louder tone, whereupon he turned upon his monitor a reproving look, grimaced and gesticulated ludicrously, and motioned to the man to be silent. He then set off rapidly down the mountain. His white comrade, unwilling to leave him, ran after him, and reached his side just as he leveled his gun at a big Indian standing tiptoe on a log and peering into the thick woods. At the crack of Ben's rifle the savage bounded into the air and fell. The others set up a fierce yell, and, as the fearless Negro said, 'skipped from tree to tree like grasshoppers.' He bawled out: 'Take dat to 'member Ben—de black white man!' and the two beat a hasty retreat.
>
> "In the family of Capt. James Estill, who established a station about fifteen miles south of Boonesborough, was a Negro slave, Monk, who was intelligent, bold as a lion, and as faithful to his pioneer friends as though he were a free white settler defending his own rights. About daylight, March 20, 1782, when all the men of the fort except four were absent on an Indian trail, a body of the savages came upon Miss Jennie Glass, who was outside, but near the station, milking—Monk being with her. They killed and scalped Miss Glass and captured Monk. When questioned as to the force inside the walls, the shrewd and self-possessed Negro represented it as much greater than it was and told of preparations for defense. The Indians were deceived, and after killing the cattle, they retreated across the river. When the battle of Little Mountain opened two days later, Monk,

who was still a prisoner with the Indians cried out: 'Don't give way, Mas' Jim! There's only about twenty-five redskins and you can whip 'em!' This was valuable and encouraging information to the whites. When the Indians began to advance on Lieutenant Miller, when he was sent to prevent a flank movement and guard the horse-holders, Monk called also to him to hold his ground and the white men would win. Instead of being instantly killed as was to be apprehended, even though the savages might not understand his English, he made his escape before the fight closed and got back to his friends. On their return to the station, twenty-five miles, without sufficient horses for the wounded, he carried on his back, most of the way, James Berry, whose thigh was broken. He had learned to make gunpowder, and obtaining saltpetre from Peyton's Cave, in Madison county, he frequently furnished this indispensable article to Estill's Station and Boonesborough. He has been described as being five feet five inches high and weighing two hundred pounds. He was a respected member of the Baptist church, when whites and blacks worshipped together. He was held in high esteem by the settlers and his young master, Wallace Estill, gave him his freedom and clothed and fed him as long as he lived thereafter—till about 1835.

"A year or two after the close of the Revolutionary war, a Mr. Woods was living near Crab Orchard, Kentucky, with his wife, one daughter (said to be ten years old), and a lame Negro man. Early one morning, her husband being away, Mrs. Woods when a short distance from the house, discovered seven or eight Indians in ambush. She ran back into the house, so closely pursued that before she could fasten the door one of the savages forced his way in. The Negro instantly seized him. In the scuffle the Indian threw him, falling on top. The Negro held him in a strong grasp and called to the girl to take an axe which was in the room and kill him. This she did by two well-aimed blows; and the Negro then asked Mrs. Woods to let in another that he with the axe might dispatch him as he came and so, one by one, kill them all. By this time, however, some men from the station nearby, having discovered that the house was attacked, had come up and opened fire on the savages, by which one was killed and the others put to flight."

CHAPTER X

From Lexington to Carrizal

Negro in War of 1812—Incident of the Chesapeake—Battle of Lake Erie—Perry's Fighters 10 Percent Negroes—Incident of the "Governor Tompkins"—Colonists Form Negro Regiments—Defense of New Orleans—Andrew Jackson's Tribute—Negroes in Mexican and Civil Wars—In the Spanish-American War—Negroes in the Philippines—Heroes of Carrizal—General Butler's Tribute to Negroes—Wendell Phillips on Toussaint L'ouverture

Prior to the actual war of 1812 and one of the most conspicuous causes leading to it, was the attack on the Chesapeake, an American war vessel. Here the Negro in the Navy figured in a most remarkable degree. The vessel was hailed, fired upon and forced to strike her colors by the British. She was boarded, searched and four persons taken from the crew charged with desertion from the English navy. Three of these were Negroes and one white. The charge against the Negroes could not have been very strong, for they were dismissed, while the white man was hanged.

The naval history of our second war with Great Britain is replete with incidents concerning the participation of the Negro. Mackenzie's history of the life of Commodore Perry states that at the famed battle of Lake Erie, fully ten percent of the American crews were blacks. Perry spoke highly of their bravery and good conduct. He said they seemed to be absolutely insensible to danger. His fighters were a motley collection of blacks, soldiers and boys. Nearly all had been afflicted with sickness. Mackenzie says that when the defeated British commander was brought aboard the "Niagara" and beheld the sickly and parti-colored beings around him, an expression of chagrin escaped him at having been conquered by such men.

The following extract is from a letter written by Commodore Nathaniel Shaler of the armed schooner "Governor Tompkins", dated January 1, 1813. Speaking of a fight with a British frigate, he said:

> "The name of one of my poor fellows who was killed ought to be registered in the book of fame and remembered with reverence as long as bravery is considered a virtue. He was a black man by the name of John Johnson. A twenty-four-pound shot struck him in the hip and tore away all the lower part of his body. In this state the poor brave fellow lay on the deck and several times exclaimed to his shipmates: 'Fire away, boys; don't haul the colors down.' Another black man by the name of John Davis was struck in much the same way. He fell near me and several times requested to be thrown overboard, saying he was only in the way of the others. When America has such tars, she has little to fear from the tyrants of the ocean."

With the history fresh in mind of the successful Negro insurrection in St. Domingo, bringing out so conspicuous a military and administrative genius as Toussaint L'Ouverture, it is not surprising that the services of Negroes as soldiers were not only welcomed, but solicited by various states during the War of 1812. Excepting the battle of New Orleans, almost all the martial glory of the struggle was on the water. New York, however, passed a special act of the legislature and organized two regiments of Negro troops, while there was heavy recruiting in other states.

When in 1814 New Orleans was in danger, the free colored people of Louisiana were called into the field with the whites. General Andrew Jackson's commendatory address read to his colored troops December 18, 1814, is one of the highest compliments ever paid by a commander to his troops. He said:

> "Soldiers!—when, on the banks of the Mobile, I called you to take up arms, inviting you to partake of the perils and glory of your white fellow-citizens, I expected much from you; for I was not ignorant that you possessed qualities most formidable to an invading enemy. I knew with what fortitude you could endure hunger and thirst, and all the fatigues of a campaign. I knew well how you loved your native country, and that you, as well as ourselves had to defend what man holds most dear—his parents, wife, children and property. You have done more than I expected. In addition to the previous qualities I before knew you to possess, I found among you a noble enthusiasm, which leads to the performance of great things.
>
> "Soldiers! The President of the United States shall hear how praiseworthy was your conduct in the hour of danger, and the representatives of the American people will give you the praise your exploits entitle you to. Your General anticipates them in applauding your noble ardor."

Many incidents are on record of the gallantry of Negro soldiers and servants also serving as soldiers, in the war with Mexico. Colonel Clay, a son of Henry Clay, was accompanied into the thick of the battle of Buena Vista, by his Negro servant. He remained by his side in the fatal charge and saw Clay stricken from his horse. Although surrounded by the murderous Mexicans he succeeded in carrying the mangled body of his master from the field.

It has been stated and the evidence seems strong, that a Negro saved the life of General Zachary Taylor at the battle of Monterey. The story is that a Mexican was aiming a deadly blow at the General, when the Negro sprang between them, slew the Mexican and received a deep wound from a lance. The Negro was a slave at the time, but was afterwards emancipated by President Taylor.

Upwards of 200,000 colored soldiers were regularly enlisted in the Federal army and navy during the Civil war. President Lincoln commissioned eight Negro surgeons for field and hospital duty. Losses sustained by the Negro troops amounting to upwards of 37,000 men, are shown to have been as heavy in proportion to the numbers engaged, as those of the white forces.

The record of the Negro troops in the Civil war is one of uniform excellence. Numerous official documents attest this fact, aside from the spoken and written commendations of many high officers. Their bravery was everywhere recognized; many distinguished themselves and several attained to the rank of regularly commissioned officers. Conspicuous in Negro annals of that time is the case of Charles E. Nash, afterwards a member of congress. He received a primary education in the schools of New Orleans, but had educated himself largely by his own efforts. In 1863 he enlisted in the 83rd regiment, United States Chasseurs d'Afrique and became acting sergeant-major of that command. At the storming of Fort Blakely he lost a leg and was honorably discharged.

Another, William Hannibal Thomas, afterwards became prominent as an author, teacher, lawyer and legislator. His best known book was entitled, "The American Negro: What he was, what he is, and what he may become." He served as a soldier during the Civil War and lost an arm in the service.

The exploit of Robert Smalls was so brilliant that no amount of unfairness or prejudice has been able to shadow it. It is well known to all students of the War of the Rebellion and is recorded in the imperishable pages of history.

Smalls was born a slave at Beaufort, South Carolina, but managed to secure some education. Having led a sea-faring life to some extent, the early part of the war found him employed as pilot of the Rebel transport Planter. He was thoroughly familiar with the harbors and inlets of the South Atlantic coast. On May 31, 1862, the Planter was in Charleston harbor. All the white officers and crew went ashore, leaving on board a colored crew of eight men in charge of Smalls. He summoned aboard his wife and three children and at 2 o'clock in the morning steamed out of the harbor, passed the Confederate forts by giving the proper signals, and when fairly out of reach, ran up the Stars and Stripes and headed a course for the Union fleet, into whose hands he soon surrendered the ship. He was appointed a pilot in the United States navy and served as such on the monitor Keokuk in the attack on Fort Sumter; was promoted to captain for gallant and meritorious conduct, December 1, 1863, and placed in command of the Planter, a position which he held until the vessel was taken out of commission in 1866. He was a member of the South Carolina Constitutional Convention, 1868; elected same year to the legislature, to the state senate 1870 and 1872, and was a member of the Forty-fourth and Forty-fifth Congresses.

Among the most inspiring pages of Civil War history written by the Negro, were the campaigns of Port Hudson, Louisiana; Fort Wagner, South Carolina and Fort Pillow, Kentucky. Negro troops participated in the siege of the former place by the Federal forces under General Banks, which began in May 1863, and ended in the surrender of the fort July 8, 1863. Fort Wagner was one of the defenses of Charleston. It was reduced by General Gilmore, September 6, 1863 and Negro troops contributed in a glorious and heroic manner to the result. Fort Pillow had been taken by the Federals and was garrisoned by a Negro regiment and a detachment of cavalry. It was recaptured April 12, 1864 by the Confederates under General Forrest. Practically the entire garrison was massacred, an act that will stain forever the name of Forrest, and the cause for which he struggled.

By the close of the Civil war, the value and fitness of the Negro as a soldier had been so completely demonstrated that the government decided to enlarge the Regular army and form fifty percent of the increase from colored men. In 1866 eight new infantry regiments were authorized of which four were to be Negroes and four new cavalry regiments of which two were to be Negroes. The Negro infantry regiments were numbered the 38th 39th, 40th and 41st. The cavalry regiments were known as the 9th and 10th.

In 1869 there was a general reduction in the infantry forces of the Regular army and the 38th and 41st were consolidated into one regiment numbered the 24th and the 39th and 40th into one regiment numbered the 25th. The strength and numerical titles of the cavalry were not changed. For over forty years the colored American was represented in our Regular Army by those four regiments. They have borne more than their proportionate share of hard service, including many Indian campaigns. The men have conducted themselves so worthily as to call forth the best praise of the highest military authorities. General Miles and General Merritt, actively identified with the Indian wars, were unstinting in their commendation of the valor and skill of Negro fighters.

Between 1869 and 1889, three colored men were regularly graduated and commissioned from the United States military academy at West Point and served in the Regular Army as officers. They were John H. Alexander, Charles Young and H.O. Flipper. The latter was dismissed. All served in the cavalry. Alexander died shortly before the Spanish-American war and up to the time of his demise, enjoyed the confidence and esteem of his associates, white and black. Young became major in the volunteer service during the Spanish-American war and was placed in command of the Ninth Battalion of Ohio volunteers. After the Spanish-American war he returned to the Regular Army with a reduced rank, but ultimately became a Major in that service. Upon America's entry into the European war he was elevated to the rank of Colonel.

At the breaking out of the Spanish-American war in 1898, Negro military organizations existed principally in the Regular Army. These were soon filled to their maximum strength and the desire of Negroes north and south to enlist, seemed likely to meet with disappointment. Congress, to meet the insistence of colored men for service, authorized the raising of ten Negro volunteer regiments of "immunes"—men who had lived in sections where the yellow fever and other malignant or malarial visitations had occurred, and who had suffered from them or shown evidences that they in all probability would be immune from the diseases. The plan to place white men in all commands above the grade of second lieutenant, prevented Negroes from enlisting as they otherwise would have done. Four immune regiments were organized—the 7th, 8th, 9th and 10th.

Several of the states appreciating the value of the Negro as a soldier and in response to his intense desire to enlist, placed volunteer Negro organizations at the disposal of the government. There were the Third Alabama and Sixth Virginia Infantry; Eighth Illinois Infantry; Companies A and B Indiana Infantry; Thirty-third Kansas Infantry, and a battalion of the Ninth Ohio Infantry. The Eighth Illinois was officered by colored men throughout. J.R. Marshall its first colonel commanded the regiment during the Spanish-American war and did garrison duty in Santiago province for some time after the war; being for a while military governor of San Luis.

Gov. Russell of North Carolina, called out a Negro regiment, the Third Infantry, officered by colored men throughout. Colonel Charles Young commanding. It was not mustered into the service.

Company L. Sixth Massachusetts Infantry, was a Negro company serving in a white regiment. John L. Waller, deceased, a Negro formerly United States Consul to Madagascar, was a captain in the Kansas regiment.

About one hundred Negro second-lieutenants were commissioned in the volunteer force during the Spanish-American war. There was a Negro paymaster, Major John R. Lynch of Mississippi, and two Negro chaplains, the Rev. C.T. Walker of Georgia and the Rev. Richard Carroll of South Carolina.

Owing to the briefness of the campaign in Cuba, most of the service of Negro troops devolved upon the Regulars who were fit and ready. But all troops were at mobilization or training bases and willing and anxious to serve. No pages in the history of this country are more replete with the record of good fighting, military efficiency and soldierly conduct, than those recording the story of Negro troops in Cuba. Colonel Roosevelt said that the conduct of the Ninth and Tenth Cavalry reflected honor upon the whole American people, especially on their own race. He could hardly say otherwise in view of the splendid support given by those two regiments that—such is, and will continue to be the verdict of history, saved him and his "Rough Riders" from annihilation at San Juan Hill.

Cuba, in her struggles for freedom, had among her own people two splendid Negro leaders, Antonio and Jose Maceo.

Following the Cuban campaign, Negro troops saw distinguished service in the Philippine Islands uprisings. They have from time to time since garrisoned and preserved order in those possessions. A very limited number of Negro officers have been attached to their racial contingents in the Philippines, and there will be found but a few of competent military authority in this country, who will deny that educated, intelligent and qualified Negroes, are fitted for positions of leadership and command.

The Negro of this country is primarily and essentially concerned with the destiny and problems of his race. His work encouraged as it must be, by the laws and spirit of the age, will determine his future and mark the commencement of the elimination of the shameful prejudice against him in the land, for which, from Lexington to the bloody trenches of France, he has given of his blood to preserve.

Before leaving the subject of the Negro in previous wars, it is highly fitting to review the heroic incident of June 21, 1916, at Carrizal, Mexico. Here is a tale of daring that to duplicate, would tax the imagination of war fiction writers, and among incidents of fact will range along with the Texans' defense of the Alamo, where men fought and perished against great odds.

The occasion was the celebrated expedition conducted by General J.J. Pershing into Mexico in pursuit of the bandit leader Villa. A picked detachment consisting of portions of Troops C and K of the colored Tenth Cavalry, was dispatched from Pershing's main force towards the town of Villa Ahumada. The force was commanded by Captain Charles T. Boyd of Troop C and Captain Lewis Morey of Troop K. Lieutenant Adair was second in command in Troop C to Captain Boyd. Including officers and civilian scouts, the force numbered about 80 men.

Early on the morning of June 21, the detachment wishing to pass through the garrisoned town of Carrizal, sought the permission of the Mexican commander. Amidst a show of force, the officers were invited into the town by the commander, ostensibly for a parley. Fearing a trap they refused the invitation and invited the Mexicans to a parley outside the town. The Mexican commander came out with his entire force and began to dispose them in positions which were very threatening to the Americans. Captain Boyd informed the Mexican that his orders were to proceed eastward to Ahumada and protested against the menacing position of the Mexican forces. The Mexican replied that his orders were to prevent the Americans from proceeding in any direction excepting northward, the direction from which they had just come.

Captain Boyd refused to retreat, but ordered his men not to fire until they were attacked. The Mexican commander retired to the flank and almost immediately opened with machine gun fire from a concealed trench. This was quickly followed by rifle fire from the remainder of the force. The Mexicans outnumbered the troopers nearly two to one and their most effective force was intrenched. The Americans were on a flat plain, unprotected by anything larger than bunches of cactus or sage brush. They dismounted, laid flat on the ground and responded to the attack as best they could. The horses were mostly stampeded by the early firing.

The spray of lead from the machine gun had become so galling that Captain Boyd decided to charge the position. Not a man wavered in the charge. They took the gun, the Captain falling dead across the barrel of it just as the last Mexican was killed or put to flight. Lieutenant Adair was also killed. The Mexicans returned in force and recaptured the position.

Captain Morey had been concerned in warding off a flank attack. His men fought no less bravely than the others. They finally were driven to seek refuge in an adobe house, that is; all who were able to reach it. Here they kept the Mexicans at bay for hours firing through windows and holes in the walls. Captain Morey seriously wounded, with a few of his survivors, finally escaped from the house and hid for nearly two days in a hole. The soldiers refused to leave their officer. When they finally were able to leave their place of concealment, the several that were left assisted their Captain on the road towards the main force. Arriving at a point where reinforcements could be summoned, the Captain wrote a report to his commander and sent his men to headquarters with it. They arrived in record time and a party was sent out, reaching the wounded officer in time to save his life.

About half of the American force was wiped out and most of the others were taken prisoners. They inflicted a much heavier loss on the Mexicans. Among the killed was the Mexican commander who had ordered the treacherous attack.

It may be that "someone had blundered." This was not the concern of the black troopers; in the face of odds they fought by the cactus and lay dead under the Mexican stars.

In closing this outline of the Negro's participation in former wars, it is highly appropriate to quote the tributes of two eminent men. One, General Benjamin F. Butler, a conspicuous military leader on the Union side in the Civil War, and Wendell Phillips, considered by many the greatest orator America ever produced, and who devoted his life to the abolition movement looking to the freedom of the slave in the United States. Said General Butler on the occasion of the debate in the National House of Representatives on the Civil Rights bill; ten years after the bloody battle of New Market Heights; speaking to the bill, and referring to the gallantry of the black soldiers on that field of strife:

> *"It became my painful duty to follow in the track of that charging column, and there, in a space not wider than the clerk's desk and three hundred*

yards long, lay the dead bodies of 543 of my colored comrades, fallen in defense of their country, who had offered their lives to uphold its flag and its honor, as a willing sacrifice; and as I rode along among them, guiding my horse this way and that way, lest he should profane with his hoofs what seemed to me the sacred dead, and as I looked on their bronzed faces upturned in the shining sun, as if in mute appeal against the wrongs of the country whose flag had only been to them a flag of stripes, on which no star of glory had ever shone for them—feeling I had wronged them in the past and believing what was the future of my country to them—among my dead comrades there I swore to myself a solemn oath, 'May my right hand forget its cunning and my tongue cleave to the roof of my mouth, if I ever fail to defend the rights of those men who have given their blood for me and my country this day, and for their race forever,' and, God helping me, I will keep that oath."

Mr. Phillips in his great oration on Toussaint L'Ouverture, the Black of St. Domingo; statesman, warrior and LIBERATOR,—delivered in New York City, March 11, 1863, said among other things, a constellation of linguistic brilliants not surpassed since the impassioned appeals of Cicero swept the Roman Senate to its feet, or Demosthenes fired his listeners with the flame of his matchless eloquence;

"You remember that Macaulay says, comparing Cromwell with Napoleon, that Cromwell showed the greater military genius, if we consider that he never saw an army till he was forty; while Napoleon was educated from a boy in the best military schools in Europe. Cromwell manufactured his own army; Napoleon at the age of twenty-seven was placed at the head of the best troops Europe ever saw. They were both successful; but, says Macaulay, with such disadvantages, the Englishman showed the greater genius. Whether you allow the inference or not, you will at least grant that it is a fair mode of measurement.

"Apply it to Toussaint. Cromwell never saw an army until he was forty; this man never saw a soldier till he was fifty. Cromwell manufactured his own army—out of what? Englishmen—the best blood in Europe. Out of the middle class of Englishmen, the best blood of the island. And with it he conquered what? Englishmen—their equals. This man manufactured his army out of what? Out of what you call the despicable race of Negroes, debased, demoralized by two hundred years of slavery, 100,000 of them imported into the island within four years, unable to speak a dialect intelligible even to each other. Yet out of this mixed, and, as you say, despicable mass, he forged a thunderbolt, and hurled it at what? At the proudest blood in Europe, the Spaniard, and sent him home conquered; at the most

warlike blood in Europe, the French, and put them under his feet; at the pluckiest blood in Europe, the English, and they skulked home to Jamaica."

The world is acquainted with the treacherous infamy inspired by the great Napoleon, that inveigled the Black Chieftain and liberator of his people on shipboard, the voyage to France, and his subsequent death—STARVED!—in the dungeon of the prison castle of St. Joux.

Whittier, the poet evangelist, whose inspired verse contributed much to the crystallization of the sentiment and spirit that finally doomed African slavery in America, thus referred to the heartless tragedy and the splendid Black who was its victim:

> *"Sleep calmy in thy dungeon-tomb,*
> *Beneath Besancon's alien sky,*
> *Dark Haytien!—for the time shall come,*
> *Yea, even now is nigh—*
> *When, everywhere, thy name shall be*
> *Redeemed from color's infamy;*
> *And men shall learn to speak of thee,*
> *As one of earth's great spirits, born*
> *In servitude, and nursed in scorn,*
> *Casting aside the weary weight*
> *And fetters of its low estate,*
> *In that strong majesty of soul,*
> *Which knows no color, tongue or clime,*
> *Which still hath spurned the base control*
> *Of tyrants through all time!"*

CHAPTER XI

Hour of his Nation's Peril

Negro's Patriotic Attitude—Selective Draft in Effect—Features and Results—Bold Reliance on Faith in A People—No Color Line Drawn—Distribution of Registrants by States—Negro and White Registrations Compared—Negro Percentages Higher—Claimed Fewer Exemptions—Inductions by States—Better Physically than Whites—Tables, Facts and Figures

As stated in a previous chapter, the Negro's real opportunity to show his patriotic attitude did not come until the passage of the compulsory service law; selective draft, was the name attached to it later and by which it was generally known.

On May 18, 1917, the day the law was enacted by congress, no advocate of preparedness could with confidence have forecasted the success of it. There were many who feared the total failure of it. The history of the United States disclosed a popular adherence to the principle of voluntary enlistment, if not a repudiation of the principle of selection or compulsory military service.

It was to be expected that many people would look upon the law as highly experimental; as an act that, if it did not produce grave disorders in the country, would fall short of the results for which it was intended. It was fortunate for the country at this time, that the military establishment possessed in the person of General Crowder, one who had made a special study of selective drafts and other forms of compulsory service, not alone in this country, but throughout the nations of the world and back to the beginning of recorded history. He had become as familiar with all phases of it as though it had been a personal hobby and lifetime pursuit.

The law was extremely plain and permitted of no guessing or legal quibbling over its terms. It boldly recited the military obligations of citizenship. It vested the president with the most complete power of prescribing regulations calculated to strike a balance between the industrial, agricultural and economic needs of the nation on the one hand and the military need on the other.

Within 18 days between May 18, when the law was approved, and June 5, the day the president had fixed as registration day, a great, administrative machine was built. Practically the entire male citizenship of the United States within the age limits fixed by law, twenty-one to thirty years inclusive, presented itself at the 4,000 enrollment booths with a registered result of nearly 10,000,000 names. The project had been so systematized that within 48 hours almost complete registration returns had been assembled by telegraph in Washington.

The order in which the ten-million registrants were to be called was accomplished on July 20 by a great central lottery in Washington.

The boards proceeded promptly to call, to examine physically and to consider claims for exemption of over one and one half million men, a sufficient number to fill the first national quota of 687,000. Thus in less than three and one-half months the nation had accepted and vigorously executed a compulsory service law.

On June 5, 1918, 753,834 men were added to the rolls. On August 24, 1918, that number was increased by 159,161; finally on September 12, 1918, under the provision of the act of August 31,1918, 13,228,762 were added to the lists of those available for military service, which, including interim and other accessions, amounted to a grand total of 24,234,021 enrolled and subject to the terms of the Selective Service law. This tremendous exhibition of man power struck terror to the heart of the Hun and hastened him to, if possible, deliver a telling blow against the Allies before the wonderful strength and resources of the American nation could be brought to bear against him.

Commenting on the facility with which the selective draft was put into effect, the report of the Provost Marshall General stated in part:

> *"The expedition and smoothness with which the law was executed emphasized the remarkable flexibility, adaptability and efficiency of our system of government and the devotion of our people. Here was a gigantic project in which success was staked not on reliance in the efficiency of a man, or an hierarchy of men, or, primarily, on a system. Here was a bold reliance on faith in a people. Most exacting duties were laid with perfect confidence on the officials of every locality in the nation, from the governors of states to the registrars of elections, and upon private citizens of every condition, from men foremost in the industrial and political life of the nation to those who had never before been called upon to participate in the functions of govern-*

ment. *By all administrative tokens, the accomplishment of their task was magic."*

No distinction regarding color or race was made in the selective draft law, except so far as non-citizen Indians were exempt from the draft. But the organization of the army placed Negro soldiers in separate units; and the several calls for mobilization, were, therefore, affected by this circumstance, in that no calls could be issued for Negro registrants until the organizations were ready for them. Figures of total registration given previously in this chapter include interim accessions and some that automatically went on the rolls after September 12, 1918. Inasmuch as the tables prepared by the Provost Marshall General's department deal only with those placed on the rolls on regular registration days and do not include the accessions mentioned, comparisons which follow will be based on those tables. They show the total registration as 23,779,997, of which 21,489,470 were white and 2,290,527 were black. Following is a table showing the distribution of colored and white registrants by states:

	Total Colored and white registrants.	Colored registrants June 5, 1917 Colored to Sept 11, 1918.	Colored registrants Sept 12, 1918.	Total colored registrants.
United States	23,779,097	1,078,331	1,212,196	2,290,527
Alabama	444,692	81,963	81,410	163,373
Arizona	93,078	295	680	975
Arkansas	365,754	51,176	53,659	104,835
California	787,676	3,308	6,404	9,712
Colorado	215,178	1,103	1,867	2,970
Connecticut	373,676	3,524	4,659	8,183
Delaware	55,215	3,798	4,448	8,246
District of Columbia	89,808	11,045	15,433	26,478
Florida	208,931	39,013	43,019	82,032
Georgia	549,020	112,593	108,183	220,781
Idaho	103,740	254	255	509
Illinois	1,571,717	21,816	35,597	57,413
Indiana	639,431	11,289	16,549	27,838
Iowa	523,957	2,959	3,022	5,981
Kansas	381,315	5,575	7,448	13,023
Kentucky	486,599	25,850	30,182	56,032
Louisiana	391,654	76,223	82,256	158,479
Maine	159,350	163	179	342
Maryland	313,255	26,435	32,736	59,171
Massachusetts	884,030	6,044	8,056	14,100
Michigan	871,410	6,979	8,950	15,929
Minnesota	540,003	1,541	1,809	3,350
Mississippi	344,506	81,548	91,534	173,082
Missouri	764,428	22,796	31,524	54,320
Montana	196,999	320	494	814
Nebraska	286,147	1,614	2,417	4,031
Nevada	29,465	69	112	172
New Hampshire	95,035	77	98	175
New Jersey	761,238	14,056	19,340	33,396
New Mexico	80,158	235	350	595

State				
New York	2,503,290	25,974	35,299	61,273
North Carolina	480,901	73,357	69,168	142,525
North Dakota	159,391	65	165	230
Ohio	1,387,830	28,831	35,156	63,987
Oklahoma	423,864	14,305	23,253	37,563
Oregon	176,010	144	534	678
Pennsylvania	2,067,023	39,363	51,111	90,474
Rhode Island	134,232	1,573	1,913	3,486
South Carolina	307,229	74,265	74,912	149,177
South Dakota	142,783	144	171	315
Tennessee	474,253	43,735	51,059	94,794
Texas	989,571	83,671	82,775	166,446
Utah	100,038	169	392	561
Vermont	71,464	63	89	152
Virginia	464,903	64,358	75,816	140,174
Washington	319,337	373	1,353	1,726
West Virginia	324,975	13,292	14,652	27,944
Wisconsin	584,639	718	1,117	1,835
Wyoming	58,700	280	570	850

	Percent of total registrants	White registrants June 5, 1917 to Sept 11 1918	White registrants Sept 12, 1918	Total white registrants	Percent of total registrants
United States	9.83	9,562,515	11,926,955	21,480,470	90.37
Alabama	36.74	124,247	157,072	281,319	63.26
Arizona	1.05	39,884	52,219	92,103	98.95
Arkansas	28.66	117,111	143,808	260,919	71.34
California	1.23	312,994	464,970	777,964	98.77
Colorado	1.38	90,453	121,755	212,208	98.62
Connecticut	2.19	171,296	194,197	365,493	97.81
Delaware	14.93	20,761	26,208	46,969	85.07
District of Columbia	29.45	25,625	37,795	63,420	70.56
Florida	39.26	55,572	71,327	126,899	60.74
Georgia	40.22	147,604	180,635	328,239	59.78
Idaho	0.49	45,224	58,007	103,231	99.51
Illinois	3.65	685,254	829,050	1,514,304	96.35
Indiana	4.35	272,442	339,151	611,593	95.65
Iowa	1.14	237,744	280,232	517,976	98.86
Kansas	3.41	161,691	206,602	368,293	96.59
Kentucky	11.52	190,060	240,507	430,567	88.43
Louisiana	40.46	103,718	129,467	233,185	59.54
Maine	0.22	67,941	91,067	159,008	99.73
Maryland	18.89	110,066	144,018	254,084	81.11
Massachusetts	1.60	391,654	478,276	869,930	93.40
Michigan	1.83	404,040	451,441	855,481	98.17
Minnesota	0.62	247,750	288,903	538,653	99.38
Mississippi	50.24	75,977	95,447	171,424	49.76
Missouri	7.11	372,106	398,002	710,108	92.89
Montana	0.41	96,753	101,432	198,185	99.59
Nebraska	1.42	130,493	151,623	282,116	98.58
Nevada	0.58	12,581	16,712	29,293	99.42
New Hampshire	0.18	41,617	53,243	94,860	99.82
New Jersey	4.39	18,615	409,225	727,840	95.61
New Mexico	0.74	36,776	42,787	79,563	99.26
New York	2.44	1,092,061	1,349,956	2,442,617	97.56
North Carolina	29.63	155,102	183,274	338,376	70.37
North Dakota	0.15	72,837	85,324	159,161	98.85

Ohio	4.61	588,170	735,673	1,323,843	95.39
Oklahoma	8.86	173,851	212,450	386,301	91.15
Oregon	0.38	69,376	105,956	175,332	99.62
Pennsylvania	4.38	353,106	1,113,443	1,976,549	95.62
Rhode Island	2.59	57,433	73,313	130,746	12
South Carolina	48.56	70,395	87,657	158,052	51.44
South Dakota	0.23	64,896	77,572	142,468	99.77
Tennessee	19.99	169,674	209,785	379,459	80.01
Texas	16.82	376,385	446,740	823,125	83.18
Utah	0.56	45,930	53,547	99,477	99.44
Vermont	0.21	30,819	40,493	71,312	99.79
Virginia	30.15	141,714	183,015	324,727	69.85
Washington	0.54	123,752	193,859	317,611	99.46
West Virginia	8.60	128,852	168,179	297,031	91.40
Wisconsin	0.31	265,501	317,303	582,804	99.69
Wyoming	1.45	24,612	33,238	57,850	98.56

Results of the classification of December 15, 1917 to September 11, 1918, in respect to colored and white registrants are shown in the following table:

Colored and white classification compared	Number	Percent of total classified	Percent of classified.
Total colored and white registered:			
June 5, 1917, to Sept. 11, 1918	10,640,846	100.00	-----
Total colored registered	1,078,331	10.13	100.00
Class I	556,917	-----	51.65
Deferred classes	521,414	-----	-----
Total white registered	9,562,515	89.87	100.00
Class I	3,110,659	-----	32.53
Deferred classes	6,451,856	-----	-----
Percentage accepted for service on calls before Dec. 15, 1917 (report of 1917).			
Colored	-----	-----	36.23
White	-----	-----	24.75

It will be seen that a much higher percentage of Negroes were accepted for service than of white men. It is true that enlistments which were permitted white men but denied Negroes, depleted the whites eligible to Class 1 to some extent. Probably there were more Negro delinquents in proportion to their numbers in the south than white delinquents. The conditions under which they lived would account for that. Delinquents, under the regulations, were placed in Class 1. Then there is the undoubted fact that the Negro sought and was granted fewer exemptions on the ground of dependency. Many Negroes in the south, where the rate of pay was low, were put in Class 1 on the ground that their allotment and allowances while in the army, would furnish an equivalent support to their dependents. But whatever the reason, the great fact stands out that a much greater percentage of colored were accepted for service than white men. The following table gives the colored and white inductions by states:

	Total colored and white registrants, June 5, 1917, to Sept. 11, 1918.	Colored registrants, June 5, 1917, to Sept. 11, 1918.	Percentage of colored and white registrants.	Colored inducted June 5, 1917, to Nov. 11, 1918.	Per Percent of colored registrants.
United States	10,640,846	1,078,331	10.13	367,710	34.10
Alabama	206,210	81,963	39.75	25,874	31.57
Arizona	40,179	295	.73	77	26.10
Arkansas	168,287	51,176	30.41	17,544	34.28
California	316,302	3,308	1.05	919	27.78
Colorado	91,556	1,103	1.20	317	28.74
Connecticut	174,820	3,524	2.02	941	26.70
Delaware	24,559	3,798	15.46	1,365	35.93
District of Columbia	36,670	11,045	30.12	4,000	36.22
Florida	94,585	39,013	41.25	12,904	33.08
Georgia	260,197	112,593	43.27	34,303	30.47
Idaho	45,478	254	.56	95	37.40
Illinois	707,070	21,816	3.09	8,754	40.13
Indiana	283,731	11,289	3.98	4,579	40.56
Iowa	240,703	2,959	1.23	929	31.40
Kansas	167,266	5,575	3.33	2,127	38.15
Kentucky	215,910	25,850	11.98	11,320	43.79
Louisiana	179,941	76,223	42.36	28,711	37.67
Maine	68,104	163	.24	50	30.67
Maryland	136,501	26,435	19.37	9,212	34.85
Massachusetts	397,698	6,044	1.52	1,200	19.85
Michigan	411,019	6,979	1.70	2,395	34.32
Minnesota	249,291	1,541	.62	511	53.16
Mississippi	157,525	81,548	51.77	24,066	29.51
Missouri	334,902	22,796	6.81	9,219	40.44
Montana	97,073	320	.33	198	61.87
Nebraska	132,107	1,614	1.22	642	39.78
Nevada	12,640	59	.47	26	44.07
New Hampshire	41,694	77	.18	27	35.07
New Jersey	332,671	14,056	4.23	4,863	34.60
New Mexico	37,011	235	.63	51	21.70
New York	1,118,035	25,974	2.32	6,193	23.84
North Carolina	228,459	73,357	32.11	20,082	27.38
North Dakota	72,902	65	.09	87	-----
Ohio	617,001	28,831	4.67	7,861	27.27
Oklahoma	188,156	14,305	7.60	5,694	39.80
Oregon	69,520	144	.21	68	47.22
Pennsylvania	902,469	39,363	4.36	15,392	39.10
Rhode Island	59,006	1,573	2.67	291	18.50
South Carolina	144,660	74,265	51.34	25,798	34.74
South Dakota	65,040	144	.22	62	43.06
Tennessee	213,409	43,735	20.59	17,774	40.64
Texas	460,056	83,671	18.19	31,506	37.65
Utah	46,099	169	.37	77	45.56
Vermont	30,882	63	.20	22	34.92
Virginia	206,072	64,358	31.23	23,541	36.57
Washington	124,125	373	.30	173	46.38
West Virginia	142,144	13,292	9.35	5,492	41.32
Wisconsin	266,219	718	.27	224	31.20
Wyoming	24,892	280	1.12	95	23.93
Alaska				5	
Hawaii					
Porto Rico					

History of the American Negro in the Great World War

	White registrants, June 5, 1917, to Sept. 11, 1918.	Percent of colored and white registrants.	White inductions, June 5, 1917, to Nov. 11, 1918.	Percent of white registrants.
United States	9,562,515	89.87	2,299,157	24.04
Alabama	124,247	60.25	33,881	27.27
Arizona	39,884	99.27	8,036	20.15
Arkansas	117,111	69.59	31,768	27.13
California	312,994	98.95	60,148	21.13
Colorado	90,453	98.80	22,487	24.86
Connecticut	171,296	97.98	31,598	18.45
Delaware	20,761	84.54	3,628	17.48
District of Columbia	25,625	69.88	5,631	21.97
Florida	55,572	58.75	12,012	21.62
Georgia	147,604	56.73	32,538	32.04
Idaho	45,224	99.44	12,471	27.58
Illinois	685,254	96.91	68,729	24.62
Indiana	272,442	96.02	65,170	23.92
Iowa	237,744	98.77	65,935	27.73
Kansas	161,691	96.67	39,778	21.60
Kentucky	190,060	88.02	47,010	24.60
Louisiana	103,718	57.64	27,494	26.51
Maine	67,941	99.76	15,216	22.40
Maryland	110,066	80.63	24,655	22.40
Massachusetts	391,654	98.48	75,367	19.24
Michigan	404,040	98.30	94,085	23.29
Minnesota	247,750	99.38	73,169	29.53
Mississippi	75,977	48.23	19,296	25.40
Missouri	312,106	93.19	83,624	26.79
Montana	96,753	99.67	27,142	28.05
Nebraska	130,493	98.78	29,165	22.35
Nevada	12,581	99.53	8,138	24.94
New Hampshire	41,617	99.82	8,377	20.13
New Jersey	318,615	95.77	66,527	20.88
New Mexico	36,776	99.37	8,811	23.96
New York	1,092,061	97.68	247,396	22.65
North Carolina	155,102	67.89	38,359	24.73
North Dakota	72,837	99.91	18,508	25.41
Ohio	568,170	95.83	130,287	22.15
Oklahoma	173,851	92.40	59,247	34.08
Oregon	69,376	99.79	16,090	23.19
Pennsylvania	863,106	95.64	185,819	21.53
Rhode Island	57,433	97.33	10,885	18.95
South Carolina	70,395	48.66	18,261	25.94
South Dakota	64,896	99.78	21,193	32.66
Tennessee	169,674	79.51	42,104	24.81
Texas	376,385	81.81	85,889	22.82
Utah	45,930	99.63	10,711	23.32
Vermont	30,819	99.80	6,607	21.44
Virginia	141,714	68.77	34,796	24.55
Washington	123,752	99.70	28,513	23.04
West Virginia	128,852	90.65	39,863	30.94
Wisconsin	265,501	99.73	70,758	26.65
Wyoming	24,612	98.88	7,828	31.81
Alaska			1,957	
Hawaii			5,406	
Porto Rico			15,734	

Further light on the question of more Negroes in proportion to their numbers being selected for service than white men, is found in a comparison of the Negroes and whites rejected for physical reasons. The following table gives the figures for the period between December 15, 1917 and September 11, 1918:

Colored and white physical rejections compared.	Number.	Percent of examined	Percent of partial disqualifications.
Total, colored and white examined Dec. 15, 1917, to Sept. 11, 1918	3,208,446	100.00	-----
Group A	2,259,027	70.41	-----
Disqualified partly or totally	949,419	-----	100.00
Group B	88,436	2.76	9.31
Group C	339,377	10.58	35.75
Group D	521,606	16.25	54.94
Total, colored examined	458,838	100.00	-----
Group A	342,277	74.60	-----
Disqualified partly or totally	116,561	-----	100.00
Group B	9,605	2.09	8.24
Group C	27,474	5.99	23.57
Group D	79,482	17.32	68.19
Total white examined	2,749,608	100.00	-----
Group A	1,916,750	69.71	-----
Disqualified partly or totally	832,858	-----	100.00
Group B	78,831	2.87	9.47
Group C	311,903	11.34	37.45
Group D	442,124	16.08	53.08

The percentage of Negroes unqualifiedly accepted for service, was 74.60% of the number examined; the white men accepted numbered 69.71% of the number examined. The Negroes it will be seen rated about 5% higher physically than the whites. No better refutation could be desired of the charge, having its inspiration in the vanquished, but unrepentant defenders of Negro slavery, mourning about its dead carcass, that the Negro is deteriorating physically, or that the so-called degenerative influences of civilization affect him in greater degree than they do the white man.

CHAPTER XII

Negro Slackers and Pacifists Unknown

Such Words not in his Vocabulary—Desertions Explained—General Crowder Exonerates Negro—No Willful Delinquency—Strenuous Efforts to Meet Regulations—No "Conscientious Objectors"—No Draft Evaders or Resisters—Negro's Devotion Sublime—Justifies his Freedom—Forgets his Sorrows—Rises Above his Wrongs—Testimony of Local Boards—German Propaganda Wasted—A New Americanism

The only phase of the selective draft in which the Negro seemed to be discredited in comparison with his white brother, was in the matter of desertions. At first glance and without proper analysis, the record appeared to be against the Negro. Upon detailed study, however, the case takes on a different aspect. The records of the Provost Marshall General show that out of 474,861 reported deserters, 369,030 were white registrants, and 105,831 colored, the ratio of white reported deserters to white registrants being 3.86, and the ratio of colored reported deserters to colored registrants being 9.81. Everyone knows now that many, yes, the bulk of the reported desertions among both whites and blacks, were not desertions at all. Circumstances simply prevented the men from keeping in touch with their local boards or from reporting when called.

Desertions among white registrants might have shown a greater percentage had they not availed themselves of the exemption feature of the law. Negroes did not understand this clause in the act so well. Besides, as previously stated, many Negroes were placed in Class 1, even where they had dependants, because their rate of pay in the army would enable them to contribute as much to the support of their dependants as would their earnings outside of army service.

This was a policy with many draft boards, but it is not exactly clear in view of the increased earning power of the Negroes through wartime demands for their labor. Following are the complete figures on so-called desertions, the variances in the several states being given:

W. Allison Sweeney

	Total white and colored registrants, June 5, 1917, to Sept. 11, 1918.	Total white registrants	Reported desertions, white	Percent of total registrants	Percent of white registrants
United States	10,640,846	9,562,515	380,030	3.47	3.86
Alabama	206,210	194,247	3,672	1.78	2.96
Arizona	40,179	39,884	6,930	17.36	17.40
Kansas	168,287	117,111	2,476	1.47	2.11
California	316,302	313,994	15,323	4.84	4.90
Colorado	91,556	90,463	4,910	5.38	5.43
Connecticut	174,820	171,296	12,416	7.10	7.25
Delaware	24,559	20,761	686	2.79	3.30
District of Columbia	36,670	25,625	390	1.06	1.52
Florida	94,585	55,572	1,823	1.93	3.28
Georgia	260,197	147,001	4,499	1.73	3.05
Idaho	45,478	45,224	2,242	4.93	4.96
Illinois	707,070	685,254	21,673	3.07	3.16
Indiana	283,731	272,442	5,252	1.85	1.93
Iowa	240,703	237,744	5,283	2.19	2.21
Kansas	167,266	161,691	3,172	1.90	1.96
Kentucky	215,910	190,060	2,830	1.03	1.23
Louisiana	179,941	103,718	2,250	1.25	2.17
Maine	68,104	67,941	2,553	3.74	3.76
Maryland	136,501	110,066	3,831	2.81	3.48
Massachusetts	397,698	391,654	19,841	4.99	5.07
Michigan	411,019	404,040	17,222	4.19	4.26
Minnesota	249,291	247,750	10,108	4.05	4.08
Mississippi	157,525	75,977	1,713	1.09	2.25
Missouri	334,902	312,106	10,549	3.14	3.38
Montana	97,073	96,753	7,835	8.13	8.16
Nebraska	132,107	130,493	2,608	1.97	2.00
Nevada	12,640	12,581	1,392	1.10	11.06
New Hampshire	41,694	41,617	1,428	3.42	3.43
New Jersey	332,671	318,815	15,114	4.54	4.74
New Mexico	37,011	36,776	3,217	8.69	8.75
New York	1,118,035	1,092,061	57,021	5.10	5.22
North Carolina	228,459	155,102	1,175	5.14	.76
North Dakota	72,902	72,837	2,520	3.46	3.46
Ohio	617,001	588,170	22,846	3.70	3.88
Oklahoma	188,156	173,851	5,860	3.11	3.37
Oregon	69,520	69,376	2,023	2.91	2.92
Pennsylvania	902,469	863,106	31,739	3.52	3.68
Rhode Island	59,006	57,433	2,340	3.97	4.07
South Carolina	144,660	70,395	1,107	.77	1.57
South Dakota	65,040	64,896	1,243	1.91	1.92
Tennessee	213,409	169,674	4,389	2.05	2.58
Texas	460,056	376,385	19,209	4.18	5.10
Utah	46,099	45,930	1,735	3.76	3.78
Vermont	30,882	30,819	690	2.23	2.71
Virginia	206,072	141,714	3,090	1.50	2.18
Washington	124,125	123,752	7,261	5.85	5.87
West Virginia	142,144	128,852	4,803	3.38	3.73
Wisconsin	266,219	265,501	4,663	1.75	1.76
Wyoming	24,892	24,612	1,734	6.96	7.05
Alaska			601		
Hawaii			184		
Porto Rico			15		

History of the American Negro in the Great World War

	Total colored registrants.	Reported desertions, colored.	Percent of total registrants.	Percent of colored registrants.
United States	1,078,331	105,831	.99	9.81
Alabama	81,963	10,835	5.25	13.22
Arizona	295	64	.16	21.69
Arkansas	51,176	4,770	2.83	9.32
California	3,303	268	.08	8.10
Colorado	1,103	91	.10	8.25
Connecticut	3,524	682	.39	19.35
Delaware	3,798	303	1.23	7.98
District of Columbi	11,045	616	1.68	5.58
Florida	39,013	8,319	8.71	21.32
Georgia	112,593	8,969	3.45	7.97
Idaho	254	108	.23	42.51
Illinois	21,816	2,911	.41	13.34
Indiana	11,289	1,199	.42	10.62
Iowa	2,959	517	.21	17.47
Kansas	5,575	255	.15	4.57
Kentucky	25,850	1,524	.71	5.90
Louisiana	76,223	5,962	3.31	7.82
Maine	163	29	.04	17.79
Maryland	26,435	2,410	1.77	9.12
Massachusetts	6,044	665	1.67	11.00
Michigan	6,979	1,015	.25	14.54
Minnesota	1,541	621	.25	40.30
Mississippi	81,548	8,112	5.15	9.95
Missouri	22,796	1,791	.53	7.86
Montana	320	114	.12	35.63
Nebraska	1,614	229	.17	14.19
Nevada	59	3	.02	6.08
New Hampshire	77	3	.01	3.90
New Jersey	14,056	1,535	.46	10.92
New Mexico	235	40	.11	17.02
New York	25,974	4,062	.36	15.64
North Carolina	73,357	4,937	2.16	6.73
North Dakota	65	19	.03	29.23
Ohio	28,831	4,048	.66	14.04
Oklahoma	14,305	1,223	.65	8.56
Oregon	144	18	.03	12.59
Pennsylvania	39,363	6,599	.73	16.76
Rhode Island	1,573	251	.43	15.96
South Carolina	74,265	4,589	3.14	6.18
South Dakota	144	27	.04	18.75
Tennessee	43,735	3,573	1.67	8.17
Texas	83,671	5,388	1.17	6.44
Utah	169	11	.02	6.51
Vermont	63	4	.01	6.35
Virginia	64,358	4,935	2.39	7.67
Washington	373	30	.02	8.04
West Virginia	13,292	2,013	1.41	15.14
Wisconsin	718	73	.03	10.17
Wyoming	280	63	.25	22.50

Negro troops newly arrived in France, lined up for inspection.

Negro troops on a practice run near their camp in France.

Official photographs, U.S. Army presentation of banner to negro Stevedores for winning first week's "Race to Berlin", Marseilles, France.

Official photographs, U.S. Army negro winners in stevedore contest being entertained by 134th infantry quartet and band at Marseilles, France.

Going to fight for Uncle Sam. Typical group of negro selective service men leaving for the training camp.

Negro troops arriving in France. A comparison with the upper picture shows the rapid transformation from civilians to fighting men.

"Moss's buffaloes" (367th Infantry), serenading famous military chieftains in France. In window at left stands General John J. Pershing, Commander-in-Chief of American expeditionary forces; at right General Gouraud, Commander of the Fourth French Army.

Heroes of the brawny arm whose service was no less effective than that of the combatants. A detail of negro railway builders engaged on the line from Brest to Tours.

Negro engineers building roads in France. An indispensable feature of the service of supply.

Negro troops in France enjoy an old-fashioned meal.

Negro machine gunners on the road near Maffrecourt, France. Part of 369th Infantry.

Captain Hinton and officers of 1st Battalion. 369th Negro Infantry on road near Maffrecourt, France.

W. Allison Sweeney

Auto horn warns Americans of coming gas attack. Soldiers don masks and sound the alarm. Insert, left corner, machine gunners.

No elaborate defense of the Negro will be attempted in the matter of the desertion record. It is not necessary. The words of Provost Marshall General Crowder, the man who knew all about the selective draft and who engineered it through its wonderfully successful course, completely absolved the Negro in this connection. The following quotation in reference to the above figures is taken verbatim from the report of General Crowder to the Secretary of War, dated December 20, 1918.

> *"These figures of reported desertions, however, lose their significance when the facts behind them are studied. There is in the files of this office, a series of letters from governors and draft executives of southern states, called forth by inquiry for an explanation of the large percentage of Negroes among the reported deserters and delinquents. With striking unanimity the draft authorities replied that this was due to two causes; first, ignorance and illiteracy; especially in the rural regions, to which may be added a certain shiftlessness in ignoring civic obligations; and secondly, the tendency of the Negroes to shift from place to place. The natural inclination to roam from one employment to another has been accentuated by unusual demands for labor incident to the war, resulting in a considerable flow of colored men to the north and to various munition centers. This shifting reached its height in the summer of 1917, shortly after the first registration, and resulted in the failure of many men to keep in touch with their local boards, so that questionnaires and notices to report did not reach them.*

> *"With equal unanimity the draft executives report that the amount of willful delinquency or desertion has been almost nil. Several describe the strenuous efforts of the Negroes to comply with the regulations, when the requirements were explained to them, many registrants travelling long distances to report in person to the adjutant general of the state. 'The conviction resulting from these reports' says General Crowder, 'is that the colored men as a whole responded readily and gladly to their military obligations once their duties were understood."*

So far as the records show, there were neither "slackers" nor "pacifists" among the Negroes. Hon. Emmett J. Scott, Special Assistant to the Secretary of War, said that the war department had heard of only two colored "conscientious objectors". When those two were cross-examined it was revealed that they had misinterpreted their motives and that their objections proceeded from a source very remote from their consciences.

Pacifists and conscientious objectors came principally from the class who held religious scruples against war or the taking up of arms. The law permitted these to enter a special so-called non-combatant classification.

It is a well known fact that Negro religionists are members of the church militant, so they could not be included in the self-declared conscientious pacifistic sects.

Neither was the Negro represented in that class known as draft resisters or draft evaders. A very good reason exists in the fact that opposition to the draft came from a class which did not admit the Negro to membership. Practically all draft resistance was traceable to the activities of radicals, whose fantastic dreams enchanted and seduced the ignorant and artless folk who came under their influence.

The resisters were all poor whites led by professional agitators. Negroes had no such organizations nor leaders.

The part played by the Negro in the great world drama upon which the curtain has fallen, was not approached in sublime devotion by that displayed by any other class of America's heterogeneous mixture of tribe and race, hailing from all the ends of the earth, that composes its great and wonderful population. Blind in a sense; unreasoning as a child in the sacredness and consecration of his fealty; clamoring with the fervor of an ancient crusader; his eye on heaven, his steps turned towards the Holy Sepulchre, for a chance to go; a time and place to die, HIS was a distinct and marked patriotism; quite alone in "splendid isolation" but shining like the sun; unstreaked with doubt; unmixed with cavil or question, which, finally given reign on many a spot of strife in "Sunny France"; the Stars and Stripes above him; a prayer in his heart; a song upon his lips, spelt death, but death glorious; where he fell—HOLY GROUND!

"The fittest place where man can DIE Is where he dies for man!"

A product of slavery, ushered into a sphere of civil and political activity, clouded and challenged by the sullen resentment of his former masters; his soul still embittered by defeat; slowly working his way through many hindrances toward the achievement of success that would enable both him and the world to justify the new life of freedom that had come to him; faced at every hand by the prejudice born of tradition; enduring wrongs that "would stir a fever in the blood of age"; still the slave to a large extent of superstition fed by ignorance, is it to be wondered at that some doubt was felt and expressed by the best friends of the Negro, when the call came for a draft upon the man power of the nation; whether, in the face of the great wrongs heaped upon him; the persecutions he had passed through and was still enduring, he would be able to forgive and forget; could and would so rise above his sorrows as to reach to the height and the full duty of citizenship; would give to the Stars and Stripes the response that was due? On the part of many leaders among the Negroes, there was apprehension that the sense of fair play and fair dealing, which is so essentially an American characteristic, when white men are involved, would not be meted out to the members of their race.

How groundless such fears, may be seen from the statistical record of the draft with relation to the Negro. His race furnished its quota uncomplainingly and cheerfully. History, indeed, will be unable to record the fullness and grandeur of his spirit in the war, for the reason that opportunities, especially for enlistment, as heretofore mentioned, were not opened to him to the same extent as to the whites. But enough can be gathered from the records to show that he was filled not only with patriotism, but of a brand, all things considered, than which there was no other like it.

That the men of the Negro race were as ready to serve as the white is amply proved by the reports of local boards. A Pennsylvania board, remarking upon the eagerness of its Negro registrants to be inducted, illustrated it by the action of one registrant, who, upon learning that his employer had had him placed upon the Emergency Fleet list, quit his job. Another registrant who was believed by the board to be above draft age insisted that he was not, and in stating that he was not married, explained that he "wanted only one war at a time."

The following descriptions from Oklahoma and Arkansas boards are typical, the first serving to perpetuate one of the best epigrams of the war:

> *"We tried to treat the Negroes with exactly the same consideration shown the whites. We had the same speakers to address them. The Rotary Club presented them with small silk flags, as they did the whites. The band turned out to escort them to the train; and the Negroes went to camp with as cheerful a spirit as did the whites. One of them when asked if he were going to France, replied: 'No, sir; I'm not going "to France". I am going "through France".'"*

> *"In dealing with the Negroes,"* the *Arkansas board report says, "the southern boards gained a richness of experience that is without parallel. No other class of citizens was more loyal to the government or more ready to answer the country's call. The only blot upon their military record was the great number of delinquents among the more ignorant; but in the majority of cases this was traced to an ignorance of the regulations, or to the withholding of mail by the landlord, often himself an aristocratic slacker, in order to retain the man's labor."*

Many influences were brought to bear upon the Negro to cause him to evade his duty to the government. Some effort in certain sections of the country was made to induce them not to register. That the attempt to spread German propaganda among them was a miserable failure may be seen from the statement of the Chief of the Bureau of Investigation of the Department of Justice, made to the United States Senate committee:

> *"The Negroes didn't take to these stories, however, as they were too loyal. Money spent in the south for propaganda was thrown away."*

Then too, these evil influences were more than offset by the various publicity and "promotion of morale" measures carried on through the office of the special assistant to the Secretary of War, the Hon. Emmet J. Scott, and his assistants. Correspondence was kept up with influential Negroes all over the country. Letters, circulars and news items for the purpose of effecting and encouraging continued loyalty of Negro citizens, were regularly issued to the various papers comprising both the white and Negro press. A special committee of 100 colored speakers was appointed to deliver public patriotic addresses all over the country, under the auspices of the Committee on Public Information, stating the war aims of the government and seeking to keep unbroken the spirit of loyalty of Negro American citizens. A special conference of Negro editors was summoned to Washington in June, 1918 by the same committee in order to gather and disseminate the thought and public opinion of the various leaders of the Negro race. Such was only a part of the work of the department of the special assistant to the Secretary of War in marshalling the man power of the nation.

Negro troops of u.s. army receiving holy baptism while in training for overseas duty at norcross rifle range. Camp cordon, ga.

It is only fair to quote the opinion and appreciation of this representative of the Negro race of the selective service administration, especially as it affected the Negro and in reference to occasional complaints received. The extract is from a memorandum addressed to the office of the Provost Marshal General on September 12, 1918 and is copied from the report of that official to the Secretary of War:

> *"Throughout my tenure here I have keenly appreciated the prompt and cordial cooperation of the Provost Marshall General's office with that particular section of the office of the Secretary of War especially referred to herein. The Provost Marshall General's office has carefully investigated and has furnished full and complete reports in each and every complaint or case referred to it for attention, involving discrimination, race prejudice, erroneous classification of draftees, etc., and has rectified these complaints whenever it was found upon investigation that there was just ground for same. Especially in the matter of applying and carrying out the selective service regulations, the Provost Marshall General's office has kept a watchful eye upon certain local exemption boards which seemed disinclined to treat the Negro draftees on the same basis as other Americans subject to*

> *the draft law. It is an actual fact that in a number of instances where flagrant violations have occurred in the application of the draft law, to Negro men in certain sections of the country, local exemption boards have been removed bodily and new boards have been appointed to supplant them. In several instances these new boards so appointed have been ordered by the Provost Marshall General to reclassify colored men who had been unlawfully conscripted into the army or who had been wrongfully classified; as a result of this action hundreds of colored men have had their complaints remedied and have been properly reclassified."*

It is also valuable to note the opinion of this representative of his race as to the results of the negroes' participation in the war:

"In a word, I believe the Negro's participation in the war, his eagerness to serve, and his great courage and demonstrated valor across the seas, have given him a new idea of Americanism and likewise have given to the white people of our country a new idea of his citizenship, his real character and capabilities, and his 100 per cent Americanism. Incidentally the Negro has been helped in many ways physically and mentally and has been made into an even more satisfactory asset to the nation."

Of the Negroes inducted into service, nearly all were assigned to some department of the army or to special work in connection with the army. Of the few who were permitted to enlist, a very small percentage was permitted to enlist in the Navy. Of this small number only a few were allowed the regular training and opportunities of combatants, to the DISCREDIT of our nation, not as yet, grown to that moral vision and all around greatness, NOT to be small.

CHAPTER XIII

Roster Of Negro Officers

Commissioned at Fort Des Moines—Only Exclusive Negro Training Camp—Mostly from Civilian Life—Names, Rank and Residence

Fort Des Moines, Iowa, was the only training camp established in the United States exclusively for Negro officers. A few were trained and commissioned at Camps Hancock, Pike and Taylor, and a few received commissions at officers' training camps in France, but the War Department records do not specify which were white and which Negro. The Fort Des Moines camp lasted from June until October 1917. Following is the roster of Negro officers commissioned. With the exception of those specified as from the United States Army or the National Guard, all came from civilian life:

Cleve L. Abbott, first lieutenant, Watertown, S.D.

Joseph L. Abernethy, first lieutenant, Prairie View, Tex.

Ewart G. Abner, second lieutenant, Conroe, Tex.

Charles J. Adams, first lieutenant, Selma, Ala.

Aurelious P. Alberga, first lieutenant, San Francisco, Calif.

Ira L. Aldridge, second lieutenant, New York, N.Y.

Edward I. Alexander, first lieutenant, Jacksonville, Fla.

Fritz W. Alexander, second lieutenant, Donaldsville, Ga.

Lucien V. Alexis, first lieutenant, Cambridge, Mass.

John H. Allen, captain, U.S. Army.

Levi Alexander, Jr., first lieutenant, Ocala, Fla.

Clarence W. Allen, second lieutenant, Mobile, Ala.

Richard S. Allen, second lieutenant, Atlantic City, N.J.

James W. Alston, first lieutenant, Raleigh, N.C.
Benjamin E. Ammons, first lieutenant, Kansas City, Mo.
Leon M. Anderson, first lieutenant, Washington, D.C.
Levi Anderson, first lieutenant, Washington, D.C.
Robert Anderson, first lieutenant, U.S. Army.
David W. Anthony, Jr., first lieutenant, St. Louis, Mo.
James C. Arnold, first lieutenant, Atlanta, Ga.
Russell C. Atkins, second lieutenant, Winston-Salem, N.C.
Henry O. Atwood, captain, Washington, D.C.
Charles H. Austin, second lieutenant, U.S. Army.
George J. Austin, first lieutenant. New York, N.Y.
Herbert Avery, captain, U.S. Army.
Robert S. Bamfield, second lieutenant, Wilmington, N.C.
Julian C. Banks, second lieutenant, Kansas City, Mo.
Charles H. Barbour, captain, U.S. Army.
Walter B. Barnes, first lieutenant, U.S. Army.
William I. Barnes, first lieutenant, Washington, D.C.
Stephen B. Barrows, second lieutenant, U.S. Army.
Thomas J. Batey, first lieutenant, Oakland, Cal.
Wilfrid Bazil, second lieutenant, Brooklyn, N.Y.
James E. Beard, first lieutenant, U.S. Army.
Ether Beattie, second lieutenant, U.S. Army.
William H. Benson, first lieutenant, Atlanta, Ga.
Albert P. Bentley, first lieutenant, Memphis, Tenn.
Benjamin Bettis, second lieutenant, U.S. Army.
Harrison W. Black, first lieutenant, Lexington, Ky.
Charles J. Blackwood, first lieutenant, Trinidad, Colo.
William Blaney, first lieutenant, U.S. Army.

Isaiah S. Blocker, first lieutenant, Atlanta, Ga.

William D. Bly, first lieutenant, Leavenworth, Kans.

Henry H. Boger, second lieutenant, Aurora, Ill.

Elbert L. Booker, first lieutenant, Wymer, Wash.

Virgil M. Boutte, captain, Nashville, Tenn.

Jas. F. Booker, captain, U.S. Army.

William R. Bowie, second lieutenant, Washington, D.C.

Clyde R. Brannon, first lieutenant, Fremont, Neb.

Lewis Broadus, captain, U.S. Army.

Deton J. Brooks, first lieutenant, Chicago, Ill.

William M. Brooks, second lieutenant, Des Moines, Ia.

Carter N. Brown, first lieutenant, Atlanta, Ga.

Emmet Brown, first lieutenant, St. Louis, Mo.

George E. Brown, second lieutenant, New York City, N.Y.

Oscar C. Brown, first lieutenant, Edwards, Miss.

Rosen T. Brown, first lieutenant, U.S. Army.

Samuel C. Brown, second lieutenant, Delaware, Ohio.

William H. Brown, Jr., first lieutenant, U.S. Army.

Arthur A. Browne, first lieutenant, Xenia, Ohio.

Howard R.M. Browne, first lieutenant, Kansas City, Kans.

Sylvanus Brown, first lieutenant, San Antonio, Tex.

Charles C. Bruen, first lieutenant, Mayslick, Ky.

William T. Burns, first lieutenant, U.S. Army.

James A. Bryant, first lieutenant, Indianapolis, Ind.

William L. Bryson, captain, U.S. Army.

John E. Buford, second lieutenant, Langston, Okla.

Thomas J. Bullock, second lieutenant, New York City, N.Y.

John W. Bundrant, second lieutenant, Omaha, Neb.

John P. Burgess, first lieutenant, Mullens, S.C.

Dace H. Burns, first lieutenant, Chicago, Ill.

William H. Burrell, second lieutenant, Washington, D.C.

John M. Burrell, second lieutenant, East Orange, N.J.

Herman L. Butler, first lieutenant, U.S. Army,

Homer C. Butler, first lieutenant, New York, N.Y.

Felix Buggs, second lieutenant, U.S. Army.

Napoleon L. Byrd, first lieutenant, Madison, Wis.

John B. Cade, second lieutenant, Ellerton, Ga.

Walter W. Cagle, first lieutenant, U.S. Army.

Charles W. Caldwell, second lieutenant, Orangeburg, S.C.

Andrew B. Callahan, second lieutenant, Montgomery, Ala.

Alvin H. Cameron, first lieutenant, Nashville, Tenn.

Alonzo Campbell, captain, U.S. Army.

Lafayette Campbell, second lieutenant, Union, W. Va.

Robert L. Campbell, first lieutenant, Greensboro, N.C.

William B. Campbell, first lieutenant, Austin, Tex.

Guy W. Canady, first lieutenant, Atlanta, Ga.

Lovelace B. Capehart, Jr., second lieutenant, Raleigh, N.C.

Adolphus F. Capps, second lieutenant, Philadelphia, Pa.

Curtis W. Carpenter, second lieutenant, Baltimore, Md.

Early Carson, captain, U.S. Army.

John O. Carter, first lieutenant, Washington, D.C.

Wilson Cary, second lieutenant, U.S. Army.

Robert W. Cheers, second lieutenant, Baltimore, Md.

David K. Cherry, captain, Greensboro, N.C.

Frank R. Chisholm, first lieutenant, Brooklyn, N.Y.

Robert B. Chubb, captain, U.S. Army.

Ewell W. Clark, first lieutenant, Giddings, Tex.

Frank C. Clark, second lieutenant, National Guard, Washington, D.C.

William H. Clarke, first lieutenant, Birmingham, Ala.

William H. Clarke, first lieutenant, Helena, Ark.

Roscoe Clayton, captain, U.S. Army.

Lane G. Cleaves, second lieutenant, Memphis, Tenn.

Joshua W. Clifford, first lieutenant, Washington, D.C.

Sprigg B. Coates, captain, U.S. Army.

Frank Coleman, first lieutenant, Washington, D.C.

William Collier, second lieutenant, U.S. Army.

William N. Colson, second lieutenant, Cambridge, Mass.

Leonard O. Colston, first lieutenant, U.S. Army.

Jones A. Coltrane, first lieutenant, Spokane, Wash.

John Combs, first lieutenant, U.S. Army.

Barton W. Conrad, first lieutenant, Cambridge, Mass.

Lloyd F. Cook, first lieutenant, U.S. Army.

Charles C. Cooper, captain, National Guard, District of Columbia.

George P. Cooper, first lieutenant, U.S. Army.

Joseph H. Cooper, first lieutenant, Washington, D.C.

Chesley E. Corbett, first lieutenant, Wewoka, Okla.

Harry W. Cox, first lieutenant, Sedalia, Mo.

James W. Cranson, captain, United States Army.

Horace R. Crawford, first lieutenant, Washington, D.C.

Judge Cross, first lieutenant, U.S. Army.

Clarence B. Curley, first lieutenant, Washington, D.C.

Merrill H. Curtis, first lieutenant, Washington, D.C.

Edward L. Dabney, first lieutenant, Hampton, Va.

Joe Dabney, captain, U.S. Army.

History of the American Negro in the Great World War

Victor R. Daly, first lieutenant, Corona, Long Island, N.Y.

Eugene A. Dandridge, first lieutenant, National Guard, District of Columbia.

Eugene L.C. Davidson, first lieutenant, Cambridge, Mass.

Henry G. Davis, first lieutenant, Atlanta, Ga.

Irby D. Davis, first lieutenant, Sumter, S.C.

William E. Davis, captain, Washington, D.C.

Charles C. Dawson, first lieutenant, Chicago, Ill.

William S. Dawson, first lieutenant, Chicago, Ill.

Aaron Day, Jr., captain, Prairie View, Tex.

Milton T. Dean, captain, U.S. Army.

Francis M. Dent, first lieutenant, Washington, D.C.

Thomas M. Dent, Jr., first lieutenant, Washington, D.C.

James B. Dickson, second lieutenant, Asheville, N.C.

Spahr H. Dickey, captain, San Francisco, Cal.

Elder W. Diggs, first lieutenant, Indianapolis, Ind.

William H. Dinkins, first lieutenant, Selma, Ala.

Beverly L. Dorsey, captain, U.S. Army.

Edward C. Dorsey, captain, U.S. Army.

Harris N. Dorsey, first lieutenant, U.S. Army.

Seaborn Douglas, second lieutenant, Hartford, Conn.

Vest Douglas, first lieutenant, U.S. Army.

Frank L. Drye, first lieutenant, Little Rock, Ark.

Edward Dugger, first lieutenant, Roxbury, Mass.

Jackson E. Dunn, first lieutenant, U.S. Army.

Benjamin F. Dunning, second lieutenant, Norfolk, Va.

Charles J. Echols, Jr., captain, U.S. Army.

Charles Ecton, captain, U.S. Army.

George E. Edwards, first lieutenant, U.S. Army.

Leonard Edwards, second lieutenant, Augusta, Ga.

James L. Elliott, second lieutenant, Atlanta, Ga.

Charles J. Ellis, second lieutenant, Springfield, Ill.

Harry C. Ellis, first lieutenant, Patrick, Ia.

Roscoe Ellis, captain, U.S. Army.

Leslie H. Engram, second lieutenant, Montezuma, Ga.

Alexander E. Evans, first lieutenant, Columbia, S.C.

Will H. Evans, second lieutenant, Montgomery, Tex.

Norwood C. Fairfax, second lieutenant, Eagle Rock, Va.

John R. Fairley, first lieutenant, Kansas City, Mo.

Clifford L. Farrer, first lieutenant, El Paso, Tex.

Leonard J. Faulkner, first lieutenant, Columbus, O.

William H. Fearence, first lieutenant, Texarkana, Tex.

Charles H. Fearing, first lieutenant, St. Louis, Mo.

Robert W. Fearing, second lieutenant, Brooklyn, N.Y.

Alonzo G. Ferguson, first lieutenant, Washington, D.C.

Gurnett E. Ferguson, captain, Dunbar, W. Va.

Thomas A. Firmes, captain, U.S. Army.

Dillard J. Firse, first lieutenant, Cleveland, O.

Octavius Fisher, first lieutenant, Detroit, Mich.

James E. Fladger, second lieutenant, Kansas City, Mo.

Benjamin F. Ford, first lieutenant, U.S. Army.

Edward W. Ford, second lieutenant, Philadelphia, Pa.

Frank L. Francis, second lieutenant, U.S. Army.

Henry O. Franklin, second lieutenant, San Francisco, Cal.

Ernest C. Frazier, second lieutenant, Washington, D.C.

Arthur Freeman, first lieutenant, U.S. Army.

Sewell G. Freeman, second lieutenant, Aragon, Ga.

Edward S. Gaillard, first lieutenant, Indianapolis, Ind.

Tacitus E. Gaillard, second lieutenant, Kansas City, Mo.

James H.L. Gaines, second lieutenant, Little Rock, Ark.

Ellsworth Gamblee, first lieutenant, Cincinnati, O.

Lucian P. Garrett, second lieutenant, Louisville, Ky.

William L. Gee, first lieutenant, Gallipolis, Ohio.

Clayborne George, first lieutenant, Washington, D.C.

Warmith T. Gibbs, second lieutenant, Cambridge, Mass.

Howard C. Gilbert, first lieutenant, Columbus, Ohio.

Walter A. Giles, first lieutenant, St. Louis, Mo.

Archie H. Gillespie, captain, U.S. Army

William Gillum, captain, U.S. Army.

Floyd Gilmer, first lieutenant, U.S. Army.

William Glass, captain, U.S. Army.

Jesse J. Gleeden, second lieutenant, Little Rock, Ark.

Leroy H. Godman, captain, Columbus, Ohio.

Edward L. Goodlett, second lieutenant, Atlanta, Ga.

Nathan O. Goodloe, second lieutenant, Washington, D.C.

Frank M. Goodner, first lieutenant, U.S. Army.

Elijah H. Goodwin, first lieutenant, U.S. Army.

James A. Gordon, first lieutenant, St. Joseph, Mo.

Herbert R. Gould, first lieutenant, Dedham, Mass.

James E. Gould, first lieutenant, Dedham, Mass.

Francis H. Gow, first lieutenant, Charleston, W. Va.

William T. Grady, second lieutenant, Dudley, N.C.

Jesse M.H. Graham, second lieutenant, Clarksville, Tenn.

William H. Graham, captain, U.S. Army.

Towson S. Grasty, first lieutenant, Pittsburgh, Pa.

Thornton H. Gray, first lieutenant, Fairmount Heights, Md.

Miles M. Green, captain, U.S. Army.

Thomas E. Green, first lieutenant, U.S. Army.

Walter Green, captain, U.S. Army.

Jesse J. Green, first lieutenant, Georgetown, Ky.

Thomas M. Gregory, first lieutenant, Newark, N.J.

Jefferson E. Grigsby, second lieutenant, Chapelle, S.C.,

Thomas Grundy, captain, U.S. Army.

William W. Green, captain, U.S. Army.

George B. Greenlee, first lieutenant, Marion, N.C.

Nello B. Greenlee, second lieutenant, New York, N.Y.

Herbert H. Guppy, second lieutenant, Boston, Mass.

George C. Hall, captain, U.S. Army.

Leonidas H. Hall, Jr., second lieutenant, Philadelphia, Pa.

George W. Hamilton, Jr., first lieutenant, Topeka, Kans.

Rodney D. Hardeway, second lieutenant, Houston, Tex.

Clarence W. Harding, first lieutenant, U.S. Army.

Clifton S. Hardy, second lieutenant, Champaign, Ill.

Clay Harper, first lieutenant, U.S. Army.

Ted O. Harper, second lieutenant, Columbus, Ohio.

Tillman H. Harpole, first lieutenant, Kansas City, Mo.

Bravid W. Harris, Jr., first lieutenant, Warrenton, N.C.

Edward H. Harris, first lieutenant, U.S. Army.

Eugene Harris, captain, U.S. Army.

William Harris, first lieutenant, U.S. Army.

Byrd McD. Hart, captain, U.S. Army.

Albert L. Hatchett, first lieutenant, San Antonio, Tex.

Lawrence Hawkins, second lieutenant, Bowie, Md.

Charles M. Hayes, second lieutenant, Hopkinsville, Ky.

Merriam C. Hayson, first lieutenant, Kenilworth, D.C.

Alonzo Heard, captain, U.S. Army.

Almando Henderson, first lieutenant, U.S. Army.

Douglas J. Henderson, first lieutenant, Washington, D.C.

Robert M. Hendrick, first lieutenant, Tallahassee, Fla.

Thomas J. Henry, Jr., first lieutenant, Atlanta, Ga.

Vodrey Henry, first lieutenant, U.S. Army.

Jesse S. Heslip, first lieutenant, Toledo, Ohio.

Lee J. Hicks, captain, Ottawa, Kans.

Victor La Naire Hicks, second lieutenant, Columbia, Mo.

Arthur K. Hill, first lieutenant, Lawrence, Kans.

Daniel G. Hill, Jr., second lieutenant, Cantonsville, Md.

Walter Hill, first lieutenant, U.S. Army.

William Hill, captain, U.S. Army.

Clarence O. Hilton, first lieutenant, Farmville, Va.

Lowell B. Hodges, first lieutenant, Houston, Tex.

Horatio B. Holder, first lieutenant, Cairo, Ga.

George A. Holland, captain, U.S. Army.

James G. Hollingsworth, captain, U.S. Army.

George C. Hollomand, second lieutenant, Washington, D.C.

Wayne L. Hopkins, second lieutenant, Columbus, Ohio.

James L. Horace, second lieutenant, Little Rock, Ark.

Reuben Homer, captain, U.S. Army.

Charles S. Hough, second lieutenant, Jamestown, Ohio.

Charles H. Houston, first lieutenant, Washington, D.C.

Henry C. Houston, captain, U.S. Army.

Cecil A. Howard, first lieutenant, Washington, D.C.

Clarence K. Howard, second lieutenant, Montgomery, Ala.

Charles P. Howard, first lieutenant, Des Moines, Ia.

Arthur Hubbard, first lieutenant, U.S. Army.

Jerome L. Hubert, first lieutenant, Houston, Tex.

William H. Hubert, second lieutenant, Mayfield, Ga.

Jefferson E. Hudgins, first lieutenant, U.S. Army.

Samuel M. Huffman, first lieutenant, Columbus, Ohio.

Samuel A. Hull, first lieutenant, Jacksonville, Fla.

John R. Hunt, first lieutenant, Washington, D.C.

Bush A. Hunter, second lieutenant, Lexington, Ky.

Benjamin H. Hunton, first lieutenant, Newport News, Va.

Frederick A. Hurt, first lieutenant, Washington, D.C.

Walter L. Hutcherson, first lieutenant, Amherst, Va.

Samuel B. Hutchinson, Jr., second lieutenant, Boston, Mass.

James E. Ivey, second lieutenant, Atlanta, Ga.

Beecher A. Jackson, first lieutenant, Texarkana, Tex.

George W. Jackson, first lieutenant, Ardmore, Mo.

Joseph T. Jackson, first lieutenant, Charleston, W. Va.

Landen Jackson, first lieutenant, U.S. Army.

Matthew Jackson, captain, U.S. Army.

Maxey A. Jackson, second lieutenant, Marian, Ky.

Joyce G. Jacobs, second lieutenant, Chicago, Ill.

Wesley H. Jamison, second lieutenant, Topeka, Kans.

Charles Jefferson, second lieutenant, U.S. Army.

Benjamin R. Johnson, first lieutenant, New York, N.Y.

Campbell C. Johnson, first lieutenant, Washington, D.C.

Ernest C. Johnson, second lieutenant, Washington D.C.

Everett W. Johnson, first lieutenant, Philadelphia, Pa.

Hanson Johnson, captain, U.S. Army.

Hillery W. Johnson, second lieutenant, Philadelphia, Pa.

Joseph L. Johnson, second lieutenant, Philadelphia, Pa.

Merle O. Johnson, first lieutenant, U.S. Army.

Robert E. Johnson, second lieutenant, Washington, D.C.

Thomas Johnson, captain, U.S. Army.

Virginius D. Johnson, first lieutenant, Richmond, Va.

William N. Johnson, second lieutenant, Omaha, Neb.

William T. Johnson, first lieutenant, U.S. Army.

Willie Johnson, first lieutenant, U.S. Army.

Charles A. Jones, second lieutenant, San Antonio, Tex.

Clifford W. Jones, first lieutenant, U.S. Army.

Dee Jones, captain, U.S. Army.

Edward D. Jones, second lieutenant, Hartford, Conn.

James W. Jones, captain, Washington, D.C.

James O. Jones, second lieutenant, Paulding, Ohio.

Paul W. Jones, first lieutenant, Washington, D.C.

Percy L. Jones, second lieutenant, U.S. Army.

Vivian L. Jones, second lieutenant, Des Moines, Ia.

Warren F. Jones, captain, U.S. Army.

William Jones, first lieutenant, U.S. Army.

Charles G. Kelly, captain, Tuskegee, Ala.

Elliott H. Kelly, first lieutenant, Camden, S.C.

John B. Kemp, captain, U.S. Army.

John M. Kenney, captain, U.S. Army.

Will Kernts, first lieutenant, U.S. Army.

Otho E. Kerr, first lieutenant, Hampton, Va.

Orestus J. Kincaid, first lieutenant, U.S. Army.

Jesse L. Kimbrough, first lieutenant, Los Angeles, Cal.

Moses King, first lieutenant, U.S. Army.

Laurence E. Knight, first lieutenant, U.S. Army.

Edward C. Knox, first lieutenant, U.S. Army.

John W. Knox, second lieutenant, Washington, D.C.

Azzie B. Koger, first lieutenant, Reidsville, N.C.

Linwood G. Koger, first lieutenant, Washington, D.C.

Charles E. Lane, Jr., first lieutenant, Washington, D.C.

David A. Lane, Jr., first lieutenant, Washington, D.C.

Frank L. Lane, second lieutenant, Houston, Tex.

Benton R. Latimer, first lieutenant, Warrenton, Ga.

Ernest W. Latson, first lieutenant, Jacksonville, Fla.

Laige I. Lancaster, first lieutenant, Hampton, Va.

Oscar G. Lawless, first lieutenant, New Orleans, La.

Samuel Lawson, second lieutenant, Philadelphia, Pa.

Wilfred W. Lawson, first lieutenant, Washington, D.C.

Geo. E. Lee, second lieutenant, Washington, D.C.

George W. Lee, second lieutenant, Memphis, Tenn.

Lawrence A. Lee, second lieutenant, Hampton, Va.

John E. Leonard, first lieutenant, U.S. Army.

Garrett M. Lewis, first lieutenant, San Antonio, Tex.

Henry O. Lewis, first lieutenant, Boston, Mass.

Everett B. Liggins, second lieutenant, Austin, Tex.

Victor C. Lightfoot, second lieutenant, South Pittsburg, Tenn.

John Q. Lindsey, first lieutenant, U.S. Army.

Redden L. Linton, second lieutenant, Boston, Ga.

Glenda W. Locust, second lieutenant, Sealy, Tenn.

Aldon L. Logan, first lieutenant, Lawrence, Kans.

James B. Lomack, first lieutenant, National Guard, Dist. of Columbia.

Howard H. Long, first lieutenant, Washington, D.C.

Victor Long, first lieutenant, U.S. Army.

Lonnie W. Lott, second lieutenant, Austin, Tex.

Charles H. Love, second lieutenant, Atlanta, Ga.

Edgar A. Love, first lieutenant, Baltimore, Md.

Frank W. Love, captain, U.S. Army.

George B. Love, first lieutenant, Greensboro, N.C.

John W. Love, first lieutenant, Baltimore, Md.

Joseph Lowe, captain, U.S. Army.

Walter Lowe, first lieutenant, St Louis, Mo.

Charles C. Luck, Jr., second lieutenant, San Marcus, Tex.

Walter Lyons, first lieutenant, U.S. Army.

Harry J. Mack, second lieutenant, Cheney, Pa.

Amos B. Madison, first lieutenant, Omaha, Neb.

Edgar F. Malone, second lieutenant, U.S. Army.

Edgar O. Malone, captain, U.S. Army.

Earl W. Mann, first lieutenant, Champaign, Ill.

Vance H. Marchbanks, captain, U.S. Army.

Leon F. Marsh, first lieutenant, Berkeley, Cal.

Alfred E. Marshall, second lieutenant, Greenwood, S.C.

Cyrus W. Marshall, second lieutenant, Baltimore, Md.

Cuby Martin, first lieutenant, U.S. Army.

Joseph H. Martin, first lieutenant, Washington, D.C.

Eric P. Mason, first lieutenant, Giddings, Tex.

Denis McG. Matthews, first lieutenant, Los Angeles, Cal.

Joseph E. Matthews, second lieutenant, Cleburne, Tex.

Anderson N. May, captain, Atlanta, Ga.

Walter H. Mazyck, first lieutenant, Washington, D.C.

Peter McCall, captain U.S. Army.

Milton A. McCrimmon, captain, U.S. Army.

Robert A. McEwen, second lieutenant, E. St. Louis, Ill.

Osceola E. McKaine, first lieutenant, U.S. Army.

James E. McKey, first lieutenant, U.S. Army.

Carey McLane, first lieutenant, U.S. Army.

Archie McLee, first lieutenant, New York, N.Y.

Leonard W. McLeod, first lieutenant, Hampton, Va.

Albert McReynolds, first lieutenant, U.S. Army.

Marshall Meadows, first lieutenant, U.S. Army.

Louis R. Mehlinger, captain, Washington, D.C.

Louis R. Middleton, first lieutenant, Washington, D.C.

Benjamin H. Mills, first lieutenant, U.S. Army.

Harry W. Mills, captain, U.S. Army.

Warren N. Mims, first lieutenant, U.S. Army.

J. Wardlaw Mitchell, second lieutenant, Milledgeville, Ga.

Pinkney L. Mitchell, second lieutenant, Austin, Tex.

John H. Mitcherson, first lieutenant, U.S. Army.

Ralph E. Mizell, second lieutenant, Champaign, Ill.

Hubert M. Moman, second lieutenant, Tougaloo, Miss.

John M. Moore, first lieutenant, Meridian, Miss.

Loring B. Moore, second lieutenant, Brunswick, Ga.

Elias A. Morris, first lieutenant, Helena, Ark.

Thomas E. Morris, captain, U.S. Army.

James B. Morris, second lieutenant, Des Moines, Ia.

Cleveland Morrow, first lieutenant, U.S. Army.

Henry Morrow, first lieutenant, U.S. Army.

Abraham Morse, first lieutenant, U.S. Army.

Benjamin H. Mosby, first lieutenant, St. Louis, Mo.

Benedict Mosley, first lieutenant, U.S. Army.

Scott A. Moyer, second lieutenant, U.S. Army.

Albert C. Murdaugh, second lieutenant, Columbia, S.C.

Alonzo Myers, captain, Philadelphia, Pa.

Thomas J. Narcisse, second lieutenant, Jeanerette, La.

Earl H. Nash, second lieutenant, Atlanta, Ga.

Homer G. Neely, first lieutenant, Palestine, Tex.

Gurney E. Nelson, second lieutenant, Greensboro, N.C.

William S. Nelson, first lieutenant, Washington, D.C.

William F. Nelson, first lieutenant, Atlanta, Ga.

James P. Nobles, first lieutenant, U.S. Army.

Grafton S. Norman, first lieutenant, Atlanta, Ga.

Richard M. Norris, first lieutenant, U.S. Army.

Ambrose B. Nutt, second lieutenant, Cambridge, Mass.

Benjamin L. Ousley, second lieutenant, Tougaloo, Miss.

Charles W. Owens, captain, United States Army.

Charles G. Owlings, second lieutenant, Norfolk, Va.

William W. Oxley, first lieutenant, Cambridge, Mass.

Wilbur E. Pannell, second lieutenant, Staunton, Va.

Charles S. Parker, second lieutenant, Spokane, Wash.

Walter E. Parker, second lieutenant, Little Rock, Ark.

Clemmie C. Parks, first lieutenant, Ft. Scott, Kans.

Adam E. Patterson, captain, Chicago, Ill.

Humphrey C. Patton, first lieutenant, Washington, D.C.

Clarence H. Payne, first lieutenant, Chicago, Ill.

William D. Peeks, captain, U.S. Army.

Robert R. Penn, first lieutenant, New York, N.Y.

Marion R. Perry, second lieutenant, Pine Bluff, Ark.

Hanson A. Person, second lieutenant, Wynne, Ark.

Harry B. Peters, second lieutenant, Atlanta, Ga.

James H. Peyton, second lieutenant, Montgomery, Ala.

Joseph Phillips, captain, Columbus, Ohio.

David A. Pierce, second lieutenant, Clarksville, Tenn.

Harrison J. Pinkett, first lieutenant, Omaha, Nebr.

James C. Pinkston, first lieutenant, U.S. Army.

Percival R. Piper, first lieutenant, Washington, D.C.

Anderson F. Pitts, first lieutenant, Chicago, Ill.

Fisher Pride, first lieutenant, U.S. Army.

Herman W. Porter, second lieutenant, Cambridge, Mass.

James C. Powell, first lieutenant, Washington, D.C.

Wade H. Powell, second lieutenant, Atlanta, Ga.

William J. Powell, first lieutenant, Chicago, Ill.

Gloucester A. Price, second lieutenant, Fort Meyer, Fla.

John F. Pritchard, first lieutenant, U.S. Army.

Henry H. Proctor, first lieutenant, Atlanta, Ga.

John H. Purnell, first lieutenant, Trappe, Md.

Howard D. Queen, captain, U.S. Army.

Richard R. Queen, second lieutenant, Washington, D.C.

Harold L. Quivers, first lieutenant, Washington, D.C.

Washington H. Racks, second lieutenant, U.S. Army.

John E. Raiford, second lieutenant, Atlanta, Ga.

Hazel L. Raine, first lieutenant, U.S. Army.

Fred D. Ramsey, first lieutenant, Wedgefield, S.C.

James O. Redmon, second lieutenant, Newton, Iowa.

Charles G. Reed, first lieutenant, Charleston, S.C.

Rufus Reed, captain, U.S. Army.

Lightfoot H. Reese, second lieutenant, Newman, Ga.

William L. Reese, second lieutenant, Bennetsville, S.C.

Robert S. Reid, second lieutenant, Newman, Ga.

Samuel Reid, captain, U.S. Army.

Adolph Reyes, second lieutenant, Philadelphia, Pa.

Elijah Reynolds, captain, U.S. Army.

John F. Rice, first lieutenant, Chicago, Ill.

Douglas C. Richardson, second lieutenant, Washington, D.C.

Harry D. Richardson, first lieutenant, Washington, D.C.

Leonard. H. Richardson, first lieutenant, Oakland, Cal.

Maceo A. Richmond, second lieutenant, Des Moines, Ia.

Francis E. Rivers, first lieutenant, New Haven, Conn.

Marion C. Rhoten, first lieutenant, U.S. Army.

Charles E. Roberts, first lieutenant, Atlantic City, N.J.

Clyde Roberts, second lieutenant, U.S. Army.

Edward Robertson, second lieutenant, U.S. Army.

Charles W. Robinson, second lieutenant, Cleveland, Ohio.

George C. Robinson, first lieutenant, Atlanta, Ga.

Peter L. Robinson, first lieutenant, Washington, D.C.

William W. Robinson, first lieutenant, U.S. Army.

Julian P. Rogers, first lieutenant, Montgomery, Ala.

John W. Rowe, first lieutenant, Danville, Ky.

Thomas Rucker, captain, U.S. Army.

Edward P. Rudd, first lieutenant, New York City.

Mallalieu W. Rush, first lieutenant, Atlanta, Ga.

John Russell, captain, U.S. Army.

Louis H. Russell, second lieutenant, New York, N.Y.

Earl Ryder, second lieutenant, Springfield, Ill.

Chester Sanders, captain, U.S. Army.

Joseph B. Sanders, second lieutenant, U.S. Army.

Walter R. Sanders, captain, U.S. Army.

Clifford A. Sandridge, captain, U.S. Army.

Lorin O. Sanford, captain, U.S. Army.

Elliott D. Saunders, second lieutenant, U.S. Army.

Walker L. Savoy, second lieutenant, Washington, D.C.

Elmer P. Sawyer, second lieutenant, Providence, R.I.

George S. Schuyler, first lieutenant, U.S. Army.

James E. Scott, second lieutenant, Washington, D.C.

James E. Scott, first lieutenant, Hampton, Va.

Joseph H. Scott, first lieutenant, Darlington, S.C.

Walter W. Scott, second lieutenant, Brooksville, Miss.

William F. Scott, captain, U.S. Army.

Fletcher Sewell, captain, U.S. Army.

Shermont R. Sewell, first lieutenant, Washington, D.C.

Charles A. Shaw, first lieutenant, Atlanta, Ga.

Warren B. Shelton, second lieutenant, Hot Springs, Ark.

Robert T. Shobe, first lieutenant, U.S. Army.

Hal Short, first lieutenant, Iowa City, Ia.

Harry W. Short, second lieutenant, Iowa City, Ia.

Ogbon N. Simmons, first lieutenant, Waldo, Fla.

Richard Simmons, captain, U.S. Army.

William E. Simmons, first lieutenant, Burlington, Vt.

Austin Simms, second lieutenant, Darien, Ga.

John H. Simms, Jr., first lieutenant, Jacksonville, Fla.

Artillery at work in a French forest. This was a phase of operation in which the negro units of the 167th Brigade distinguished themselves in the closing days of the war.

Sentry box outside of regimental headquarters with warning horn for gas attacks. Camouflaged gate on the left.

One of the huge guns, 16-inch caliber of the American railway artillery, which did such frightful execution near the close of the war. Camouflaged throughout.

A railroad in France. This one was used by a portion of the 93rd Division in the Champagne to transport troops and supplies to the front.

Passenger cars used by famous 93rd. Negro Division in Champagne, France.

Sending message by carrier pigeon. Officer and soldiers of 369th Infantry outside of dugout in France.

Kitchen and dining quarters at the front. Soldiers belong to famous 93rd Division American negro soldiers brigaded with the French.

Infantry and gunners at close grips. Drawing represents a brilliant counter-attack in a shell-torn wood in France.

History of the American Negro in the Great World War

A typical trench scene. Negroes of the 93rd division serving with French in the Champagne.

Secret organizations present at the breaking of the ground for Mcdonough memorial hospital, W. 133rd street, New York. Named in honor of Mr. David Kearney Mcdonough, pioneer negro physician of that city. To be used as a base unit for colored soldiers.

Lieut. John a Applebee of the red cross home service, comforting and reassuring soldiers anxious about the welfare of their families. Camp no. 43. Gievres. France.

Crown Prince and Kaiser Bill. Two German dogs and their captors. The soldiers are Privates Robinson Cleve, 539th Engineers and Daniel Nelson, 372nd Infantry.

Types of negro engineers who were such important factors in our overseas forces.

Four caverns, studded with ivory, furnish harmony in the training camp.

Abraham L. Simpson, captain, Louisville, Ky.

Lawrence Simpson, first lieutenant, Chicago, Ill.

William R. Smalls, first lieutenant, Manassas, Va.

Daniel Smith, captain, U.S. Army.

Enos B. Smith, second lieutenant, U.S. Army.

Ernest Smith, second lieutenant, Philadelphia, Pa.

Fairel N. Smith, first lieutenant, Orangeburg, S.C.

Joseph W. Smith, second lieutenant, Concord, S.C.

Oscar H. Smith, first lieutenant, U.S. Army.

Pitman E. Smith, first lieutenant, Columbus, Ohio.

Russell Smith, first lieutenant, U.S. Army.

Walter H. Smith, first lieutenant, Chattanooga, Tenn.

Levi E. Southe, second lieutenant, Chicago, Ill.

Carlos Sowards, second lieutenant, U.S. Army.

Edward W. Spearman, captain, U.S. Army.

Walter R. St. Clair, second lieutenant, Philadelphia, Pa.

Lloyd A. Stafford, captain, U.S. Army.

Moody Staten, captain, U.S. Army.

Percy H. Steele, first lieutenant, Washington, D.C.

Waddell C. Steele, first lieutenant, U.S. Army.

Grant Stewart, first lieutenant, U.S. Army.

Robert K. Stephens, captain, U.S. Army.

Leon Stewart, first lieutenant, U.S. Army.

Thomas R. Stewart, first lieutenant, Ft. Wayne, Ind.

William A. Stith, first lieutenant, U.S. Army.

James M. Stockett, Jr., first lieutenant, Providence, R.I.

Wilbur F. Stonestreet, second lieutenant, Topeka, Kans.

Daniel T. Taylor, second lieutenant, U.S. Army.

Hannibal B. Taylor, second lieutenant, Guthrie, Okla.

Pearl E. Taylor, first lieutenant, St. Louis, Mo.

Benjamin F. Thomas, captain, U.S. Army.

Bob Thomas, captain, U.S. Army.

Vincent B. Thomas, second lieutenant, Washington, D.C.

Charles M. Thompson, first lieutenant, Columbia, S.C.

Joseph Thompson, captain, U.S. Army.

Pierce McN. Thompson, first lieutenant, Albany, Ga.

Richard C. Thompson, first lieutenant, Harrisburg, Pa.

Toliver T. Thompson, first lieutenant, Houston, Tex.

William H. Thompson, first lieutenant, Jacksonville, Fla.

William W. Thompson, captain, United States Army.

James W. Thornton, first lieutenant, West Raleigh, N.C.

Leslie J. Thurman, captain, U.S. Army.

Samuel J. Tipton, captain, U.S. Army.

Frederick H. Townsend, second lieutenant, Newport, R.I.

Anderson Trapp, first lieutenant, U.S. Army.

Charles A. Tribbett, first lieutenant, New Haven, Conn.

Joseph E. Trigg, captain, Syracuse, N.Y.

Archibald R. Tuck, second lieutenant, Oberlin, O.

Victor J. Tulane, first lieutenant, Montgomery, Ala.

William J. Turnbow, first lieutenant, U.S. Army.

Allen Turner, first lieutenant, U.S. Army.

Edward Turner, first lieutenant, Omaha, Nebr.

Samuel Turner, second lieutenant, U.S. Army.

Shadrach W. Upshaw, second lieutenant, Austin, Tex.

Ferdinand S. Upshur, second lieutenant, Philadelphia, Pa.

George L. Vaughn, first lieutenant, St. Louis, Mo.

Austin T. Walden, captain, Macon, Ga.

John P. Walker, first lieutenant, U.S. Army.

Lewis W. Wallace, captain, U.S. Army.

Thomas H. Walters, first lieutenant. New York, N.Y.

Robert L. Ward, first lieutenant, Detroit, Mich.

James H.N. Waring, Jr., first lieutenant, Washington, D, C.

Genoa S. Washington, captain, U.S. Army.

George G. Washington, second lieutenant, U.S. Army.

Bolivar E. Watkins, first lieutenant, St. Louis, Mo.

Alstyne M. Watson, second lieutenant, Tallapoosa, Ga.

Baxter W. Watson, second lieutenant, U.S. Army.

Louis L. Watson, first lieutenant, Washington, D.C.

William H. Weare, first lieutenant, U.S. Army.

Walter T. Webb, first lieutenant, Baltimore, Md.

Carter W. Wesley, first lieutenant, Houston, Tex.

Harry Wheeler, first lieutenant, U.S. Army.

Chauncey D. White, first lieutenant, Mathews, Va.

Emmett White, captain, U.S. Army.

Journee W. White, second lieutenant, Los Angeles, Cal.

Lorenzo C. White, second lieutenant, Hampton, Va.

Johnson C. Whittaker, first lieutenant, Lawrence, Kans.

Horace G. Wilder, second lieutenant, U.S. Army.

Arthur R. Williams, second lieutenant, Edwards, Miss.

Everett B. Williams, first lieutenant, Syracuse, N.Y.

Gus Williams, first lieutenant, U.S. Army.

James B. Williams, first lieutenant, Baltimore, Md.

John Williams, second lieutenant, U.S. Army.

Oscar H. Williams, second lieutenant, New York, N.Y.

Richard A. Williams, captain, Lawnside, N.J.

Robert G. Williams, first lieutenant, U.S. Army.

Seymour E. Williams, second lieutenant, Muskogee, Okla.

Major Williams, second lieutenant, U.S. Army.

Walter B. Williams, captain, U.S. Army.

William H. Williams, captain, U.S. Army.

Elmore S. Willie, first lieutenant, U.S. Army.

Harry E. Wilson, first lieutenant, Des Moines, Ia.

John E. Wilson, first lieutenant, Leavenworth, Kans.

William H. Wilson, second lieutenant, Greensboro, N.C.

Meredith B. Wily, first lieutenant, El Paso, Tex.

Christopher C. Wimbish, first lieutenant, Atlanta, Ga.

Hugh H. Wimbish, second lieutenant, Atlanta, Ga.

Rolland T. Winstead, second lieutenant, Rocky Mount, N.C.

George W. Winston, captain, United States Army.

Ernest M. Wood, second lieutenant, Mebane, N.C.

Benjamin F. Wright, second lieutenant, New York, N.Y.

Elbert S. Wright, second lieutenant, Baldwin, Kans.

John Wynn, second lieutenant, U.S. Army.

Edward York, captain, United States Army.

Charles Young, first lieutenant, U.S. Army.

William A. Young, second lieutenant, Sumter, S.C.

Charles G. Young, first lieutenant, Washington, D.C.

CHAPTER XIV

Across Dividing Seas

Black Thousands Assemble—Soldiers of Liberty—Severing Home Ties—Man's Work Must Be Done—First Negroes in France—Meeting with French Colonials—Early History of15th New York—They Sail Away—Become French Fighting Men—Hold 20% ofAmerican Lines—Terror to Germans—Only Barrier Between Boche and Paris—Imperishable Record of New Yorkers—Turning Point of War

> *"Doan you see the black clouds ris'n ober yondah*
> *Like as tho we's gwan ter hab a storm?*
> *No, you's mistaken, dem's "Loyal BLACK FOLKS*
> *Sailing off ter fight fer Uncle Sam."*

From the plantations of the South, from the mines, the workshops and factories; from the levees of the Mississippi, the cities, villages, farms of the North, the East, the South, the West; from the store, the counting house, the office and the institution of learning they came—the black thousands to strike for their altars and their homes; to fight for Uncle Sam. How splendid was the spectacle of their response! "Their's not to ask the WHY; their's but to do and die."

Bearing the burden placed upon them by white men as they have for centuries, nevertheless, in this supreme moment of their country's life; "a day that shall live in story"; many of them did not know what it all was about; where Germany was located, nor the significance attaching to the word Hun. In a vague way they understood that across the sea an armed and powerful nation was threatening the happiness of mankind; the freedom of the world.

In the presence of this contemplated crime, they were wide-eyed, open-souled, awake! Their sires had known bondage, and they, their children, had felt and knew the effects of it. America which for centuries had oppressed their forefathers had finally through the arbitrament of war, freed them. White men and black men; in the dark days of '61-'65, numbering many thousands, had lain down their lives to save the Union, and in doing so had brought them freedom.

They had been told that America was threatened; that was enough. It was to them a summons; sharp, quick, incisive to duty. It was, although one hundred and forty years after, the voice of Washington at Valley Forge; the call of Perry to their fathers, needing soldiers at the battle of Lake Erie; of Jackson at New Orleans. It was to their listening ears the echo of Bull Run, of Santiago, of Manila, and later of Carrizal; Uncle Sam needed them! That was enough; what more was to be said?

Denied the opportunity to enlist, the Negro's patriotic, patient soul asserted itself; if he must go as a drafted soldier, it would be in the same fine spirit that would have inspired him as a loyal enlisted man.

Life, as to all men, was sweet to them. They had mothers, fathers, sisters and brothers, wives and sweethearts; the ties of association; of home, from all of which they would be separated and for all of which they cherished that love, which alone of human fires: "Burns and burns, forever the same, for nature feeds the pyre."

Above and over all these things, tending to augment the seriousness of the sacrifice he was to be called upon to make, was the spirit, the optimism, the joy of life that attends vigorous youth and young manhood.

Nature in all of its enticing charm and beauty, was smiling in the home places these men were leaving; flowers bloomed; birds sang; insects buzzed cheerily. There were green fields and babbling brooks; the stately beauty of trees, and the delights of lake, river and vale. The cities from which they came, were many of them, splendid monuments of the work of man. The sun clothed in glory the days, moon and stars gave a loveliness to the nights. Leaving these things to face suffering and hardship; possible death in strange lands, caused many a pang; but a man's work had to be done, and they were there to do it.

Well they knew there would be no chance in France to follow the wild bee to its tree; to track the fox or hunt the 'possum or the coon. The hum they would hear would be that of machine gun bullets; their sting, death or serious wounding. For game they would hunt the Hun; would kill or be by him killed.

There were busy times in thousands of homes when the young Negroes of the land; from East, West, North and South went forth to war.

Bright faces hiding the pangs of parting; happy, singing lads left their homes to enter a new life on earth or, the tragedy of it; also the glory; a new life in the great Beyond; beyond the stars and flaming suns. The training camp was their first destination and was to be their home for months.

Correspondents in France wrote of Negro soldiers being among the first expeditionary force to set foot upon the soil of the battle torn Republic. This force arrived there in June, 1917, and was composed of marines and infantry from the Regular army. Floyd Gibbons, the intrepid representative of the Chicago Tribune, speaking of the first Negro contingents in his remarkable book entitled, "And They Thought We Wouldn't Fight", said:

> "There was to be seen on the streets of St. Nazaire that day some representative black Americans, who had also landed in that historical first contingent. There was a strange thing about these Negroes. It will be remembered that in the early stages of our participation in the war it had been found that there was hardly sufficient khaki cloth to provide uniforms for all of our soldiers. That had been the case with these American negro soldiers.
>
> "But somewhere down in Washington, somehow or other, someone resurrected an old, large heavy iron key and this, inserted into an ancient rusty lock, had opened some long forgotten door in one of the Government arsenals. There were revealed old dust-covered bundles wrapped up in newspapers, yellow with age, and when these wrappings of the past were removed, there were seen the uniforms of old Union blue that had been laid away back in '65—uniforms that had been worn by men who fought and bled and died to save the Union, and ultimately free those early 'Black Americans'.
>
> "And here on this foreign shore, on this day in June more than half a century later, the sons and grandsons of those same freed slaves wore those same uniforms of Union blue as they landed in France to fight for a newer freedom; freedom for the white man no less than themselves, throughout all the earth.
>
> "Some of these Negroes were stevedores from the lower Mississippi levees; who sang as they worked in their white army undershirts, across the chest of which were penciled in blue and red, strange mystic devices, religious phrases and other signs, calculated to contribute the charm of safety to the running of the submarine blockade.
>
> "Two of these American Negroes, walking up the main street of St. Nazaire, saw on the other side of the thoroughfare a brother of color wearing the lighter blue uniform of a French soldier. This French Negro was a

colonial black from the north of Africa and of course had spoken nothing but French from the day he was born. One of the American Negroes crossed the street and accosted him.

"'Looka here, boy', he inquired good-naturedly, 'what can you all tell me about this here wah?'

"'Comment, monsieur?' responded the non-understanding French black, and followed the rejoinder with a torrent of excited French.

"The American Negro's mouth fell open. For a minute he looked startled, and then he bulged one large round eye suspiciously at the French black while he inwardly debated on the possibility that he had become color-blind. Having reassured himself, however, that his vision was not at fault, he made a sudden decision and started on a new tack.

"'Now, never mind that high-faluting language' he said, 'you all just tell me what you know about this here wah and quit you' putting on aihs.'

"The puzzled French Negro could only reply with another explosion of French interrogations, coupled with vigorous gesticulations. The American Negro tried to talk at the same time and both of them endeavoring to make the other understand, increased the volumes of their tones until they were standing there waving their arms and shouting into one another's faces. The American gave it up.

"'My Gawd', he said shaking his head as he recrossed the street and joined his comrades, 'this is sure some funny country. They got the ignorantest colored people here I ever saw.'"

It has been noted that the first Negro combatant regiment to reach France was the celebrated National Guard organization known as the 15th New York Infantry, rechristened the 369th when made a part of the 93rd division of the United States army. This was such a well drilled and equipped regiment that early in the war it was permitted to go across with the first 100,000; all of which was due to the aggressiveness and insistence of its white commander, Colonel William Hayward. He simply gave the war department no rest, stating that he was willing his men should unload ships, fell trees and build docks or cantonments so long as they were permitted to sail.

The regiment had been organized by Colonel Hayward at the suggestion of Governor Whitman of New York. It was to be patterned after the 8th Illinois where colored men of means sufficient to support commissions, were the officers. The regiment was started in June 1916 and by October had 1,000 in the ranks. Colonel Hayward was the only white officer, the Negro commission-holders at that time being Captain Marshall, Captain Fillmore, Lieutenant Lacey, Lieutenant Reed and Lieutenant Europe. The latter was attached to the Machine Gun section but became later the famous musician of the outfit. He was the only Negro officer who remained with the regiment throughout, the others being superseded or transferred after several months service in France.

Early in 1917, the Federal government said it would recognize the regiment if it could muster fifty-one officers. As recruiting had been slow and a Negro regiment in New York was looked upon as an experiment, Colonel Hayward was obliged to secure the needed officers from among his friends in the 7th New York, the Motor Battery, Squadron A and other organizations. By this time the enlisted strength had grown to 1,200. On April 8, 1917, two days after the United States entered the war, the regiment was inspected by Federal officers and a week later was recognized as a regular unit of the Federal Guard.

But, as the Colonel expressed it, they were a "street urchin of a regiment." They had no armory, no place to drill except in the open and no place where more than a single company at a time could meet. In his post-war observations, the Colonel has noted that when the regiment returned to these shores and was feasted and entertained by the people of New York in the 71st regiment armory, it was the first occasion on which the old 15th was ever assembled under one roof.

After its Federal recognition the regiment was sent to the Peekskill rifle range to learn to shoot, a valuable experience as developed later. Many of the boys became expert marksmen, a skill that became of precious value to them and their comrades. In June, 1917, they went to a war strength of 2,000 men and 56 officers. One battalion did pioneer work at Camp Upton, another at Camp Dix. A third guarded 600 miles of railroads in New York, New Jersey and Pennsylvania. The Machine Gun company guarded 2,000 interned spies and pro-German prisoners at Ellis Island. Colonel Hayward has pointed with pride to the fact that in all their territory there was not a wreck, an explosion, an escaped prisoner or any other trouble. Two battalions later went to Spartanburg for training, but remained there only a couple of weeks.

"I wonder what got those colored boys to volunteer" someone asked their colonel as they were embarking for France. He replied: "I have often thought of that. With many the cause was sheer patriotism. Others said they had gone into the 15th for social reasons, to meet with their friends. One—this seemed to me a most pathetic touch—said: 'I j'ined up because when Colonel Hayward asked me it was the first time anyone had ever asked me to j'ine up with anything in my whole lifetime.'"

If any great amount of superstition had existed among the men or officers of the New York regiment, they would have been greatly depressed over the series of incidents that preceded their arrival in France. In the first place they had been assigned to police and pioneer duty at camps near New York, a duty which no fighting man relishes. They embarked on the transport Pocahontas November 12, 1917. Two hundred miles at sea a piston rod was bent and the vessel put back to port. They got away again December 3, were out a day and had to return on account of fire in the coal bunkers. A third attempt on December 12, in a blizzard, was frustrated by a collision with a tanker in New York harbor.

After this series of bad starts, anyone inclined to indulge in forebodings would have predicted the certainty of their becoming prey for the submarines on the way over. But the fourth attempt proved successful and they landed in France on December 27, 1917. They had hoped to celebrate Christmas day on French soil, but were forced by the elements and the precautions of convoys and sailing master to observe the anniversary on board the ship.

The Colonel undoubtedly thought that those first in France would be the first to get a chance at the Boche, but the department took him at his word, and for over two months his men were kept busy in the vicinity of St. Nazaire, largely as laborers and builders. Early in 1918 they went into training quarters near St. Nazaire. The 371st, another Negro regiment, made up of draft selectives principally from South Carolina, was later given quarters nearby.

The black soldiers of the 369th were brigaded as a part of the 16th division of the 8th Corps of the 4th French Army. From St. Nazaire they went to Givrey-En-Argonne, and there in three weeks the French turned them into a regulation French regiment. They had Lebel rifles, French packs and French gas masks. For 191 days they were in the trenches or on the field of battle. In April, 1918, the regiment held 20 percent of all the territory held by American troops, though it comprised less than one percent of all the American soldiers in France.

Officers of the 369th reported for an entire year only six cases of drunkenness, and twenty-four of serious disease. The regiment fought in the Champagne, in the Vosges mountains, on the Aisne, at Main de Massiges, Butte de Mesnil, Dormouse, Sechault, the Argonne, Ripont, Kuppinase, Tourbe, and Bellevue Ridge. It was the first unit of any of the

Allied armies to reach the left bank of the Rhine following the signing of the armistice, moving from Thann on November 17th and reaching Blodesheim the next day.

Negro soldiers were a source of terror to the Germany throughout the war, and objects of great curiosity to the German people afterwards. Wherever they appeared in the area occupied by the Americans they attracted great attention among the civilians. In Treves, Coblenz and other places during the early days of the occupation, crowds assembled whenever Negro soldiers stopped in the streets and it became necessary for the military police to enforce the orders prohibiting gatherings in the public thoroughfares.

Returning soldiers have told how they were followed in the German towns by great troops of stolid, wide-eyed German children who could not seem to decide in their minds just what sort of being these Negro fighters were. The curiosity of the children no doubt was inspired by stories told among their elders of the ferocity of these men.

The Associated Press has related a conversation with a discharged German soldier in Rengsdorf, in which it is stated that the German army early in the war offered a reward for the capture alive of each Negro. The soldier said that throughout the war the Germans lived in great terror of the Negroes, and it was to overcome this fear that rewards were offered.

One evening on the front a scouting party composed of ten Germans including the discharged soldier, encountered two French Negroes. In the fight which followed two of the scouting party were killed. One of the Negroes escaped the other being taken prisoner. During the fight two of the Germans left their comrades and ran to the protection of their own trenches, but these it was explained, were young soldiers and untrained. The reward of 400 marks subsequently was divided among the remaining six Germans for capturing the one French Negro.

The 93rd division, which was made up of the 369th, 370th, 371st and the 372nd regiments of infantry, was put into service green, so green they did not know the use of rockets and thought a gas alarm and the tooting of sirens meant that the Germans were coming in automobiles. The New York regiment came largely from Brooklyn and the district around West 59th street in New York City, called San Juan Hill in reference to certain notable achievements of Negro troops at a place of that name in the Spanish-American war.

They learned the game of war rapidly. The testimony of their officers was to the effect that it was not hard to send them into danger—the hard part being to keep them from going into it of their own accord. It was necessary to watch them like hawks to keep them from slipping off on independent raiding parties.

The New York regiment had a band of 40 pieces, second to none in the American army. It is stated that the officers and men in authority in the French billeting places had difficulty in keeping the villagers from following the band away when it played plantation airs and syncopations as only Negroes can play them.

On April 12, 1918, the 369th took over a sector of 5-1/2 kilometers in the Bois de Hauzy on the left of a fringe of the Argonne Forest. There they stayed until July 1st. There was no violent fighting in the sector, but many raids back and forth by the Negroes and the Germans, rifle exchanges and occasionally some artillery action.

One important engagement occurred June 12th, which the soldiers called the million dollar raid, because they thought the preparatory barrage of the Germans must have cost all of that. The Germans came over, probably believing they would find the Negro outfit scared stiff. But the Negro lads let them have grenades, accurate rifle fire and a hail from some concealed machine gun nests. Sergt. Bob Collins was later given the Croix de Guerre for his disposition of the machine guns on that occasion.

While holding the sector of Hauzy Wood, the 369th was the only barrier between the German army and Paris. However, had there been an attempt to break through, General Gouraud, the French army commander, would have had strength enough there at once to stop it. About this time everyone in the Allied armies knew that the supreme German effort was about to come. It was felt as a surety that the brunt of the drive would fall upon the 4th French Army, of which the 369th regiment and other portions of the American 93rd Division were a part. This army was holding a line 50 kilometers long, stretching between Rheims and the Argonne Forest. It was the intention of the Germans to capture Chalons and then proceed down the Marne Valley to Paris. It was expected that the big German drive would begin on July 4th, but as it turned out it did not begin until the night of the 14th—the French national holiday.

On July 1st, the 369th had been moved from its sector further toward the east where the center of the attack was expected. Upon the 14th of July the French made a raid for the purpose of getting prisoners and information. This had a tremendous effect upon the whole course of the war, for through it General Gouraud's staff learned that at midnight the

Boche artillery preparation was to begin, and at 5:25 o'clock on the morning of the 15th the Germans were coming over the top.

This phase of the operation is described by Col. Hayward as follows:

> "This is what Gen. Gouraud—Pa Gouraud we called him—did: He knew the Boche artillery would at the appointed hour start firing on our front lines, believing as was natural, that they would be strongly held. So he withdrew all his forces including the old 15th, to the intermediate positions, which were at a safe distance back of the front lines. Then, at the point where he expected would be the apex of the drive he sent out two patrols, totalling sixteen men.
>
> "These sixteen had certain camouflage to perform. They were to set going a certain type of French machine gun which would fire of its own accord for awhile after being started off. They were to run from one of these guns to the other and start them. Also the sixteen were to send up rockets, giving signals, which the Germans of course knew as well as we. Then again they were to place gas shells—with the gas flowing out of them—in all the dugouts of the first line. Meanwhile the French artillery had registered directly on our own front trenches, so that it could slaughter the Germans when they came across, believing those trenches to be occupied as usual.
>
> "Everything worked out as expected, and as luck had it, most of those gallant sixteen Frenchmen got back safely.
>
> "Five minutes before the Germans started their artillery preparation for the drive Gen. Gouraud started his cannon going and there was a slaughter in the German lines. Then when the German infantry crossed to our front line trenches (now entirely vacant) they were smashed up because the French guns were firing directly upon these positions, which they knew mathematically. And those of the Boche who went down in the dugouts for safety were killed by the gas which the Frenchmen had left there for them.
>
> "This battle—the supreme German drive—raged over eighty-five kilometers (51 miles). West of Rheims the enemy broke through the line, but they did not break through anywhere in Gen. Gouraud's sector. Stonewall Gouraud stopped them. The American units which took in the defense that was so successful were the 42nd Division, including the gallant 69th of New York, who were to the west of us, our own little regiment, and the American Railroad Artillery.
>
> "That was the turning point of the war, because soon thereafter began Marshal Foch's great counter thrust, in which the 1st and 2nd American

> *Divisions participated so wonderfully about Belleau Wood, Chateau-Thierry and that district. Gouraud in my belief, turned the tide of the war, and I am proud that the New York City colored boys had a share of that vital fight.*
>
> *"Right here I may say that this orphan, urchin regiment of ours placed in the pathway of the Boche in the most significant battle the world has ever known, had only thirty-seven commissioned officers, and four of those wounded, had to be carried in stretchers to their positions in the trenches in order to direct the fighting."*

Colonel Hayward was himself in the hospital with a broken leg. Disregarding the orders of the surgeons he went to the front line on crutches and personally directed his men in the fight. In all of his written and quoted utterances since the war, he has refrained from mentioning this fact, but it is embodied in the regimental records.

Shortly after the French national holiday, the 369th was sent about 15 kilometers west to a position in front of the Butte de Mesnil, a high hill near Maison en Champagne, occupied by the Germans. Around that district they held half a dozen sectors at different times with only one week of rest until September 26th.

Artillery duels were constant. It is related that near the Butte de Mesnil the regiment lost a man an hour and an officer a day from the shell fire of the Boche. So accurate were the gunners handling the German 77s that frequently a solitary soldier who exposed himself would actually be "sniped" off by a cannoneer.

In the September fighting the 369th saw the toughest period of its entire service. In company with a Moroccan Negro unit and others, the regiment participated in the attack on the Butte de Mesnil. The New Yorkers took the important town of Sechault and it was for that exploit that their flag was decorated with the Croix de Guerre.

Throughout the western Argonne fighting and the various sectors of the Champagne in which the 369th operated, especially during the months of July, August and September, their service was typical of that of other units of the 93rd Division. The going was tough for all of them and each contributed everlasting fame to American arms and undying renown to the Negro race.

Heroes of the Old 15th Infantry.

Officers and men of the 369th New York colored regiment awarded the Croix de Guerre for gallantry in Action:

Sergt. A.A. Adams

Corp. John Allen

Lieut. R.R. DeArmond

Lieut. G.A. Arnston

Corp. Farrandus Baker

Sergt. E.W. Barrington

Sergt M.W. Barron

Sergt. William D. Bartow

Capt. Aaron T. Bates

Corp. Fletcher Battle

Corp. R. Bean

Corp. J.S. Beckton

Pvt. Myril Billings

Sergt. Ed. Bingham

Lieut. J.C. Bradner

Pvt. Arthur Brokaw

Pvt. H.D. Brown

Pvt. T.W. Brown

Lieut. Elmer C. Bucher

Pvt. Wm. H. Bunn

Sergt. Wm. Butler

Pvt. J.L. Bush

Sergt. Joseph Carmen

Corp. T. Catto

Corp. G.H. Chapman

Sergt. Major Benedict W. Cheesman

Capt. John H. Clarke, Jr.

Lieut. P.M. Clendenin

Capt. Frederick W. Cobb

Sergt. Robert Collins

Lieut. J.H. Connor

Sergt. Wm. H. Cox

Sergt C.D. Davis

Lieut. Charles Dean

Pvt. P. Demps

Wagoner Martin Dunbar

Corp. Elmer Earl

Pvt. Frank Ellis

Sergt. Sam Fannell

Capt. Robt. F. Ferguson, Jr.

Capt. Charles W. Fillmore

Capt. Edward J. Farrell

Capt. Hamilton Fish, Jr.

Capt Edwin R.D. Fox

Lieut. Conrad Fox

Sergt. Richard W. Fowler

Pvt. Roland Francis

Pvt. B. Freeman

Pvt. I. Freeman

Sergt Wm. A. Gains

Wagoner Richard O. Goins

Pvt. J.J. Gordon

Lieut. R.C. Grams

Pvt. Stillman Hanna

Pvt. Hugh Hamilton

Pvt. G.E. Hannibal

Pvt. Frank Harden
Pvt. Frank Hatchett
Corp. Ralph Hawkins
Colonel Wm. Hayward
Lieut. E.H. Holden
Sergt. Wm. H. Holliday
Corp. Earl Horton
Pvt. G. Howard
Lieut. Stephen H. Howey
Sergt. Major Clarence C. Hudson
Pvt. Ernest Hunter
Sergt. S. Jackson
Corp. Clarence Johnson
Sergt. D.F. Johnson
Pvt. Gilbert Johnson
Sergt. George Jones
Lieut. Gorman R. Jones
Sergt. James H. Jones
Pvt. Smithfield Jones
Pvt. J.C. Joynes
Lieut. W.H. Keenan
Lieut. Elwin C. King
Lieut. Harold M. Landon
Lieut. Nils H. Larsen
Major David A. L'Esperance
Lieut. W.F. Leland
Pvt. D.W. Lewis
Pvt. W.D. Link

Major Arthur W. Little

Lieut. Walter R. Lockhart

Sergt. B. Lucas

Pvt. Lester A. Marshall

Pvt. Lewis Martin

Sergt. A.J. McArthur

Capt. Seth B. MacClinton

Pvt. Elmer McGowan

Pvt. Herbert McGirt

Capt. Comerford McLoughlin

Pvt. L. McVea

Sergt. H. Matthews

Sergt. Jesse A. Miller

Sergt Wm. H. Miller

Sergt. E. Mitchell

Pvt. Herbert Mills

Corp. M. Molson

Lieut. E.D. Morey

Sergt. W. Morris

Sergt. G.A. Morton

Lieut. E.A. Nostrand

Sergt. Samuel Nowlin

Capt. John O. Outwater

Lieut. Hugh A. Page

Lieut. Oliver H. Parish

Sergt. C.L. Pawpaw

Pvt. Harvey Perry

Sergt. Clinton Peterson

Lieut. Col. W.A. Pickering

Lieut. Richardson Pratt

Sergt. John Pratt

Sergt. H.D. Primas

Pvt. Jeremiah Reed

Lieut. Durant Rice

Pvt. John Rice

Sergt. Samuel Richardson

Sergt Charles Risk

Pvt. F. Ritchie

Lieut. G.S. Robb

Corp. Fred Rogers

Pvt. Lionel Rogers

Pvt. George Rose

Lieut. R.M. Rowland

Sergt. Percy Russell

Sergt. L. Sanders

Pvt. William Sanford

Lieut. H.J. Argent

Pvt. Marshall Scott

Capt. Lewis E. Shaw

Capt. Samuel Shethar

Lieut. Hoyt Sherman

Major G. Franklin Shiels

Pvt. A. Simpson

Sergt. Bertrand U. Smith

Pvt. Daniel Smith

Sergt. Herman Smith

Corp. R.W. Smith
Major Lorillard Spencer
Sergt. J.T. Stevens
Corp. Dan Storms
Lieut. George F. Stowell
Corp. T.W. Taylor
Lieut. Frank B. Thompson
Sergt. Lloyd Thompson
Sergt. A.L. Tucker
Sergt. George Valaska
Lieut. D.H. Vaughan
Capt. Edward A. Walton
Capt Charles Warren
Sergt. Leon Washington
Pvt. Casper White
Capt. James D. White
Sergt. Jay White
Sergt. Jesse J. White
Sergt. C.E. Williams
Pvt. Robert Williams
Sergt. Reaves Willis
Pvt. H. Wiggington
Sergt. L. Wilson
Pvt. Tim Winston
Sergt. E. Woods
Pvt. George Wood
Lieut. A.D. Worsham
Sergt. E.C. Wright

Sergt. Henry Johnson
Pvt. Needham Roberts

CHAPTER XV

Over There

Henry Johnson and Needham Roberts—The Tiger's Cubs—Negro First to Get Palm—Johnson's Graphic Story—Smashes the Germans—Irvin Cobb's Tribute—Christian and Mohammedan Negroes Pals—Valor of 93rd Division—Laughter in Face of Death—Negro and Poilu Happy Together—Butte De Mesnil—Valiant and Humorous Elmer Mccowin—Winning War Crosses—Verdict of The French—The Negro's Faith

A most conspicuous Negro hero of the war, and for that matter of any race serving with the American army, was Sergeant Henry Johnson of Albany, N.Y. His exploit was shared by a company mate, Needham Roberts. For pure bull dog grit and tigerish fighting, the exploit has seldom, if ever, been equalled in the annals of any war. It resulted in the War Crosses for each with a special citation, and the whole French force in that section of the Champagne lined up to see them get the decorations. Across the red and green ribbon of Johnson's decoration was a golden palm, signifying extraordinary valor. Johnson was the first private of any race in the American army to get the palm with his Croix de Guerre. Here is the story as told in Johnson's own words after his arrival back in New York:

"There isn't so much to tell", said Johnson with characteristic modesty. *"There wasn't anything so fine about it. Just fought for my life. A rabbit would have done that.*

"Well, anyway, me and Needham Roberts were on patrol duty on May 15. The corporal wanted to send out two new drafted men on the sentry post for the midnight-to-four job. I told him he was crazy to send untrained men out there and risk the rest of us. I said I'd tackle the job, though I needed sleep.

"German snipers had been shooting our way that night and I told the corporal he wanted men on the job who knew their rifles. He said it was imagination, but anyway he took those green men off and left Needham

and me on the posts. I went on at midnight. It was moonlight. Roberts was at the next post. At one o'clock a sniper took a crack at me from a bush fifty yards away. Pretty soon there was more firing and when Sergeant Roy Thompson came along I told him.

"'*What's the matter men*' *he asked, 'You scared?*'

"'*No I ain't scared*', *I said*, '*I came over here to do my bit and I'll do it. But I was jes' lettin' you know there's liable to be some tall scrappin' around this post tonight*'. *He laughed and went on, and I began to get ready. They'd a box of hand grenades there and I took them out of the box and laid them all in a row where they would be handy. There was about thirty grenades, I guess. I was goin' to bust that Dutch army in pieces if it bothered me.*

"*Somewhere around two o'clock I heard the Germans cutting our wire out in front and I called to Roberts. When he came I told him to pass the word to the lieutenant. He had just started off when the snippin' and clippin' of the wires sounded near, so I let go with a hand grenade. There was a yell from a lot of surprised Dutchmen and then they started firing. I hollered to Needham to come back.*

"*A German grenade got Needham in the arm and through the hip. He was too badly wounded to do any fighting, so I told him to lie in the trench and hand me up the grenades.*

"'*Keep your nerve*' *I told him*. '*All the Dutchmen in the woods are at us, but keep cool and we'll lick 'em.*' *Roberts crawled into the dugout. Some of the shots got me, one clipped my head, another my lip, another my hand, some in my side and one smashed my left foot so bad that I have a silver plate holding it up now.*

"*The Germans came from all sides. Roberts kept handing me the grenades and I kept throwing them and the Dutchmen kept squealing, but jes' the same they kept comin' on. When the grenades were all gone I started in with my rifle. That was all right until I shoved in an American cartridge clip—it was a French gun—and it jammed.*

"*There was nothing to do but use my rifle as a club and jump into them. I banged them on the dome and the side and everywhere I could land until the butt of my rifle busted. One of the Germans hollered, 'Rush him! Rush him!' I decided to do some rushing myself. I grabbed my French bolo knife and slashed in a million directions. Each slash meant something, believe me. I wasn't doing exercises, let me tell you.*

"I picked out an officer, a lieutenant I guess he was. I got him and I got some more of them. They knocked me around considerable and whanged me on the head, but I always managed to get back on my feet. There was one guy that bothered me. He climbed on my back and I had some job shaking him off and pitching him over my head. Then I stuck him in the ribs with the bolo. I stuck one guy in the stomach and he yelled in good New York talk: 'That black —— got me.'

"I was still banging them when my crowd came up and saved me and beat the Germans off. That fight lasted about an hour. That's about all. There wasn't so much to it."

No, there was not much to it, excepting that next morning the Americans found four German bodies with plentiful indications that at least thirty-two others had been put on the casualty list and several of the German dead probably had been dragged back by their comrades. Thirty-eight bombs were found, besides rifles, bayonets and revolvers.

It was Irvin Cobb, the southern story writer, who first gave to the world a brief account of the exploit of Johnson and Roberts in the Saturday Evening Post during the summer of 1918. He commented as follows:

"If ever proof were needed, which it is not, that the color of a man's skin has nothing to do with the color of his soul, this twain then and there offered it in abundance."

Mr. Cobb in the same article paid many tributes to the men of the 369th and 371st serving at that time in that sector. Among other things he said:

"They were soldiers who wore their uniforms with a smartened pride; who were jaunty and alert and prompt in their movements; and who expressed as some did vocally in my hearing, and all did by their attitude, a sincere heartfelt inclination to get a whack at the foe with the shortest possible delay."

Continuing, Mr. Cobb uttered a sentiment that is sure to awaken a glow in the hearts of all sympathizers and friends of the Negro race. "I am of the opinion personally," he said, "and I make the assertion with all the better grace, I think, seeing that I am a Southerner with all the Southerner's inherited and acquired prejudices touching on the race question—that as a result of what our black soldiers are going to do in this war, a word that has been uttered billions of times in our country, sometimes in derision, sometimes in hate, sometimes in all kindliness—but which I am sure never fell on black ears but it left behind a sting for the heart—is going to have a new meaning for all of us, South and North too, and that hereafter n-i-g-g-e-r will merely be another way of spelling the word American."

Many a man in the four regiments comprising the 93rd division when he heard about the exploit of May 15th, oiled his rifle, sharpened his bayonet and whetted his trench knife, resolved to go Henry Johnson and Needham Roberts one better if the opportunity came to him. It did come to many of them in the days that followed and although none got a chance to distinguish himself in equal degree with the redoubtable Johnson, it was because the Boche had become too wary. They had cultivated a healthy respect for the colored men and called them "blutlustige schwartze manner," meaning "blood-thirsty black men." Another nickname they had was "Hell Fighters."

When the 93rd division was brigaded with the French on the Aisne, at least two of the component regiments were under a French general having in his command several thousand Moroccan Negroes. He placed them on the other side of the river fearing they would quarrel over religious differences. However, it was impossible to keep them from fraternizing. There were no religious disputes, nor is it of record that the Americans attempted to convert the Mohammedans. But they did initiate their turbaned comrades into the mysteries of a certain American game and it is said that the disciples of Allah experienced considerable hard luck.

Most of the 93rd division was under fire from the early days of May, 1918, until the close of the war. The 369th, which left New York with 56 officers and 2,000 men, returned with only 20 officers and 1,200 men of the original organization. A few had been transferred to casual companies and other commands, but many will never come back; their bodies being part of the soil of France—killed in action, died of wounds or disease.

The tale of the 93rd is full of deeds of valor, laughter in the face of death, of fearful carnage wrecked upon the foe, of childlike pride in the homage their Allies paid them, and now and then an incident replete with the bubbling Negro humor that is the same whether it finds its outlet on the cotton-fields of Dixie or the battlefields of France.

Between the French and the colored troops the spirit was superb. The French poilu had not been taught that the color of a man's skin made a difference. He had no prejudices. How could he have, coming from a nation whose motto is LIBERTY, FRATERNITY, EQUALITY?

He formed his judgment from bravery and Manhood and Honor. The Negro soldiers ate, slept and drank with the poilus. They were happy together.

An incident of the valor of the 93rd division was in the fight at Butte de Mesnil, as tough a spot as any in the line between the sea and Switzerland. The ground had been fought over back and forth, neither side holding it for long. The French said it was the burying place of 200,000 of their troops and Germans, and that it could not be held permanently. The Negro boys tackled the job. In four days they had advanced fourteen kilometers (8.4 miles) and they NEVER retreated.

The Negro troops to a great extent went into action with little training, but they learned quickly in the hard school of experience. They excelled in grenade throwing and machine gun work. Grenade throwing is very ticklish business. Releasing the pin lights the fuse. Five seconds after the fuse is lighted the grenade explodes. It must be timed exactly. If thrown too quickly the enemy is liable to pick it up and hurl it back in time to create the explosion in one's own lines. No one cares to hold a grenade long after the fuse is lighted so the boys sometimes threw them ahead of the signal.

"Shorty" Childress of B company, 371st Infantry, had been drilled with dummy grenades. When given the real thing he released the pin and immediately heard the fulminating fuse working its way down into the charge. It was too much for his nerves. He threw the grenade as far as he could send it. The lieutenant reprimanded him severely.

"What do you mean," he said, "by hurling that explosive ahead of the proper time. Do you want the Boches to pick it up, fire it back here and blow us all to smithereens?"

"Shorty" was properly abashed. He hung his head and responded: "Lieutenant, I begs your pardon, I didn't mean to heave it so soon, but I could actually feel that thing a swellin' in my hand."

But they soon acquired the idea, and after a short time very few of the grenades reached the enemy either ahead of or behind time.

Here is the valiant and humorous story of Elmer McCowin, 669 Lenox Avenue, New York City, a private in Company K, 369th infantry, and how he won the Distinguished Service Cross. He said:

> "On September 26th, the captain asked me to carry dispatches. The Germans pumped machine gun bullets at me all the way, but I made the trip and got back safely. Then I was sent out again. As I started the captain

hollered to bring him back a can of coffee. He was joking but I didn't know it.

"Being a foot messenger I had some time ducking those German bullets. Those bullets seemed very sociable but I didn't care to meet up with any of them, so I kept on traveling on high gear. None touched my skin, though some skinned pretty close.

"On the way back it seemed the whole war was turned on me. One bullet passed through my trousers and it made me hop, skip and jump. I saw a shell hole six feet deep. Take it from me I dented it another six feet when I plunged into it. In my fist I held the captain's can of coffee.

"When I climbed out of the hole and started running again a bullet clipped a hole in the can and the coffee started to run out. But I turned around stopped a second, looked the Kaiser in the face and held up the can of coffee with my finger plugging up the hole to show the Germans they were fooled. Just then another bullet hit the can and another finger had to act as a stopper. I pulled out an old rabbit's foot that my girl had given me and rubbed it so hard the hair almost came off.

"It must have been the good luck thing that saved my life because the bullets were picking at my clothes and so many hit the can that at the end all my fingers were in use to keep the coffee in. I jumped into shell holes and wriggled along the ground and got back safely. And what do you think? When I got back into our own trenches I stumbled and spilled the coffee."

Not only did Lieutenant George Miller, battalion adjutant, confirm the story, but he added:

"When that boy came back with the coffee his clothes were riddled with bullets. Yet half an hour later he went out into no man's land and brought back a number of wounded until he was badly gassed. Even then he refused to go to the rear and went out again for a wounded soldier. All this under fire. That's the reason he got the D.S.C."

Corporal Elmer Earl, also of Company K, living in Middletown, N.Y., won the D.S.C. He explained:

"We had taken a hill Sept. 26 in the Argonne. We came to the edge of a swamp when the enemy machine guns opened fire. It was so bad that of the 58 of us who went into a particular strip, only 8 came out without being killed or wounded. I made a number of trips out there and brought back about a dozen wounded men."

The proudest recollection which Negro officers and privates will carry through life is that of the whole-hearted recognition given them in the matter of decorations by the French army authorities. Four colored regiments of the 93rd division attained the highest record in these awards. These regiments being brigaded with the French, their conduct in action was thus under their observation. Not only was each of these regiments cited as a unit for the Croix de Guerre, but 365 individual soldiers received the coveted decoration. A large number of Distinguished Service Crosses were also distributed to the 93rd division by General Pershing. The verdict pronounced by critical French commanders may be considered as an unquestionable confirmation that the Negro troops were under all conditions brave fighters. This fact and the improved status of the Negro as a result of it was pointed to by the New York Tribune, in a leading editorial in its issue of February 14, 1919. It said:

> *"The bas-relief of the Shaw Memorial became a living thing as the dusky heroes of the 15th cheered the Liberty statue and happily swarmed down the gangplank. Appropriately the arrival was on the birthday of the "revered Lincoln," and never was the young and martyred idealist of Massachusetts filled with greater pride than swelled in Colonel Hayward as he talked of his men the best regiment, he said, with pardonable emphasis, 'of all engaged in the great war.'*
>
> *"These were men of the Champagne and the Argonne whose step was always forward; who held a trench ninety days without relief, with every night a raid night; who won 171 medals for conspicuous bravery; who saw the war expire under their pressure in a discouraged German cannonade. First class fighting men! Hats off to them! The tribunal of grace does not regard skin color when assessing souls.*
>
> *"The boys cheered the Bartholdi statue. It makes some whites uncomfortable. It converts into strange reading glib eulogies of democratic principles.*
>
> *"A large faith possesses the Negro. He has such confidence in justice,—the flow—of which he believes will yet soften hard hearts. We have a wonderful example of a patience that defies discouragement; the "Souls of Black Folk"! When values are truly measured, some things will be different in this country."*

CHAPTER XVI

Through Hell and Suffering

Negro Officers Make Good—Wonderful Record of the 8th Illinois—"Black Devils" Win Decorations Galore—Tribute of French Commander—His Farewell to Prairie Fighters—They Fought After War Was Over—Hard to Stop Them—Individual Deeds of Heroism—Their Dead, Their Wounded and Suffering—A Poem

In the past when the subject of the Negro's fighting ability was under discussion, there were always found those whose grudging assent to his merits as a soldier was modified by the assertion that he had to be properly commanded; in other words must have white officers. Never having been given a conspicuous opportunity to demonstrate his capacity for leadership in battle, until the formation of the 8th Illinois infantry in the Spanish-American war, the Negro was forced to rest under the imputation that as a follower he did fairly well, but as a leader he was a failure.

Let anyone who still holds that view study the record of the 8th Illinois, or the 370th, as it was rechristened when entering the service of the general government in the recent war. Seventy-one War Crosses with special citations for valor and merit, and twenty-one Distinguished Service Crosses were awarded officers and men of the regiment. Many men in the 370th were veterans of the Spanish-American war as well as the campaign of 1916 on the Mexican border, which, while not an actual war, was for some months a locality of service and hard service at that; the regiment passing through it with great credit.

It was organized as a single battalion in 1891, increased to a regiment and sent to Cuba in 1898, every officer and man in the regiment being a Negro. Upon its return, over half of the city of Chicago turned out in greeting. Until July 12th, 1918, the regiment had never had a white officer. Then its Colonel, F.A. Denison, was relieved on account of illness and a white officer in the person of Colonel Thomas A. Roberts for the first time was placed in command. Shortly before the armistice two other white officers were attached to the regiment, in the persons of Major William H. Roberts, a brother of the colonel, and Captain John F. Prout; Second Lieutenant M.F. Stapleton, white, also served as adjutant of the First battalion.

The 370th received brief training at Camp Logan, Houston, Texas, and landed in France April 22, 1918; going within a few weeks into actual service. Like nearly all of the new regiments arriving at that time its operations were confined mainly to trench warfare.

Trench warfare continued until July 6, when the men got their real baptism of fire in a section of the Argonne and were in all the important engagements of their portion of the Champagne and other fronts, fighting almost continuously from the middle of July until the close of the war, covering themselves with a distinction and glory, as Knights in the warfare for Mankind, that will endure as long as the story of valorous deeds are recorded.

Like the other regiments of the 93rd Division, the 370th was brigaded with the French; first with the 73rd French Division and later under direct command of General Vincendon of the 59th Division, a part of the famous 10th French army under General Mangin. Shortly after the signing of the armistice, the division commander sent the regiment the following communication:

Officers, non-commissioned officers and men:

Your efforts have been rewarded. The armistice is signed. The troops of the Entente to whom the armies of the American Republic have nobly come to join themselves, have vanquished the most powerful instrument of conquest that a nation could forge—the haughty German Army acknowledges itself conquered. However hard our conditions are, the enemy government has accepted them all.

The 370th R.I.U.S. has contributed largely to the success of the 59th Division, and has taken in bitter strife both cannon and machine guns. Its units, fired by a noble ardor, got at times even beyond the objectives given them by the higher command; they have always wished to be in the front line, for the place of honor is the leading rank.

They have shown in our advance that they are worthy of being there.

VINCENDON.

"Black Devils" was the name the Prussian Guard who faced them gave to the men of the 370th. Their French comrades called them "The Partridges," probably on account of their cockiness in action (a cock partridge is very game), and their smart, prideful appearance on parade.

A general outline of the service of the Illinois men after coming out of the trenches, as well as an illustration of the affection and high appreciation in which they were held by the French, is contained in the following order issued by General Vincendon in December:

Officers and soldiers of the 370th R.I.U.S.:

You are leaving us. The impossibility at this time that the German Army can recover from its defeat, the necessity which is imposed on the people of the Entente of taking up again a normal life, leads the United States to diminish its effectiveness in France. You are chosen to be among the first to return to America. In the name of your comrades of the 59th Division I say to you, au revoir. In the name of France, I thank you.

The hard and brilliant battles of Chavigny, Leury and the Bois de Beaumont having reduced the effectiveness of the division, the American government generously put your regiment at the disposition of the French High Command. In order to reinforce us, you arrived from the trenches of the Argonne.

We at first, at Mareuil Sur Ourcq, in September, admired your fine appearance under arms, the precision of your review and the suppleness of your evolutions that presented to the eye the appearance of silk unrolling in wavy folds. We advanced to the line. Fate placed you on the banks of the Ailette in front of the Bois Mortier. October 12 you occupied the enemy trenches at Acier and Brouze. On the 13th we reached the railroad of Laon le Fere; the forest of Saint Gobain, the principal center of resistance of the Hindenburg line was ours.

November 5th the Serre was at last crossed and the pursuit became active. Major Prout's battalion distinguished Itself at the Val St. Pierre, where it captured a German battery. Major Patton's battalion was first to cross the Hirson railroad at the heights of Aubenton, where the Germans tried to resist. Duncan's battalion took Logny and, carried away by their ardor, could not be stopped short of Gue d' Hossus on November 11th, after the armistice. We have hardly time to appreciate you and already you depart.

183

W. Allison Sweeney

As Lieut. Colonel Duncan said November 28, in offering to me your regimental colors as proof of your love for France and as an expression of your loyalty to the 59th Division and our Army, you have given us of your best and you have given it out of the fullness of your hearts.

The blood of your comrades who fell on the soil of France mixed with the blood of our soldiers, renders indissoluble the bonds of affection that unite us. We have, besides, the pride of having worked together at a magnificent task, and the pride of bearing on our foreheads the ray of a common grandeur.

VINCENDON.

---

59 th DIVISION   *Quartier General Dec. 8/18*

GENERAL ORDERS
NO. 4765

Officers and Soldiers of the 370 th R. I. U. S.

You are leaving us: the impossibility at this time that that the German Army can recover from its defeat, — the necessity which is imposed upon the people of the ENTENTE of again taking up a normal life, leads the UNITED STATES to diminish its effectives in FRANCE. You are chosen to be among the first to return to America. In the name FRANCE " Thank you ". In the name of your comrades of the 59 th DIVISION, I say to you " AU REVOIR "

The hard brilliant battles of CHAVIGNY and LEURY, and of the BOIS de MORTIER generously put your regiment at the disposal of the FRENCH HIGH COMMAND to reinforce us. You have come from the trenches of the ARGONNE.

We at first at MAUBIEL sur ORCQ, in September, admired your fine appearance under arms, — the parcision of your review, the suppleness of your evolution that presented to the appearance of silk unrolling in wavy folds.

We advanced to the lines; fate placed you on the banks of the AILLETTE in front of the BOIS de MORTIER. Oct. 12 th you occupied the enemy trenches ACIER and BRAUZE. On the 13 th we reached the Railroad of LAON la FERRE, the forest of ST-GOBAIN, principal of resistance of the HINDENBURG LINE was ours.

November the 5 th SERRE was at last crossed, — the pursuit became effective. Prout's Bataillon distinguished itself at the VAL ST-PIERRE, where it captured a German Battery. Patton's Bataillon was first the cros the HIRSON RAILROAD at the heights of AUBONON whe the Germans tried to resist. Duncan's Bataillon took LOGNY and on November 11 th after Armistice, carried by their order, could not be stopped short of GUE d'HOSSUS.

We have barely time to appreciate you, an al ready you depart.

As Lieutenant COLONEL Duncan said November the 28 th in offering me your Regimental Colors, was a proof of your Ler for FRANCE. As an expression of your loyalty to the 59 th DIVISION of our Army, you have given your best, and you are given it out of the fulness of your hearths.

The blood of your comrades, who fell on the soil of FRANCE, mixet with the blood of your soldiers, renders indissoluble the bonds of affecti on that unites us. We have, besides the pride od having worked together at a magnificent task; and the pride of beering our forheads to the rays of a common grandeur.

A last time. " Au revoir "

All of us of the 59 th Division will remember the time when the 370 th R. I. U. S. under the orders of the distinguished Colonel Roberts, foormed a part of our beautiful DIVISION.

           General VINCENDON
           Commanding the 59 th Division.

Signed : VINCENDON, *facsimile*.

This is a facsimile reproduction of the original, printed hurriedly near the field of battle and also translated hurriedly without eliminating errors. Corrected on page 155.

To the 370th belongs the honor of the absolutely last engagement of the war. An objective had been set for the regiment on the morning of November 11th. General Vincendon heard of the hour at which hostilities were to end and sent an order to the regiment to shorten its objec-objective. The order failed to arrive in time and ten minutes after the fighting was over Lieut. Colonel Duncan led the third battalion over the German line and captured a train of fifty wagons. General Vincendon said:

"Colonel Duncan is the hardest man to stop fighting I ever saw. He doesn't know when to quit."

One of the most daring exploits by a member of the regiment was that performed by Sergeant Matthew Jenkins, a Chicago boy and member of Company F. On September 20, at Mont des Singes, he went ahead of his comrades and captured from the Boche a fortified tunnel which by aid of his platoon was held for thirty-six hours without food or ammunition, making use of the enemy machine gun and munitions until relieved. This gained for Sergeant Jenkins the Croix de Guerre with Palm and the Distinguished Service Cross.

A deed of remarkable bravery accompanied by clever strategy was performed by Captain Chester Sanders and twenty men mostly of Company F. It won decorations for three and the unbounded admiration of the French. Captain Sanders and his men offered themselves as sacrifices in an effort to draw the fire of about a dozen German machine guns which had been working havoc among the Americans and French. The Illinois men ran into the middle of a road knowing they were under German observation. Instantly the Germans, suspecting a raid on their lines, opened fire on the underbrush by the roadside, figuring the Americans would take refuge there. Instead they kept right in the center of the road and few were wounded. The ruse had revealed the whereabouts of the German guns, and a short time later they were wiped out by French artillery.

Another hero of Company F was Lieutenant Harvey J. Taylor, who found himself in a nest of machine guns on July 16 in the western part of the Argonne forest. He received wounds in both legs, a bullet through one arm, a bullet in his side, had a front tooth knocked out by a bullet and received a ruptured ear drum by another. After all this he was back in the lines October 24th at Soissons. The Germans were making a counter attack that day and when the battling colored men needed supplies, Lieutenant Taylor, who was regimental signal officer, proceeded to get the supplies to them, though he had to pass through a German barrage. He was badly gassed. He received the Croix de Guerre with a special citation.

Lieutenant Elmer D. Maxwell won his Cross in the Champagne, six miles northwest of Laon. He led a platoon of men against a nest of machine guns, taking four guns and eighteen prisoners, not to speak of leaving behind a number of Germans who were not in a condition to be taken prisoner.

Many of the officers of the regiment were wounded. The escape of many from death, considering the continuous fighting and unusual perils through which they passed, was miraculous. The only officer who made the supreme sacrifice was Lieutenant George L. Giles of 3833 Calumet Avenue, Chicago. He was the victim of a direct hit by a shell at Grandlut on November 1 while he was heroically getting his men into shelter. Lieut. Giles was very popular with the men and with his brother officers. He was popular among the members of the race section in which he lived in Chicago, and was regarded as a young man of great promise.

One of the engagements of the first battalion that received more than honorable mention was on the morning of November 6th, when the battalion crossed the Hindenburg line and after extremely hard fighting captured on St. Pierre Mont, three 77 guns and two machine guns. Captain James H. Smith of 3267 Vernon Avenue, Chicago, commanded the company, and Lieutenant Samuel S. Gordon of 3842 Prairie Avenue, Chicago, the assault forces making the capture. The battalion continued across the Serre river and when the armistice was signed was at a small place in Belgium.

Several of the officers passed through practically all of the fighting with hardly a scratch, only to be taken ill at the finish and invalided home. These men would have been greatly disappointed had the war continued after they were put out of action. Conspicuous among them was Lieutenant Robert A. Ward of 3728 South Wabash Avenue, Chicago, of the Trench Mortar platoon; Lieutenant Benjamin A. Browning of 4438 Prairie Avenue, Chicago, and Lieutenant Joseph R. Wheeler, 3013 Prairie Avenue, Chicago.

Major Rufus Stokes led the first battalion on the initial raid at Vauquois. They fired 300 shells from six trench mortars and scored a notable success. In that raid Private William Morris of Chicago, the only man in the regiment who was captured by the Germans, was taken. He was reported missing at the time, but weeks later his picture was found among a group of prisoners portrayed in a German illustrated newspaper found in a captured dugout.

Three men were killed and a large number of others had a miraculous escape while entering Laon a few days prior to November 1st. A German time mine exploded tearing up a section of railroad track, hurling the heavy rails into the air, where they spun around or flew like so many arrows.

First Lieutenant William J. Warfield, regimental supply officer, a Chicago man, won the Distinguished Service Cross for extraordinary heroism in action near Ferme de la Riviere, September 28th.

Sergeant Norman Henry of the Machine Gun company, whose home is in Chicago, won the Distinguished Service Cross for extraordinary heroism in action near Ferme de la Riviere, September 30th.

Other members of the regiment upon whom the D.S.C. was conferred by General Pershing were:

Captain William B. Crawford, home address, Denison, Texas; for extraordinary heroism in action at Ferme de la Riviere, September 30th.

Sergeant Ralph Gibson, Company H, a Chicago man; for extraordinary heroism at Beaume, November 8th.

Sergeant Charles T. Monroe, Headquarters Company; for extraordinary heroism in action at Mont de Singes, September 24th. His home is at Senrog, Va.

Sergeant Emmett Thompson, Company L, home in Quincy, Illinois; for extraordinary heroism at Mont de Singes, September 20th.

Supply Sergeant Lester Fossie, Company M, home at Metropolis, Illinois; for extraordinary heroism at Ferme de la Riviere, October 5th.

Private Tom Powell, deceased, Company H; for extraordinary heroism near Beaume, November 8th.

Private Spirley Irby, Company H, home at Blackstone, Va.; for extraordinary heroism in action at Beaume, November 8th.

Private Alfred Williamson, medical detachment, home at San Diego, California; for extraordinary heroism in action near Beaume, November 8th.

Private William G. Hurdle, Machine Gun Company No. 3, home at Drivers, Va.; for extraordinary heroism in action at Ferme la Folie, September 30th.

Private Harry Pearson, Machine Gun company No. 3, home at Portland, Oregon; for extraordinary heroism in action near Ferme la Folie, September 30th.

Private Alonzo Walton, Machine Gun Company No. 3, home at Normal, Illinois; for extraordinary heroism in action at Rue Lamcher and Pont D'Amy, November 7th and 9th.

Private Leroy Davis, Company L, home at Huntsville, Missouri; for extraordinary heroism in action at Mont de Singes, September 18th.

Negro warriors administering cold steel. Germans unable to stand the attack. Surrendering. In the Argonne Forest France.

About fifty percent of the 370th met casualties of some sort during their service in France. Like the New York regiment heretofore mentioned, they were singularly free from disease. Only 65 men and one officer were killed in action and about thirty died from wounds. The total number wounded and missing was 483. Probably 1,000 men were gassed and incapacitated at times, as the regiment had three replacements, necessary to make up its losses. The regiment went to France with approximately 2,500 men from Chicago and Illinois, and came back with 1,260. Of course, many of the wounded, sick and severely gassed were invalided home or came back as parts of casual companies formed at hospital bases. The replacement troops which went into the regiment were mostly from the Southern states. A few of the colored officers assigned to the regiment after its arrival in France, were men from the officers training camps in this country and France.

The 370th boasted of the only race court martial in the army. There were thirteen members, Lieutenant Colonel Duncan presiding. Captain Louis E. Johnson was the judge advocate, and Lieutenant Washington was his assistant. It is not of record that the findings of the court martial were criticized. At least there was no scandal as there was concerning court martial proceedings in other divisions of the army. The fact is that there was very little occasion for court martialing among the men of the 370th. The behavior of the men was uniformly good, as is attested by the fact that every town mayor in France where the men passed through or were billeted, complimented the officers on the splendid discipline and good behavior shown.

Colonel Roberts, a veteran cavalryman, was very fond of his men. He has repeatedly paid them the highest compliments, not only for their valor and soldierly qualities, but for their quick intelligence, amenity to discipline, and for the clean living which made them so remarkably free from disease. He has stated that he would not know where to select a better group of men for everything that goes to make up efficient, dependable soldiers. Colonel Roberts received the Croix de Guerre, with the following citation:

> *"A commander entirely devoted to duty, he succeeded by dint of working day and night in holding with his regiment a difficult sector, though the officers and men were without experience, under heavy shelling. He personally took charge of a battalion on the front line on October 12 and led it to the objectives assigned by the crossing of the Ailette canal."*

American historians may not give the Negro fighters the place to which their records entitle them; that remains to be seen. From the testimony of French commanders, however, it is evident that the pages of French history will not be printed unless they contain the valiant, patriotic, heroic deeds of the Illinois and New York regiments with their comrades of the 93rd and 92nd Divisions.

In the various sectors to which they were assigned, they were in virtually every important fight. They met the flower of the Kaiser's forces, held them and on more than one occasion made them retreat. The Hun had misjudged them and it was fortunate that he had. They endured their share of hardship, marching many weary miles, day after day, without sufficient food. Nothing could affect their spirit and dash. When the call came, they went over the top, that the world might be made safe for democracy.

Among the officers and men of the 370th were represented about every calling in which the Negro of this day engages. There were men of professional pursuits; lawyers, doctors and teachers; students, mechanics, business men, farmers and laborers. The poet of the regiment was Lieutenant Blaine G. Alston. The following little poem, if properly digested and understood, tells volumes within itself:

"OVER THERE"

Did you ever hear a bullet whiz,
  Or dodge a hand grenade?
Have you watched long lines of trenches dug
  By doughboys with a spade?
Have you seen the landscape lighted up
  At midnight by a shell?
Have you seen a hillside blazing forth
  Like a furnace room in hell?
Have you stayed all night in a ruined town
  With a rafter for a bed?
With horses stamping underneath
  In the morning when they are fed?
Have you heard the crump-crump whistle?
  Do you know the dud shell's grunt?
Have you played rat in a dugout?—
  Then you have surely seen the front.

—Lieut. Blaine G. Alston, 370th U.S. Troops.

CHAPTER XVII

Narrative of an Officer

Special Article by Captain John H. Patton, Adjutant of 8th Illinois—Summarizes Operations of the Regiment—From First Call to Mustering Out—An Eye Witness Account—In Training Camps, at Sea, in France—Service in Argonne Forest—Many Other Engagements—A Thrilling Record—Battalion Operations in Detail—Special Mention of Companies and Individuals

Captain John H. Patton, regimental adjutant of the 370th, who commanded the second battalion through most of its service, presents a summary of the operations of the regiment from the first call to the mustering out. Being in charge of the organization's records, his account is detailed, authentic and highly valuable as supplementing the data of the previous chapter; gleaned from departmental records and other sources. It carries additional interest as being the testimony of an eye-witness, one who participated in the stirring events in a marked and valorous degree. The recital in Captain Patton's own words, the phrase of a highly trained and efficient military man, follows:

Pursuant to the call of the President, under date of July 3, 1917, the 8th Illinois Infantry reported at the various rendezvous on July 25, 1917, as follows: At Chicago, Illinois regimental headquarters; Headquarters company, Machine Gun company, Supply company, Detachment Medical Department, and Companies A, B, C, D, E, F, G and H; at Springfield, Illinois, Company I; at Peoria, Illinois, Company K; at Danville, Illinois, Company L; at Metropolis, Illinois, Company M.

On the date the regiment responded to the call Colonel Franklin A. Denison commanded the regiment, the other Field Officers being Lieutenant Colonel James H. Johnson, Major Rufus M. Stokes, Major Charles L. Hunt, Major Otis B. Duncan and Captain John H. Patton, regimental adjutant.

The strength of the regiment a short time before responding to the call was approximately one thousand officers and enlisted men, and orders having been received to recruit to maximum strength, 3604 enlisted men, an active recruiting campaign was begun. On July 25, 1917, the strength was approximately 2,500. Soon afterwards orders were received that the regiment would be organized according to Minimum Strength Tables of Organization, which gave it an authorized strength of 2,138 enlisted men. After reporting that the regiment already had several hundred men in excess of that strength, authority was granted to retain the excess men. From this time until demobilized at Camp Grant in March, 1919, the regiment had from 600 to 1,300 men in excess of its authorized strength, and upon arrival in France in April, 1918, the entire personnel consisted of men who had voluntarily enlisted.

Intensive training was begun immediately after the regiment reported at the various armories and the public streets in the vicinity were utilized for this purpose until October 12, 1917, on which date the various organizations entrained for Camp Logan, Houston, Texas, arriving a few days later.

While stationed at Camp Logan, the regiment was engaged in intensive training. Officers and enlisted men attended the various schools established by the 33rd Division to which the regiment had been attached and acquitted themselves with credit.

At the end of October, 1917, on the date of the closing of the Second Liberty Loan Campaign, out of a total of 2,166 officers and enlisted men belonging to the regiment at that time, 1,482 officers and men subscribed $151,400.00.

While at Camp Logan, approximately 96 percent of the regiment took out $10,000.00 War Risk Insurance per man.

On December 1, 1917, the official designation of the regiment was changed from the 8th Illinois Infantry to the 370th Infantry.

On March 6, 1918, the regiment left Camp Logan enroute to Camp Stuart, Newport News, Va., arriving on March 10, 1918, and immediately taking up its interrupted intensive training.

While at Camp Stuart, Va., Lieutenant Colonel James H. Johnson was discharged from the service, and Major Otis B. Duncan, who had commanded the 3rd battalion, was promoted to the grade of lieutenant-colonel and Captain Arthur Williams was promoted to the grade of major and placed in command of the 3rd battalion.

On April 6, 1918, the regiment embarked on the S.S. President Grant en route overseas. In attempting to get out to sea, the vessel ran aground in Hampton Roads and three days later having been refloated, the journey overseas was resumed. On account of this delay the journey was begun without convoy, the warships assigned to this duty having departed as scheduled on or about April 6, 1918. On April 20, 1918, the steamer was met by a convoy of torpedo boats which accompanied us to Brest, France, at which place the regiment arrived on April 22, 1918.

The following day, April 23, 1918, the regiment debarked and marched to camp at Pontanezen Barracks, near Brest, and two days later entrained for Grandvillers (Haut-Rhin), arriving on April 27, 1918, and taking station.

The regiment, upon arrival at Grandvillers, was attached to the 73rd Division, French Army, and orders were given for the reorganization and equipping of the regiment to conform to that of a French regiment. All American arms, ammunition and equipment were salvaged and French rifles, machine guns, ammunition, wheel transportation, packs, helmets and other necessary equipment furnished. Except for the uniform the regiment was outfitted exactly as were the French regiments of that division. French rations were issued with the exception of the wine component, for which an extra allowance of sugar was substituted.

The Division sent officers to take charge of the instruction of the regiment in every phase of the work to be later undertaken and another period of intensive training was begun. Even French cooks were present to instruct our cooks in the preparation and conservation of the French rations.

After six weeks training at this place, the regiment entrained enroute to the front, arrived at Ligny-en-Barrios (Meuse) on June 13, 1918, and moved up toward the lines by easy stages.

On June 21, 1918, the regiment began occupying positions in the Saint Mihiel Sector, completing the occupation on June 24, 1918. This being the first time the regiment had been actually in the lines, the division commander deemed it advisable to intermingle our troops with French troops in order that officers and men might observe and profit by close association with the veteran French troops. Thus the units of the 1st and 2nd battalions, which had been assigned to the front lines were intermingled with platoons and companies of the 325th regiment of infantry.

Many valuable lessons were learned while in this sector, which was exceptionally quiet at the time. Except for occasional shelling and some scattered machine gun and rifle fire, nothing of interest occurred while in the sector, and there were no casualties.

On the night of June 30-July 1, 1918, the regiment, having been relieved in the sector, began withdrawing, and on July 3, 1918, the withdrawal had been completed without any losses.

After resting a few days in the region of Lignieres (Meuse), the regiment entrained en route to the Argonne Forest, arriving behind the lines on July 6, 1918, the 1st Battalion, under command of Major Stokes, moving up immediately into the reserve positions at Brabant (S. Groupement Courcelles) and later into the front lines in the Center of Resistance de la Foret, Sub-Sector Hermont.

The 2nd Battalion under command of Major Hunt took station at Rarecourt, the latter moved up to Locheres (Plateau of Gorgia) at which place the Major located his Commanding Post. From this position companies of the 2nd Battalion were sent into the lines alternately, the companies being relieved after a five days' tour of duty.

On July 12, 1918, Colonel Franklin A. Denison, who had commanded the regiment up to this time and had become incapacitated through illness contracted during the strenuous days incident to the preparation of the regiment for service in the lines, was relieved from command on this account and Colonel T.A. Roberts, cavalry, assumed command of the regiment.

The 3rd battalion under command of Major Williams, was held in reserve at Vraincourt, and only Company M of that battalion was sent into the front lines. This company took up positions in the supporting point at Buzemont on August 7, 1918, and remained until August 14, 1918.

On August 1, 1918, the Stokes Mortar platoon under command of Lieutenant Robert A. Ward took position in the lines in the sub-sector Vaquois, and on August 4, 1918, took an active part in a coup-de-main arranged by the French. His mission, filling in the gaps in the French artillery barrage, was so successfully accomplished that his entire platoon was highly commended for their work by the commanding general of the division.

Although patrols were operating between the lines nightly and the positions occupied were under artillery, machine gun and rifle fire a number of times, the only losses sustained during the six weeks in the Argonne Forest were 1 killed, 1 captured and 4 wounded.

On the night of August 15-16, 1918, the regiment was relieved from its positions in the Forest and marched to Rampont and entrained for villages in the vicinity of Fains (Meuse) for a period of rest, arriving on August 18, 1918.

Upon arrival at the new stations, instruction was begun again, more attention being paid to open warfare than to work incident to trench warfare. This training proved of great value to the officers and men in the latter days of the war, when the regiment was actively engaged in the pursuit of the enemy to the Belgian border.

On September 11, 1918, the regiment left its various stations and proceeded by train to Betz, where it detrained and marched to stations in villages in the vicinity of Mareuil-sur-Ourcq (Meuse). On September 11, 1918, Majors Hunt and Williams having become incapacitated through illness and injury, were relieved from command of the 2nd and 3rd Battalions, respectively, and Lieutenant Colonel Otis B. Duncan and Captain John H. Patton were assigned to the command of those battalions.

The battles of Chavigny, Leury and the Bois de Beaumont having reduced the effectives of the 59th French Division, the regiment was placed at the disposition of the division and was assigned as one of the three infantry regiments thereof. Upon joining this division the effective strength of the regiment was approximately double that of either of the two French regiments; and in future operations a large share of the work of the division fell to our lot.

On September 15, 1918, the regiment received orders to move again toward the front. From Mareuil-sur-Ourcq to the region of St. Bandry (Meuse) the movement was made in motor trucks. On September 16, 1918, the journey was resumed, the regiment proceeding by marching. Upon arrival at Tartier, Companies F and G were sent to Monte Couve (Aisne) to join the 232nd Regiment of Infantry, and Companies I and L pushed forward to Bagneux (Aisne) to join the 325th Regiment. The 1st battalion proceeded the next day to the caves in the vicinity of Les Tueries, the 3rd battalion moved up into the reserve in the region of Antioch Farm with the remainder of the 2nd battalion.

As soon as Companies F, G, I and L had moved up and taken position in the lines opposite Mont des Signes an attack was ordered. Attacks on the enemy positions on the plateau of Mont des Signes were almost continuous from the date of arrival of these companies until about September 21, 1918, when they were withdrawn and joined their battalions. These companies acquitted themselves with credit. One platoon under command of Sergeant Matthew Jenkins, Company F, took a large section of the enemy works for which the sergeant was awarded both the French Croix de Guerre and the American Distinguished Service Cross.

About the 22nd of September, the regiment for the first time took over a full regimental sector, the Battalion Stokes relieving the Battalion Garnier in the positions outlined by La Folie-l'Ecluse on the Canal l'Oise-l'Aisne and the Farm Gulliminet, the Battalion Patton going into the support positions at Mont des Tombes and the Battalion Duncan going into reserve at Tincelle Farm. Colonel Roberts located his commanding post at Antioch Farm. From the date of arrival in these positions until the enemy began to retreat on October 12, 1918, the entire area occupied by the regiment was almost constantly shelled, gas being used frequently. The front lines were almost constantly under the fire of enemy minnenwurfers and numerous machine guns located in the Bois de Mortier, a very dense wood north of the canal.

On the night of September 26-27, 1918, the Battalion Patton was ordered to relieve with like units one-half of each of the companies of the Battalion Stokes in the front lines and soon after the relief was completed an attack along the l'Oise-l'Aisne Canal was ordered. By the extreme of effort the remainder of the Battalion Patton was brought up and having completed the relief of the Battalion Stokes, the attack began as ordered. The attack continued until October 4th, on which date all objectives had been gained and the enemy pushed back across the canal. On September 30th the Battalion Duncan was thrown into the fight and two companies of the Battalion Patton withdrawn to the support. The Battalion Duncan was ordered to make a frontal attack which necessitated an advance across the open fields. This was successfully accomplished, the battalion being subjected to intense artillery, machine gun and rifle fire continuously. The Battalion Duncan, having gained its objectives, the Farm de la Riviere and the railroad south of the canal, held on tenaciously in spite of the intense fire of the enemy and held the positions gained until the pursuit began on October 12, 1918, when it passed into the reserve of the division.

During the occupancy of the sector, from September 22, 1918, to October 12, 1918, patrols from the three battalions were out night and day between the lines making necessary reconnaissances. On October 4, 1918, a volunteer patrol of twenty men under command of Captain Chester Sanders in an effort to discover whether the enemy had abandoned the woods, penetrated the Bois de Mortier to a point about 100 yards behind the enemy positions and having been discovered were fired on from all sides by numerous machine guns. The patrol returned to our lines intact. For this exploit Captain Sanders was awarded the French Croix de Guerre and the patrol received the commendation of the commanding general of the division. On October 7, 1918, after 5 minutes violent bombardment by our artillery, three raiding parties from Company F made a dash for the triangle formed by the railroad, the L'Oise-l'Aisne canal and the Vauxaillon road. One of these parties gained the enemy trenches along the canal, ejecting the enemy after a hand grenade fight. All parties returned to our lines intact though several were wounded. Lieutenant William Warfield of the Battalion Duncan single-handed took an enemy machine gun nest which had been harassing his company, and after disposing of the enemy machine gunners returned to our lines with the gun. Numerous other acts of gallantry were performed in this sector for which officers and men received both French and American decorations.

At 9:20 a.m. on October 12, 1918, the alert was given for a general advance by the entire division and the battalions assembled at the zones of assembly previously designated. The Battalion Stokes was given the mission of clearing the Bois de Mortier and the Battalion Patton was placed at the disposition of Lieutenant Colonel Lugand of the 232nd Infantry, and the 3rd battalion was placed in the divisional reserve. At about 11:00 a. m. the pursuit began, the 1st battalion clearing the Bois de Mortier and successfully reaching its first objective, Penancourt, the same date, and continuing the pursuit the next day to a point west of Molinchart.

The Battalion Patton, having been assigned as the support battalion of the 232nd Regiment of Infantry, took up the pursuit via Anizy le Chateau, Cessieres and the Bois de Oiry, bivouacing the night of October 13th in the vicinity of the Bois.

These battalions were commended by the commanding general. The Battalion Stokes for its passage of the exceedingly strong position in the Bois de Mortier and the 2nd for its well conducted march in pursuit via Anizy le Chateau.

On account of the straightening out of the lines due to the retreat of the enemy, the 59th Division was withdrawn on October 14th and sent back for rest, the regiment being sent into the St. Gobain Forest and vicinity for this purpose. Ten of the twelve days in this locality were spent in hard work on the roads and the last two were given over to the re-equipping of the regiment.

W. Allison Sweeney

On October 22, 1918, Major Rufus M. Stokes was relieved from command of the 1st battalion and assigned to duty as administrative officer of the Regimental Combat and Supply Trains. Captain John T. Prout was assigned to the command of the 1st battalion.

On October 27th, 1918, the regiment was again ordered into the lines and at midnight on that date the 2nd battalion moved up into support positions in the vicinity of Grandlup.

The 1st battalion on October 29, 1918, moved up into support positions in the vicinity of the same village. During this time the 3rd battalion was located at Manneaux Farm in reserve. The battalions remained in various positions in the vicinity of Grandlup until November 5, 1918, on which date the enemy again began to retreat, and while thus occupied were subjected to severe shelling and those units occupying front line positions to much machine gun and rifle fire; casualties were few except in Company A stationed in the vicinity of Chantrud Farm, where an enemy shell fell in the midst of the company at mess, killing thirty-five men and wounding fifty, thus causing the company to be withdrawn from the lines.

On the morning of November 5th, a general advance was ordered and the enemy retreated before it. The retreat of the enemy was so rapid that our troops did not catch up with them until about November 8th, on which date a general attack by the division was ordered. The 2nd battalion on the left of the division was given the task of clearing out the enemy from positions along the Hirshon railroad and the Heights of Aubenton. After an all day fight the battalion reached its objective about nightfall. The French division on the left did not advance as anticipated, owing to enemy resistance on their front, and the 2nd battalion having advanced about two kilometers to the front suffered severely on account of the exposed flank, three men being killed and two officers and thirty-three enlisted men being wounded. On the morning of the 9th the enemy again retreated and the 2nd battalion continued the pursuit to Goncelin, resting there for the night and on the morning of the both was ordered to cantonment at Pont d'Any, where it was located at the taking effect of the armistice.

On November 6th the 1st battalion took up the pursuit in support of the Battalion Michel of the 325th Regiment of Infantry, advancing via Brazicourt and Rapeire to Hill 150 near St. Pierremont. Company C having passed on into the front lines at the Brazicourt Farm, upon arrival near St. Pierremont were ordered on the morning of November 6, 1918, to attack and occupy St. Pierremont, cross the Serre River and take up a position along the railroad track. The mission of the company was successfully accomplished in spite of the strong resistance of the enemy, St. Pierremont being occupied, the river crossed and three pieces of enemy artillery as well as several machine guns taken. For this operation Company C was cited and awarded the French Croix de Guerre with a Palm, the highest French citation received in the regiment. The battalion continued the pursuit until arrival at Mont Plaisir, when it was ordered back to Fligny, where it was in cantonment at the taking effect of the armistice.

The 3rd Battalion took up the pursuit on November 5th, resting in the open fields the nights of the 5th and 6th. The battalion in moving up advanced via Bosmont and Mont Plaisir and passed on into the front lines at the Rue Larcher on November 7, 1918. In the afternoon of the 8th orders were received to deliver a cover fire for French units which were to make an attack on the village of Logny, which was strongly held by the enemy. Company M, having been assigned for this work, moved out from Hurtebise and advanced to a position where the cover fire could be effectively delivered, and opened fire. About this time word was received from the French commander that his troops could not advance on account of the severe shell and machine gun fire, and Company M having arrived at a position where it was safer to go ahead than to retreat, attacked the town and drove the enemy therefrom. For this action Lieutenant Osceola A. Browning, commanding Company M, and several others received the French Croix de Guerre and Sergeant Lester Fossie both the Croix de Guerre and the American Distinguished Service Cross. On November 10, 1918, the advance and pursuit was continued. At Etignieres the battalion was temporarily stopped by intense shell fire. On November 11, 1918, the pursuit was again taken up with Resinowez as the principal objective. Later the objective was changed to Gue d'Hossus, Belgium, which objective was reached a few minutes before the taking effect of the armistice, an enemy combat train of about 50 vehicles being captured about this time.

A few days after the armistice, the regiment began to move southward, taking station in villages in the vicinity of Verneuil-sur-Serre.

Some war cross winners of 8th Illinois (370th Infantry). Front row left to right: Capt. G.M. Allen. Lieut. O.A. Browning. Capt. D.J. Warner. Lieut. Roy B. Tisdell. Standing left to right: Lieut. Robt. P. Hurd, Lieut-Col. Otis B Duncan. Major J.R. White. Capt. W.B. Crawford, Lieut. Wm. Warfield. Capt. Matthew Jackson.

On December 12, 1918, the regiment formally passed from the French command and to Brest via Soissons and Le Mans, arriving at the latter place on January 10, 1919.

On February 2, 1919, the regiment embarked on the S.S. La France IV, en route to the U.S., arriving on February 9, 1919, and taking station at Camp Upton, Long Island, N.Y.

On February 17, 1919, the regiment left Camp Upton for Camp Grant, Illinois, via Chicago, where it was accorded a wonderful and never-to-be-forgotten reception by the citizens of Chicago.

After arrival at Camp Grant, work incident to the demobilization of the regiment was commenced. The majority of officers and enlisted men were discharged from the service during the latter part of February, and finally on March 12, 1919, orders were issued declaring that the regiment had ceased to exist.

The health of the regiment while in the service was exceptional. The Medical Detachment, under command of Major James R. White, worked incessantly to protect the health of the command. Before departure for France a number of cases of pneumonia of a very severe type developed, but only two deaths resulted. The Medical Detachment was divided among the various units, Captain Spencer C. Dickerson having charge of the detachment attached to the 1st battalion, Lieutenant James F. Lawson that of the 2nd battalion, and Lieutenant Claudius Ballard that of the 3rd battalion. The work of these detachments was at all times of a high order of excellence, and during engagements both officers and men in numerous instances went out into the open and rendered first aid to the wounded after terrific fire. Each man wounded, however slightly, was given an injection of anti-tetanic serum and as a result no cases of tetanus were reported, nor were any cases of gas baccilus infection reported. During the severe fighting around the Guilliminet and de la Riviere Farms, more help was needed and Lieutenant Park Tancil, dental surgeon, volunteered to take charge of one of the first aid stations which was daily receiving showers of shells from the enemy batteries. Lieutenant Claudius Ballard, though wounded during the fighting, refused to be evacuated and continued his duties administering to the wounded. Major James R. White made daily rounds of the first aid stations in the lines, disregarding the intense fire of the enemy and personally dressing numbers of wounded. For their heroic conduct in administering to the wounded under fire, Major White and Lieutenants Tancil and Ballard as well as several enlisted men of the Medical Detachment, were awarded the French Croix de Guerre, and Private Alfred Williamson of the detachment was awarded both the French Croix de Guerre and the American Distinguished Service Cross.

*****

Roster of Officers Old 8th Illinois (370th Infantry)

(All Negroes unless otherwise designated.)

Field and Staff—F.A. Denison, commanding until July 12, 1918, invalided home; Col. T.A. Roberts (white), commanding after July 12, 1918; Major James R. White, surgeon; Major W.H. Roberts (white), operation officer; Capt. Charles W. Fillmore, personnel officer; Capt. John H. Patton, commanding 2nd battalion; Capt. James E. Dunjil, assistant to adjutant; 1st Lieut. George Murphy, assistant to adjutant; 1st Lieut. Louis C. Washington, administrative officer; 2nd Lieut. Noble Sissle, assistant to administrative officer; 1st Lieut. Park Tancil, dentist; 1st Lieut. John T. Clemons, chaplain.

First Battalion—Major Rufus M. Stokes, commanding; 2nd Lieut. M.F. Stapleton (white), battalion adjutant; Capt. Spencer C. Dickerson, medical officer; 1st Lieut. Harry W. Jones, battalion supply officer.

Company A—Capt. Stewart A. Betts, 1st Lieut. John L. McDonald, 1st Lieut. Robert L. Chavis, 2nd. Lieut. Wycham Tyler, 2nd Lieut. Howard F. Bell, 2nd Lieut. Willis Stearles.

Company B—Capt. Stuart Alexander, 1st Lieut. Robert P. Hurd, 1st Lieut. Franklin McFarland, 1st Lieut. Samuel Ransom, 2nd Lieut. Fred K. Johnson, 2nd Lieut. Samuel Block.

Company C—Capt. James H. Smith, 1st Lieut. Samuel S. Gordon, 1st Lieut. Harry N. Shelton, 1st Lieut. Arthur Jones, 2nd Lieut. Elmer J. Myers, 2nd Lieut. Roy B. Tisdell.

Machine Gun Company—Captain Devere J. Warner, 1st Lieut. George C. Lacey, 2nd Lieut. Thomas A. Painter, 2nd Lieut. Bernard McGwin, 2nd Lieut. Homer C. Kelly, 2nd Lieut. Julian D. Rainey.

Second Battalion—Capt. John H. Patton, commanding; 1st Lieut. Samuel A. McGowan, battalion adjutant; 1st Lieut. James F. Lawson, medical officer; 1st Lieut. Rufus H. Bacote, medical officer; 1st Lieut. William Nichols, battalion supply officer.

Company F—Capt. Rufus Reed, 1st Lieut. Carter W. Wesley, 2nd Lieut. Edward Douglas, 2nd Lieut. Robert A.D. Birchett.

Company G—Capt. George M. Allen, 1st Lieut. Durand Harding, 1st Lieut. Gerald C. Bunn, 1st Lieut. Harvey E. Johnson, 2nd Lieut. Clarence H. Bouchane.

Company H—Capt. James C. Hall, 1st Lieut Harry L. Allen, 1st Lieut. George L. Amos, 1st Lieut Binga Dismond, 2nd Lieut Lawrence Willette, 2nd Lieut. John A. Hall.

Machine Gun Company No. 2—Capt. Lilburn Jackson, 2nd Lieut. Frank T. Logan, 2nd Lieut. Junius Walthall, 2nd Lieut. William A. Barnett.

Third Battalion—Lieut. Col. Otis B. Duncan, commanding; 2nd Lieut. Stanley B. Norvell, battalion adjutant; 1st Lieut. Claudius Ballard, medical officer; 1st Lieut. William J. Warfield, battalion supply officer.

Company I—Capt Lorin O. Sanford, 1st Lieut. Howard R. Brown, 2nd Lieut. D. Lincoln Reid, 2nd Lieut. Edmond G. White, 2nd Lieut. Oswald Des Verney, 2nd Lieut. Harry J. Douglas.

Company L—Capt. William B. Crawford, 1st Lieut. Frank Robinson, provost officer; 1st. Lieut Frank W. Bates, 2nd Lieut. James H. Peyton, 2nd Lieut Luther J. Harris.

Company M—Capt. Edward W. Spearman, 1st Lieut Osceola A. Browning, 1st Lieut. Jerome L. Hubert, 2nd Lieut. Lawson Price, 2nd Lieut. Irving T. Howe, 2nd Lieut. Larkland F. Hewitt.

Machine Gun Company No. 3—Capt. Matthew Jackson, 1st Lieut. William C.P. Phillips, 2nd Lieut. Charles C. Jackson, 2nd Lieut Clyde W. Donaldson, 2nd Lieut George F. Proctor.

Special Units

Headquarters Company—Capt. Lewis E. Johnson, 1st Lieut Robert A.J. Shaw, 1st Lieut. Benote H. Lee, 2nd Lieut Elias F.E. Williams, pioneer officer; 2nd Lieut. Rufus B. Jackson, Stokes mortar; 2nd Lieut. Reginald W. Harang, signal officer.

Supply Company—Capt. Lloyd G. Wheeler, 1st Lieut. Harry Wheeler, 1st Lieut. James A. Riggs, 1st Lieut. Dan M. Moore, medical officer; 2nd Lieut Augustus M. Fisher, veterinary surgeon.

Depot Company K—Capt Wm. H. Lewis, commanding; 2nd Lieut. Alvin M. Jordan, adjutant; 1st Lieut. Norman Garrett, 1st Lieut. Napoleon B. Roe, dentist; 1st Lieut. George W. Antoine, medical officer; 2nd Lieut Avon H. Williams; 2nd Lieut. Edward L. Goodlett, 2nd Lieut Frank Corbin, 2nd Lieut Frederick L. Slade, 2nd Lieut. Walter H. Aiken, 2nd Lieut. Rufus A. Atkins, 2nd Lieut James T. Baker, 2nd Lieut. John S. Banks, 2nd Lieut. Marcus A. Bernard, 2nd Lieut. Charles E. Bryant, 2nd Lieut Henry H. Carr, 2nd Lieut. Horace E. Colley, 2nd Lieut. Ira R. Collins, 2nd Lieut. Charles H. Conley, 2nd Lieut. Bernie B. Cowan, 2nd Lieut. Flenoid Cunningham, 2nd Lieut. Frank P. Dawson, 2nd Lieut. Samuel A. Dillard, 2nd Lieut. John W. Harris.

Roll of Honor

Heroes of Old 8th Illinois

Negro National Guardsmen known in France as the 370th Infantry, who were decorated with the Croix de Guerre. The exploits of some of these men and also of some of those in the appended list decorated with the Distinguished Service Cross, are mentioned in the chapters devoted to the regiment.

Col. T.A. Roberts (white)

Lieut. Col. Otis B. Duncan

Major James R. White

Capt. John H. Patton
Capt. Chester Sanders
Capt. John T. Prout
Capt. Samuel R. Gwynne
Capt. Devere J. Warner
Capt. Wm. B. Crawford
Capt. George M. Allen
Capt. James C. Hall
Capt. Stuart Alexander
Capt. Mathew Jackson
Capt. James H. Smith
Lieut. Park Tancil
Lieut. Osceola A. Browning
Lieut. George C. Lacey
Lieut. Frank Robinson
Lieut. Claudius Ballard
Lieut. Charles C. Jackson
Lieut. William J. Warfield
Lieut. Samuel S. Gordon
Lieut. Robert P. Hurd
Lieut. Henry N. Shelton
Lieut. Henry P. Cheatham
Lieut. Stanley B. Norvell
Lieut. Roy B. Tisdell
Lieut. Thomas A. Painter
Lieut. Lawson Price
Lieut. Lincoln D. Reid
Lieut. Elmer J. Myers

Sergt. Norman Henry

Sergt. Clarence T. Gibson

Sergt. Matthew Jenkins

Sergt. Cecil Nelson

Sergt. Howard Templeton

Sergt. Chas. T. Monroe

Sergt. Derry Brown

Corp. James R. Brown

Corp. Lewis Warner

Corp. Joseph Henderson

Corp. Maceo A. Tervalon

Corp. William Stevenson

Corp. Emil Laurent

Corp. Charles T. Brock

Pvt. Nathaniel C. White (deceased)

Pvt. Robert Pride

Pvt. George B. White

Pvt. Howard Sheffield

Pvt. Cornelius Robinson

Pvt. Ulysses Sayles

Pvt. William Cuff (deceased)

Pvt. Hugh Givens

Pvt. Arthur Johnson

Pvt. Rufus Pitts

Pvt. Olbert Dorsey

Pvt. William Hurdle

Pvt. Bee McKissic

Pvt. Jonas Paxton

Pvt. Harry Pearson

Pvt. Paul Turlington

Pvt. Reed J. Brown

Pvt. Paul Johnson

Pvt. Reedy Jones

Pvt. Alonzo Keller

Pvt. Leroy Lindsay

Pvt. Lavern Massey

Pvt. Josiah Nevees

Pvt. Ira Taylor

Pvt. Jesse Ferguson

Pvt. William M. Robinson

Awarded Distinguished Service Crosses by General Pershing:

Capt. William B. Crawford

Lieut. William J. Warfield

Sergt. Norman Henry

Sergt. Ralph Gibson

Sergt. Robert Barnes

Sergt. Charles T. Monroe

Sergt. Emmett Thompson

Sergt. Lester Fossie

Sergt. Matthew Jenkins

Pvt. Tom Powell (deceased)

Pvt. Andrew McCall

Pvt. Wm. Cuff (deceased)

Pvt. Spirley Irby

Pvt. Alfred Williamson

Pvt. William G. Hurdle

Pvt. Harry Pearson

Pvt. Alonzo Walton

Pvt. Leroy Davis

Pvt. James Fuquay

Pvt. Nathaniel C. White (deceased)

Pvt. Arthur Johnson

CHAPTER XVIII

Blood of the Black and White in One Rivulet of Departing Life

Lincoln's Prophetic Words—Negroes Alongside Best *Soldiers* in the World—Hold Their Own—The 372nd Regiment—Brigaded With Veterans of the Marne—Famous "Red Hand" Division—Occupy Hill 304 At Verdun—Nine Days Battle in "Bloody Argonne"—Admiration of the French—Conspicuous Components of 372nd—Chronology of Service

They will probably help in some trying time to keep the jewel of liberty in the family of freedom.—

Abraham Lincoln.

Prophetic words uttered by the Great Emancipator concerning the Negroes of America. The Negroes helped. They would have helped in much greater measure had they been given the opportunity.

Fighting for the first time on the soil of the world's most famous battleground—Europe—and for the first time brought into direct comparison with the best soldiers of the world, they proved themselves able to hold their own where tests of courage, endurance and aggressiveness were most severe.

They fought valiantly in the vicinity of Chateau Thierry, on the Vesle, on the Aillette, in the Argonne, and various other sectors; and in the final drive at Metz. They vanquished the Germans who opposed them; the heaviest fire of the enemy failing to stop their advance.

No part of the 93rd Division made a more gallant record than the 372nd regiment. Throughout its service in France it was a part of the famous French 157th Division known as the "Red Hand" division, under the command of General Goybet. It was this division which first opposed the Huns at the Marne in 1914. To brigade the Negro soldiers with such famous veterans was a rare mark of distinction and placed the black men on their mettle at all times.

The 372nd arrived in France on April 14 and went into training with the French eleven days later. On May 29 the regiment took over a sector in the Argonne and on June 20 was sent to the trenches just west of Verdun, occupying the famous battle-swept Hill 304, and sections at Four de Paris and Vauquois. On Hill 304 thousands of French and Germans had fallen as the battle line swung back and forward. That this hill was given to the Negroes to hold demonstrated that as soldiers they had already won the confidence of the French.

The regiment's first engagement was in the Champagne sector with Monthois as an objective. Here came the real test. The Negroes were eager to get into the fight. They cheered and sang when the announcement came that their opportunity had arrived—but the question was; back of their enthusiasm had they the staying qualities drilled into European troops through centuries of training in the science of warfare.

The answer was that some of the heaviest and most effective fighting of the day was done by the Negro regiment. From June 6th to September 10th, the 372nd was stationed in the bloody Argonne forest or in the vicinity of Verdun. On the night of September 25th they were summoned to take part in the Argonne offensive and were in that terrific drive, one of the decisive engagements of the war, from September 28th to October 7th.

In the nine days' battle the Negroes not only proved their fighting qualities in an ordeal such as men rarely have been called upon to face, but these qualities in deadly striking power and stubborn resistance in crises, stood out with such distinction that the coveted Croix de Guerre was bestowed upon the regiment.

The casualty list of the 372nd in this and previous fighting carried 500 names of men killed, wounded and gassed. For their achievements they were at once cited for bravery and efficiency in General Orders from the corps commander transmitted through their French divisional chief. It was dated October 8th and read as follows:

In transmitting you with legitimate pride the thanks and congratulations of General Garnier Duplessis, allow me, my dear friends of all ranks, American and French, to address you from the bottom of the heart of a chief and soldier, the expression of gratitude for the glory you have lent to our good 157th Division. During these nine days of hard fighting you have progressed eight kilometers (4.8 miles) through powerfully organized defenses, taken 600 prisoners, captured 15 heavy guns, 20 minenwerfers and nearly 150 machine guns, secured an enormous amount of engineering material and important supplies of artillery ammunition, and brought down by your fire three enemy aeroplanes. The "Red Hand" sign of the division, has, thanks to you, become a bloody hand which took the Boche by the throat and made him cry for mercy. You have well avenged our glorious dead. GOYBET.

In a communication delivered to the colonel of the regiment on October 1st, General Goybet said:

Your troops have been admirable in their attack. You must be proud of the courage of your officers and men, and I consider it an honor to have them under my command. The bravery and dash of your regiment won the admiration of the Moroccan Division, who are themselves versed in warfare. Thanks to you, during these hard days, the division was at all times in advance of all other divisions of the Army Corps. I am sending you all my thanks and beg you to transmit them to your subordinates. I call on your wounded. Their morale is higher than any praise.

The high honor of having its flag decorated with the Croix de Guerre was bestowed upon the regiment in the city of Brest just a few days before it embarked for the return to America. Vice Admiral Moreau, the French commander of the port of Brest, officially represented his government in, the ceremony. It was intended as France's appreciation of the services of these Negro fighters.

The decoration took place at one of the most prominent points in the city and was witnessed by thousands of French soldiers and civilians, as well as by sailors and soldiers of several nations.

One of the conspicuous components of the 372nd was the battalion, formed from what formerly was known as the 1st Separate Battalion of the District of Columbia National Guard. This famous old Washington organization has a long, proud history. Many of the members were veterans of the Spanish-American war. At the close of the European war, the organization numbered 480 men from the city of Washington, twenty of whom had been decorated one or more times for individual bravery under fire.

The battalion was first assembled at Potomac Park on the Speedway in Washington, shortly after the declaration of war. The men spent almost half a year at the camp, during which time they had the important assignment of guarding railway and highway bridges and adjacent points around the National Capitol. They also had the proud distinction of guarding the secret archives and departments at Washington, a duty which required unquestioned loyalty and for which the Negroes were well selected.

It seemed at the time an inconspicuous bit of war time soldiering, and they were long trying days to the men. But it was a service which required intelligence and nerve, as the likelihood was great that the enemy's agents in this country would strike in the vicinity of the seat of government. That such responsible duty was delegated to the Negroes was a high compliment from the military authorities. The manner in which they discharged the duty is shown in the fact that no enemy depredations of any consequence occurred in the vicinity of Washington.

After a period of training at Camp Stewart, Newport News, Va., the battalion was sent to France. Its colored commander was dead. Other colored officers were soon superseded, leaving the chaplain, Lieutenant Arrington Helm, the only colored officer attached to the organization.

Arriving at St. Nazaire, France, April 14, 1918, the battalion was soon sent to Conde en Barrois, where it underwent a period of intensive training with special preparation for sector warfare. The instructors were French. Lessons were hard and severe, but the instructors afterwards had much cause for pride in their pupils.

From the training camp the battalion and regiment proceeded to the Argonne front, at first settling in the vicinity of La Chalade. It was there the soldiers received their first taste of warfare, and it was there their first casualties occurred.

September 13th the outfit withdrew and retired to the rear for a special training prior to participation in the general attack from Verdun to the sea. On the morning of September 28th the District of Columbia battalion was sent to the front to relieve a regiment of famous Moroccan shock troops. It was at this time that the Champagne offensive took such a decided turn and the Washington men from that time on were taking a most active and important part in the general fighting. They distinguished themselves at Ripont just north of St. Menehold. They suffered greatly during their valiant support of an advanced position in that sector. Despite its losses the battalion fought courageously ahead. Prior to that it had occupied Hill 304 at Verdun. It had the distinction of being the first American outfit to take over that sector. The battalion fought doggedly and bravely at Ripont and succeeded in gaining much valuable territory, as well as enemy machine guns and supplies and ninety Hun prisoners.

Later the battalion held a front line position at Monthois, and it finally formed a salient in the line of the 9th French Army Corps. It was subjected to a long period of gruelling fire from the Boches' famous Austrian 88s and machine guns, and an incessant barrage from German weapons of high caliber.

The regiment moved south to the Vosges, where the battalion took up a position in sub-sector B, in front of St. Marie Aux Mines, where it was situated when word of the armistice came.

The record of the Negro warriors from the District of Columbia is very succinctly contained in a diary kept by Chaplain Lieutenant Arrington Helm. It relates the activities of the unit from the time they sailed from Newport News, March 30, 1917, until the end of the war. It is also a condensed account of the major operations of the 372nd regiment. The diary follows:

March 30—Embarked from Newport News, Va., for overseas duty on the U.S.S. Susquehanna.

April 17—Disembarked at St. Nazaire and marched to rest camp.

April 21—Left rest camp. Base section No. 1 and entrained for Vaubecourt.

April 23—Arrived at Vaubecourt at 7 p.m. Left Vaubecourt at 8:30 p.m. and hiked in a heavy rainstorm to Conde en Barrois.

April 25—Assigned to school under French officers.

May 26—Left Conde en Barrois at 8 a.m. in French motor trucks for Les Senades.

May 29—Our regiment today took over the sector designated as Argonne West.

May 31—In front line trenches.

June 20—Changed sectors, being assigned to the Vauquois sector, a sub-sector of the Verdun front. The 157th Division is stationed in reserve. The enemy is expected to attack.

July 13—Left for Hill 304 on the Verdun sector. Colonel Young has been relieved from command and Colonel Herschell Tupes has assumed command.

July 25—Left Sivry la Perche to take over Hill 304. Arrived at Hill 304 at 9 p.m.

August 16—Heavily shelled by regiment of Austrians opposing us. Two Americans and one Frenchman in the regiment killed.

August 20—Lieutenant James Sanford, Company A, captured by the Germans.

August 21—Fight by French and German planes over our lines. Very exciting.

September 8—Left Hill 304. Relieved by 129th infantry of the 33rd Division. Hiked in rain and mud for Brocourt.

September 14—Arrived at Juvigny at noon.

September 17—Left Juvigny for Brienne la Chateau at 8 p.m. Passed through Brienne la Chateau and reached Vitray la Francois this afternoon. The city is near the Marne.

September 18—Hiked to Jessecourt. All colored officers left the regiment today.

September 28—Arrived at Hans. The regiment was in action in the vicinity of Ripont. The third battalion took up a battle position near Ripont.

September 29—The third battalion went over the top. The Germans are in retreat. Our positions are being bombarded. The machine gun fire is terrific and 88 millimeter shells are falling as thick and fast as hailstones. We are unable to keep up with the enemy. This afternoon it is raining. This makes it bad for the wounded of whom there are many.

September 30—The first battalion is now on our right and advancing fast despite the rain and mud. The machine gun opposition is strenuous. Our casualties are small. We have captured a large number of prisoners.

October 1—Our advance is meeting with increased opposition. The enemy has fortified himself on a hill just ahead. The ground prevents active support by the French artillery. Still we are giving the Germans no rest. They are now retreating across the valley to one of their supply bases. The enemy is burning his supplies. We have taken the village at Ardeuil. Our losses have been heavy but the Germans have lost more in killed, wounded and taken prisoner than have our forces. On our right the first battalion has entered the village of Sechault, after some hard fighting by Company A.

October 4—The Second battalion is going in this morning. We are resting at Vieux three kilometers from Monthois, one of the enemy's railroad centers and base hospitals. The enemy is destroying supplies and moving wounded. We can see trains moving out of Monthois. Our artillery is bombarding all roads and railroads in the vicinity. The enemy's fire is intense. We expect a counterattack.

October 5—The enemy's artillery has opened up. We are on the alert. They have attacked and a good stiff hand to hand combat ensued. The Germans were driven back with heavy losses. We have taken many prisoners from about twelve different German regiments. We continued our advance and now are on the outskirts of Monthois.

October 6—The enemy is throwing a stiff barrage on the lines to our left where the 333rd French Infantry is attacking. We can see the Huns on the run. The liaison work of the 157th Division is wonderful; not the slightest gap has been left open. Our patrols entered Monthois early this morning and were driven out by machine gun fire, but returned with a machine gun and its crew. We will be relieved by the 76th infantry regiment at 8 p.m. We hiked over the ground we had fought so hard to take to Minnecourt, where the regiment proceeded to reorganize.

October 12—Left Valmy today and continued to Vignemont.

October 13—Arrived at Vignemont. Hiked fifteen kilometers to St. Leonard.

October 15—Left St. Leonard for Van de Laveline in the Vosges. We arrived at Van de Laveline at 10:15 p.m. and took over a sector.

November 11—A patrol of Company A took several prisoners from a German patrol. Received word of the signing of the armistice at 11 a.m. today. Martial music was played. The colors of the regiment are displayed in front of the post command.

It is related that the Washington fighters, as well as the other members of the 372nd regiment, received the news of the armistice with more of disappointment than joy, for they had made all preparations to advance with the French through Lorraine.

CHAPTER XIX

Comrades on the March. Brothers in the Sleep of Death

Policy of Substituting White Officers—Injustice to Capable Negroes—Disappointment But No Open Resentment—Showed Themselves Soldiers—Intenser Fighting Spirit Aroused—Race Forgotten in Perils of War—Both Whites and Blacks Generous—Affection Between Officers and Men—Negroes Preferred Death to Captivity—Outstanding Heroes of 371st and 372nd—Winners of Crosses

    Changing from Negro to white officers was in accordance with the military policy of the American Government; the generic inspiration and root being found in national prejudice, incident to the institution of slavery and the spirit of racial caste and narrowness, that still disgraces it. Doubt was pretended to be entertained of the ability of the colored man to command, and although there were not lacking champions for the policy of placing capable Negroes in command of Negro units, the weight of opinion; superinduced and fostered by racial prejudice, inclined to the opposite course.

    In the light of the fine record made by such Negro officers as were given responsible commands, let us hope for the future honor of the nation; preening herself as being in the vanguard of the progressive commonwealths of the age, that a policy so unjust, narrow and unworthy will; as quickly as feasible be abandoned. In favor of Negro commanders is the additional testimony of high French generals, who knew no color distinction and could see no reason why a Negro should not command his own race troops if he had intelligence, courage and military skill. Indeed there are not wanting in the annals of French warfare brilliant examples where men of African blood commanded not only mulattoes and blacks, but heroic whites as well. It is not of record that those white Frenchmen showed any reluctance to follow such leaders or viewed them with less affection than they did their white officers.

One should not say that the Negro troops would have fought any better under the men of their own race. They achieved all possible glory as it was. They simply did their duty whether their officers were white or black. But that they did not fight any the less valiantly or efficiently under men of their own race is abundantly proven by the record of the 370th, or the 8th Illinois as the soldiers and their people still prefer to call it; and other units which had Negroes in responsible positions.

That there was disappointment, chagrin and anger in the rank and file of the Negro soldiers when their own officers were taken from them and white men substituted was natural and quite to be expected.

However, there was little open murmuring. While the Negro regarded the removal of the officers who had trained him and were, in a sense, his comrades, unfair and uncalled for, his fighting spirit, seemed to burn with an intenser heat; a determination to do his best to show and shame the spirit that robbed him of his own race leaders, and at the same time convince his white commanders of the stuff he was made of.

There was much disappointment in the ranks of the District of Columbia battalion, when the place of its old leader was taken by Major Clark L. Dickson, twenty-seven years of age, one of the youngest—if not the youngest—of battalion commanders in the American army. But their disappointment was soon allayed, for Major Dickson made an enviable record. He received the Croix de Guerre with this citation:

> *"Most efficient officer, valorous and intrepid, acting in dual capacity as regimental adjutant and operation officer. Displayed the utmost energy in issuing operation orders during the period between September 26th and October 6th, 1918, and especially distinguished himself in crossing a roadway under violent artillery fire to give assistance to a wounded brother officer. His clear view of the situation at all times and the accuracy with which he issued the necessary orders required of him, contributed largely to the success of the regiment."*

Many of his men have stated that the citation only hinted at the real accomplishments of Major Dickson.

In the rigors of war and the perils of battle, men serving side by side, forget race. They simply realize that they are sharing hardships in common; are beset by a common foe and are the subjects of common dangers. Under such circumstances they become comrades. They learn to admire each other and willingly give to each other a full measure of praise and appreciation. The Negro soldiers generally, have expressed unstintedly, approbation and praise of their white officers; and the officers have been equally generous. Here is an appreciation by one of the officers of the 372nd regiment, Lieutenant Jerome Meyer of Washington, concerning the men of that organization:

> *"Casualties were heavy because the colored lads fought to the last, cheerfully accepting death in preference to captivity. Their adeptness in mastering the throwing of hand grenades and in operating the machine guns quickly won them the esteem of the French. Remember, that the colored lads were quite new to warfare. But in the Champagne they fought with a persistence and courage that enabled them to hold permanently the ground they gained and won for many of them their decorations. Not a few of the prisoners taken by the regiment declared that the Germans were in positive fear of the Negroes, who, they complained, would never quit even under terrible fire."*

One of the outstanding heroes of the 372nd regiment was Sergeant Ira Payne, of 325 Fifteenth Street, Washington, D.C. He won the Croix de Guerre and the Distinguished Service Cross, and according to his comrades, "was not afraid of the devil himself." His story as related by himself on his return home, follows:

> *"During the fighting at Sechault the Germans were picking off the men of my platoon from behind a bush. They had several machine guns and kept up a deadly fire in spite of our rifle fire directed at the bush. We did our best to stop those machine guns, but the German aim became so accurate that they were picking off five of my men every minute. We couldn't stand for that.*
>
> *"Well, I decided that I would get that little machine gun nest myself, and I went after it. I left our company, detoured, and, by a piece of luck got behind the bush. I got my rifle into action and 'knocked off' two of those German machine gunners. That ended it. The other Germans couldn't stand so much excitement. The Boches surrendered and I took them into our trenches as prisoners."*

Not a long story for such an able and courageous exploit, yet it contains the germ for an epic recital on bravery.

First Sergeant John A. Johnson a colored member of Company B, was decorated with the Croix de Guerre with palm for exceptional bravery during a charge over the top, and for capturing single-handed, two Hun soldiers who later proved valuable as sources of information. Sergeant Johnson's home was at 1117 New Jersey Avenue, Washington, D.C. He was equally reticent about boasting of his deeds.

"Near Sechault during the time the District men were making a big effort to capture the town," said Johnson, "I was put in the front lines not fifty feet away from the enemy. A greater part of the time I was exposed to machine gun fire. I suppose I got my medal because I stuck to my men in the trenches and going over the top. Quite a few of the boys were bumped off at that point."

Another hero was Benjamin Butler, a private. The citation with his Croix de Guerre read: "For displaying gallantry and bravery and distinguishing himself in carrying out orders during the attack on Sechault, September 29, 1918, under heavy bombardment and machine gun fire."

"I did very little," Butler said. "During this fight with several others, I carried dispatches to the front line trenches from headquarters. They decorated me, I suppose, because I was the only one lucky enough to escape being knocked off."

Private Charles E. Cross of 1157 Twenty-first street, Washington, D.C. was awarded the Croix de Guerre, his citation reading: "For his speed and reliability in carrying orders to platoons in the first line under the enemy's bombardment on September 29, 1918." In some cases he had to creep across No Man's Land and a greater part of the time was directly exposed to the enemy's fire.

Private William H. Braxton, a member of the machine gun company of the regiment, whose residence was at 2106 Ward Place, Washington D.C., received the Croix de Guerre for "displaying zealous bravery."

"An enemy party," reads his citation, "having filtered through his platoon and attacked same in the rear. Private Braxton displayed marked gallantry in opening fire on the enemy and killing one and wounding several others, finally dispersing the entire party."

"The men who stuck by me when death stared them in their faces," said Braxton, "deserve just as much credit as I do. I was only the temporary leader of the men."

Corporal Depew Pryor, of Detroit, Michigan, was awarded the Medal Militaire, one of the most coveted honors within the gift of the French army, as well as the American Distinguished Service Cross. Pryor saw Germans capture a Frenchman. Grabbing an armful of grenades, he dashed upon the Germans killing, wounding or routing a party of ten and liberating the Frenchman.

Sergeant Bruce Meddows, 285 Erskine street, Detroit, Michigan, brought home the Croix de Guerre with silver star, which he won for bringing down an aeroplane with an automatic rifle.

To have forty-six horses which he drove in carting ammunition up to the front lines, killed in five months was the experience of Arthur B. Hayes, 174 Pacific Avenue, Detroit, Michigan. He returned home sick, with practically no wounds after risking his life daily for months.

Sergeant George H. Jordan of Company L, whose home was in Boston, Mass., won the Croix de Guerre and palm for taking charge of an ammunition train at Verdun, when the commanding officer had been killed by a shell. He saved and brought through eight of the seventeen wagons.

Lieutenant James E. Sanford of Washington, D.C., one of the early Negro officers of the 372nd, was captured in Avocourt Woods near Verdun, August 19 , 918. He was endeavoring to gain a strategic position with his men when he was met by an overpowering force concealed behind camouflaged outposts, he was taken to Karlsruhe and transferred to three other German prison camps, in all of which he suffered from bad and insufficient food and the brutality of the German guards.

U.S. flag and 369th regiment flag, decorated with Croix de Guerre at Ungersheim, Alsace, France.

W. Allison Sweeney

The 369th Infantry in rest billets at Maffrecourt, France. Henry Johnson. One of foremost heroes of the war. With his famous smile. In right foreground.

The joke seems to be on the lad at the left.

A few of the many guns captured from the Germans.

Americans in prison camp. Prisoners are amused listeners while jovial negro fighter relates an episode of war life to a German officer.

Arthur Johnson, a doughboy of the 8th Illinois (370th Infantry), winner of Croix de Guerre and the distinguished service cross.

Game probably is strip poker as two men have already discarded their shirts. One has a large safety pin for instant use. But then, note the horseshoe on his shoe.

Kitchen police on board the celtic. There is always some duty for Uncle Sam's men on land or sea.

Minstrels on board the "Saxonia," typical group organized on the transports to entertain wounded boys returning from France.

Four caverns, studded with ivory, furnish harmony in the training camp.

Lieut. Maxom and his band, who saw distinguished service in France.

Group on edge of pier waiting to entrain for demobilization camp. Part of the 351st Artillery unit specially mentioned by General Pershing.

Salvation army lassies handing out chocolate to two soldiers of 351st Artillery. .

Heroes of 351st Artillery greeting friends after debarking from the transport Louisville.

Major Johnson led his battalion of the 372nd in an attack in the Champagne which resulted in the capture of a German trench, 100 prisoners, an ammunition dump, thirty machine guns and two howitzers. He received the Croix de Guerre and the Legion of Honor decoration from the French, as well as the Distinguished Service Cross from General Pershing.

Company B of the 372nd, took at Sechault in a raid, seventy-five prisoners and four machine guns.

One of the distinguished units of the 372nd, was the old and famous Company L of the Massachusetts National Guard. This unit was assembled at Camp Devens and left soon after the declaration of war for the south. It was stationed for a time at Newport News, and was then incorporated with the 372nd, went to France with that organization and saw its share of service throughout the campaign. Other distinguished units were the well known Ninth Ohio Battalion National Guard, and National Guard companies from Connecticut, Maryland and Tennessee.

Brigaded with the 372nd in the French "Red Hand" division, was another Negro regiment, the 371st, made up principally of selectives from South Carolina. It was commanded by Colonel P.L. Miles. Among the officers were Major Thomas Moffatt and Captain William R. Richey from Charleston.

History of the American Negro in the Great World War

The regiment saw practically the same service as the 372nd under General Goybet, was mentioned in divisional and special orders, was decorated by Vice Admiral Moreau, Maritime Prefect of Brest, at the same time the honor was conferred on the 372nd. The two regiments were together for seven months. The men of the 371st especially distinguished themselves at Crete des Observatories, Ardeuil and in the plains of Monthois. Seventy-one individual members received the Croix de Guerre and some the Distinguished Service Cross. Among the latter were the following:

Sergeant Lee R. McClelland, Medical Detachment, home address, Boston, Mass., for extraordinary heroism in action near Ardeuil, September 30, 1918.

Corporal Sandy E. Jones, Company C, home address Sumter, S.C.; for extraordinary heroism in action in the Champagne, September 28 and 29, 1918.

Private Bruce Stoney, Medical Detachment, home address, Allendale, S.C.; for extraordinary heroism in action near Ardeuil, September 29, 1918.

Private Charlie Butler, Machine Gun Company, home address, McComb, Miss.; for extraordinary heroism in action near Ardeuil, September 29, 1918.

Private Willie Boston, Machine Gun Company, home address, Roopville, Ga.; for extraordinary heroism in action near Ardeuil, September 29, 1918.

Private Tillman Webster, Machine Gun Company, home address, Alexandria, La.; for extraordinary heroism in action near Ardeuil, September 29, 1918.

Private Ellison Moses, Company C, home address, Mayesville, S.C.; for extraordinary heroism in action near Ardeuil, September 30, 1918.

Private Hunius Diggs, Company G, home address, Lilesville, N.C.; for extraordinary heroism in action near Ardeuil, September 30, 1918.

The two regiments, besides the regimental Croix de Guerre, awarded for gallantry in the Champagne, won individual decorations amounting in the aggregate to 168 Croix de Guerre, 38 Distinguished Service Crosses, four Medal Militaire and two crosses of the Legion of Honor.

An incident of the service of the 371st and particularly emphasizing the honesty and faithfulness of the Negro Y.M.C.A. and the regiment's medical detachment, was the case of Prof. H.O. Cook, a teacher in the Lincoln High School at Kansas City, Mo. Professor Cook, a Y.M.C.A. man attached to the sector which the 371st was holding during the great offensive in September, went with the men to the front line trenches and rendered valuable aid among the wounded until he was gassed. Owing to the fact that there were no facilities at that particular time, for the safe keeping of money and valuables, he carried on his person more than 150,000 francs (in normal times $30,000) which boys in the regiment had given him to keep when they went over the top.

After being gassed he was walked over for an hour before being discovered. The money was found and sent by Sergeant Major White also colored, to general headquarters at Chaumont. When Prof. Cook was discharged from the hospital and made inquiry about the money, it was returned to him. Not a cent was missing. Colonel Miles recommended that General Pershing award Prof. Cook a Distinguished Service Cross.

The men of the 93rd Division and other Negro divisions and organizations will never forget their French comrades and friends. It was a lad of the 371st regiment who wrote the following to his mother. The censor allowed the original to proceed but copied the extract as a document of human interest; in that it was a boyish and unconscious arraignment of his own country—for which he with many thousands of others, were risking their lives.

```
"Mammy,
  these French people don't bother with no color
line business. They treat us so good that the only
time I ever know I'm colored is when I look in the
glass."
```

The 371st regiment had 123 men killed in action and about 600 wounded or gassed. The casualties of the 372nd consisted of 91 killed in action and between 600 and 700 wounded or gassed. Like the other Negro regiments of the 93rd Division, there was comparatively little sickness among the men, outside of that induced by hard service conditions.

Heroes of The 371st and 372nd

The names listed below are cross and medal winners. The exploits of some are told in detail in the chapters devoted to their regiments. There are many known to have received decorations whose names are not yet on the records.

Cross of the Legion of Honor
372nd Regiment

Major Johnson

Medal Militaire
372nd Regiment

Corp. Depew Pryor   Corp. Clifton Morrison

Pvt. Clarence Van Allen

Distinguished Service Cross
371st Regiment

Sergt Lee R. McClelland   Pvt. Willie Boston
Corp. Sandy E. Jones   Pvt. Tillman Webster
Pvt. Bruce Stoney   Pvt. Ellison Moses
Pvt. Charlie Butler   Pvt. Hunius Diggs

372nd Regiment

Major Johnson   Sergt. Ira M. Payne

Corp. Depew Pryor

Croix de Guerre
372nd Regiment

Col. Herschell Tupes   Sergt. Homer Crabtree
Major Johnson   Sergt. Norman Winsmore
Major Clark L. Dickson   Sergt. William A. Carter

Lieut. Jerome Meyer
Sergt. Major Samuel B. Webster
Sergt. John A. Johnson
Sergt. Ira M. Payne
Sergt James A. Marshall
Sergt. Norman Jones
Pvt. Warwick Alexander
Pvt. George H. Budd
Pvt. Thomas A. Frederick
Pvt. John S. Parks
Pvt. Charles H. Murphy
Pvt. William N. Mathew
Pvt. Ernest Payne

Sergt. George H. Jordan
Sergt. Bruce Meddows
Sergt. Harry Gibson
Corp. John R. White
Corp. Benjamin Butler
Corp. March Graham
Pvt. Joseph McKamey
Pvt. William Dickerson
Pvt. William Johnson
Pvt. Walter Dennis
Pvt. Charles E. Cross
Pvt. William H. Braxton
Pvt. Nunley Matthews

CHAPTER XX

Mid Shot and Shell

In Trench and Valley—The Open Plain—On Mountain Top—In No Man's Land—Two Classes of Negro Soldiers Considered—Trained Guardsmen and Selectives—Gallant 92nd Division—Race can be Proud of It—Had Six Hundred Negro Officers—Sets at Rest All Doubts—Operations of the Division—At Pont A Mousson—Great Battle of Metz—Some Reflections—Casualties Considered

History, as made in France by the Negro soldier, falls naturally into two divisions; that which was made by the bodies of troops which had an organization prior to the war, and whether trained or not, could lay claim to an understanding of the first principles of military science; and that made by the raw selectives—the draft soldiers—to whom the art of war was a closed book, something never considered as likely to affect their scheme of life and never given more than a passing thought.

We have followed the first phase of it in the wonderful combat-records of the colored National Guard, its volunteers and recruits. We have seen them like a stone wall bearing the brunt of attack from the finest shock troops of the Kaiser's Army. We have seen them undaunted by shot and shell, advancing through the most terrific artillery fire up to that time ever concentrated; rout those same troops, hold their ground and even advance under the most powerful counter attack which the enemy could deliver. We have followed them from trench to plain, to valley and into the mountains and read the story of their battles under all those varying conditions. We have pitied them in their trials, sympathized with their wounded and ill, been saddened by their lists of dead and finally have seen the survivors come home; have seen them cheered and feted as no men of their race ever were cheered and feted before.

Much of the nation's pride in them was due to the fact that it knew them as fighting men; at least as men who were organized for fighting purposes before the war. When they marched away and sailed we had confidence in them; were proud of their appearance, their spirit, their willingness to serve. The country felt they would not fail to clothe with luster their race and maintain the expectations of them. That they fulfilled every expectation and more; had come back loaded with honors; finer, manlier men than ever, increased the nation's pride in them.

Now we come to a contemplation of the other class; the men who knew nothing of military life or military matters; who, most of them, wished to serve but never dreamed of getting the opportunity. Many of them employed in the cotton fields or residing in the remote corners of the country, hardly knew there was a war in progress. Some of them realized that events out of the ordinary were transpiring through the suddenly increased demand for their labor and the higher wages offered them. But that Uncle Sam would ever call them to serve in his army and even to go far across seas to a shadowy—to them, far off land, among a strange people; speaking a strange language, had never occurred to most of them even in dreams.

Then all of a sudden came the draft summons. The call soon penetrated to the farthest nooks of our great land; surprised, bewildered but happy, the black legions began to form.

It already has been noted that with the exception of the 371st regiment, which went to the 93rd Division, the selectives who saw service in the fighting areas, were all in the 92nd Division. This was a complete American division, brigaded with its own army, commanded through the greater part of its service by Major General Ballou and towards the end by Major General Martin.

While the 92nd Division as a whole, did not get into the heavy fighting until the last two weeks of the war, individual units had a taste of it earlier. Service which the division as a whole did see, was some of the most severe of the war. The Negroes of the country may well be proud of the organization, for its record was good all the way through and in the heavy fighting was characterized by great gallantry and efficiency.

One of the outstanding features of the division was the fact that it had about six hundred Negro commissioned officers. Its rank and file of course, was composed exclusively of Negro soldiers. The fine record of the division must forever set at rest any doubts concerning the ability of Negro officers, and any questions about Negro soldiers following and fighting under them. It was a splendid record all the way through, and Negro officers rendered excellent service at all times and under the most trying circumstances. Many of these officers, be it understood, were entirely new to military life. Some had seen service in the National Guard and some had come up from the ranks of the Regular Army, but the majority of them were men taken from civilian life and trained and graduat- graduated from the officer's training camps at Fort Des Moines, Camp Taylor, Camp Hancock and Camp Pike. A few received commissions from the officers' training schools in France.

The 92nd Division was composed of the 183rd Infantry Brigade, consisting of the 365th and 366th Infantry Regiments and the 350th Machine Gun Battalion; the 184th Infantry Brigade, composed of the 367th and 368th Infantry Regiments and the 351st Machine Gun Battalion; the 167th Artillery Brigade consisting of the 349th, 350th and 351st Artillery Regiments; and the 349th Machine Gun Battalion, the 317th Trench Mortar Battalion, the 317th Engineers' Regiment, the 317th Engineers' Train, the 317th Ammunition Train, the 317th Supply Train, the 317th Train Headquarters, the 92nd Military Police Company; and the Sanitary Train, comprising the 365th, 366th 367th and 368th Field Hospital and Ambulance Companies.

Briefly summarized, the operations of the 92nd Division may be stated as follows: Arrived in France the summer of 1918. After the usual period of intensive training in the back areas it was divided into several groups for training alongside the French in front line trenches.

In August they took over a sector in the St. Die region near the Lorraine border. September 2nd they repulsed an enemy raid at LaFontenelle. On September 26th the division was a reserve of the First Army Corps in the first phase of the Meuse-Argonne offensive.

On October 10th they moved to the Marbache sector in the vicinity of Pont a Mousson. November 10th they advanced, reaching Bois Frehaut and Bois Cheminot, capturing 710 prisoners. These positions were being consolidated on November 11th when the armistice put an end to the fighting. Of course there was fighting by some units of the division from the time early in the summer when they went into the trenches.

When the Marbache sector was taken over by the 92nd Division, "No Man's Land" was owned by the Germans and they were aggressively on the offensive. They held Belie Farm, Bois de Tete D'Or, Bois Frehaut, Voivrotte Farm, Voivrotte Woods, Bois Cheminot and Moulin Brook. Raids and the aggressiveness of the patrols of the 92nd Division changed the complexion of things speedily. They inflicted many casualties on the Germans and took many prisoners.

Each of the places named above was raided by the doughty black men as was also Epley, while their patrols penetrated north nearly to the east and west line through Pagny. The Germans were driven north beyond Frehaut and Voivrotte to Cheminot bridge. In their desperation they tried to check the Americans by an attempt to destroy the bridge over the Seille river. They succeeded in flooding a portion of the adjacent country; these tactics demonstrating that they could not withstand the Negro soldiers. West of the Seille river excellent results followed the energetic offensive, the Germans losing heavily in killed, wounded and prisoners. In nearly every instance the raids were conducted by Negro line officers.

Up to this time the division as a whole, had never been in a major battle. The only regiment in it that had seen a big engagement was the 368th infantry, which took part in the action in the Argonne Forest in September.

The division's chance came in the great drive on Metz, just before the end of the war. They were notified at 4 o'clock Sunday morning, November 10th. The motto "See it through" of the 367th infantry, known as the "Buffaloes," echoed through the whole division.

They began their advance at 7 o'clock from Pont a Mousson. Before them was a valley commanded by the heavy guns of Metz and by innumerable nests of German machine guns. The Negroes seemed to realize that here for the first time was the opportunity to show their mettle—that for the first time they were going to battle as a division. A sense of race pride seemed to stir and actuate every man. Here was a chance to show what this great body, composed of cotton-field Negroes, of stevedores, mechanics, general laborers, trades, professional men and those from all walks of civilian life who but recently had taken up the profession of arms, could do. An opportunity to enact a mighty role was upon them, and they played it well.

Not only were the black infantry and machine gun units up at the front; in the thickest of it, but the artillery—the 167th Brigade—was on the line behaving like veterans. They laid down a barrage for the infantry that was wonderfully effective. They established a reputation which has been made by but few, among French, British or Americans, of laying down a barrage that did not entrap; and fatally so, their own comrades.

It was a glorious day for the division. The casualty roll was heavy for the sector was strongly fortified and the enemy made a most determined resistance. Metz is considered by experts to be the strongest fortified inland city in the world.

Indeed it is almost as strong, if not quite so, as Gibraltar or the Dardanelles. But from the way the Americans hammered at it, military authorities say that only the signing of the armistice prevented the taking of it by assault. As it was, the close of fighting saw Negro troops on German soil.

The fortitude and valor of the Negroes, especially in the action against Metz, won them high praise from their commanding officers. Entire units were decorated by the French with the Croix de Guerre. Fourteen Negro officers and forty-three enlisted men were cited for bravery in action and awarded the Distinguished Service Cross by General Pershing. This is a splendid showing considering that up to November 10th, 1918, the greater portion of the division had to content itself with making daily and nightly raids on the German front line trenches to harass the foe and capture prisoners. This, however, required daring and courage and, in some ways, was more trying and dangerous than being in a big engagement. A total of 57 citations by the American military authorities, besides honors bestowed by the French, is a splendid showing for a division which won most of its honors during its first great baptism of fire.

The casualties of the 92nd Division amounted to an aggregate of 1,511 of all kinds. Six officers were killed in action and one died from wounds. Among the non-commissioned officers and privates 103 were killed in action, 50 died from wounds, 47 were missing in action and five were taken prisoner. Forty enlisted men died from disease. Sixteen officers and 543 enlisted men were wounded; thirty-nine officers and 661 enlisted men were gassed. The number of gassed was unusually large, a reason being, perhaps, that the men in the front line trenches were exceptionally daring in making raids into the enemy's territory. One of the main reliances of the Germans against these raids was poison gas, a plentiful supply of which they kept on hand at all times, and which they could utilize quickly and with great facility.

The small number in this division who were taken prisoner by the enemy verifies the assertion made before that the Negro would sacrifice his life or submit to deadly wounds rather than be captured. When only five out of a total of about 30,000 fell into the Germans' hands alive, it gives some idea of the desperate resistance they put up. Perhaps the stories they had heard about the wanton slaughter of prisoners by the Hun or the brutalities practiced on those who were permitted to live, had something to do with the attitude of the Negroes against being captured; but a more likely solution is that their very spirit to advance and win and to accept death in preference to being conquered, caused the small number in the prisoner list, and the large number in the lists of other casualties.

Considering the desperate advance made by the 92nd Division from Pont a Mousson the morning of November 10th, through a valley swept by the tremendous guns of Metz and thousands of machine guns, the casualty list really is slight.

Advancing over such dangerous ground to gain their objective, it appears miraculous that the division was not wiped out, or at least did not suffer more heavily than it did. An explanation of this seeming miracle has been offered in the rapidity of the advance.

No two battles are ever fought alike. Offensives and defensives will be planned along certain lines. Then will suddenly obtrude the element of surprise or something that could not be foreseen or guarded against, which will overturn the most carefully prepared plans.

No soldiers in the world were ever trained to a higher degree of efficiency than the Germans. Mathematical precision ruled everywhere; the ultimate detail had been considered; and all students of military matters were forced to admit that they had reduced warfare seemingly, to an exact science. But it was a mistake. The Germans were the victims of surprise times innumerable. Some of the greatest events of the war, notably the first defeat at the Marne in its strategic features, was a complete surprise to them.

Everything about war, can, it seems, be reduced to a science except strategy. Certain rules can be laid down governing strategy, but they do not always work. Generally speaking, it is psychology; something which exists in the other man's mind. To read the other man's mind or make a good guess at it, defeats the most scientifically conceived strategy. Napoleon outwitted the best military brains and was himself the greatest strategist of his time, because he invariably departed from fixed military customs and kept his opponent entirely at sea regarding what he was doing or intended to do. Very seldom did he do the thing which his enemy thought he would do; which seemed most likely and proper according to military science. He thought and acted quickly in crises, relied constantly on the element of surprise and invented new strategy on the spur of the moment.

It was the big new strategy, the big new surprises, with which the Germans found themselves unable to cope. The strategy of Foch which developed in the offensive shortly after the battle of Chateau Thierry in July and was well under way in the early part of August, was a surprise to the Germans. Pershing surprised them in his St. Mihiel and following operations, especially the battles of Argonne Forest, and had a greater surprise in store for them in the Lorraine campaign had the war continued.

Perhaps the Germans figured at Metz, that owing to the extreme difficulty of the ground to be covered, their strong fortifications and great gun power, any advance, especially of Negro troops, would be slow. They accordingly timed their artillery action and their defensive measures for a slow assault.

But they were surprised again. Officers could not hold back the Negro fighters and German guns and soldiers could not stop them. They plunged on to Preny and Pagny, and they rushed into the Bois Frehaut, and held for thirty-six hours, this place from which picked Moroccan and Senegalese troops were forced to retreat in ten minutes after they had entered it. The Bois Frehaut was an inferno under the murderous fire of the Germans. Holding it for thirty-six hours and remaining there until hostilities ceased, it is surprising that the casualty list of the 92nd Division did not amount to many times 1,511.

It is not intended to convey the impression that the Negroes were entirely responsible for the victory before Metz. Many thousands of white troops participated and fought just as valiantly. But this History concerns itself with the operations of Negro soldiers and with bringing out as many of the details of those operations as the records at this time will supply.

CHAPTER XXI

The Long, Long Trail

Operations of 368th Infantry—Negroes From Pennsylvania, Maryland and South—In Argonne Hell—Defeat Iron Cross Veterans—Valiant Personal Exploits—Lieutenant Robert Campbell—Private John Baker—Operations of 367th Infantry—"Moss's Buffaloes"—365th and 366th Regiments—The Great Divide—Their Souls are Marching on—Praised By Pershing—Some Citations

When the history of the 92nd Division is written in detail, much prominence will necessarily be given to the operations of the 368th Infantry. This unit was composed of Negroes mostly from Pennsylvania, Maryland and the Southern states. They went abroad happy, light-hearted boys to whom any enterprise outside of their regular routine was an adventure. They received adventure a plenty; enough to last most of them for their natural lives. They returned matured, grim-visaged men who had formed a companionship and a comradeship with death. For months they were accustomed to look daily down the long, long trail leading to the Great Divide. They left behind many who traveled the trail and went over the Divide. Peril was their constant attendant, danger so familiar that they greeted it with a smile.

It has been noted that this unit of the division saw real service prior to the campaign leading from Pont Mousson to Metz. Their first action was in August in the Vosges sector. This was largely day and night raiding from front line trenches. A month later they were in that bit of hell known as the Argonne Forest, where on September 26th, they covered themselves with glory.

They were excellent soldiers with a large number of Negro officers, principally men who had been promoted from the ranks of non-commissioned officers in the Regular Army.

Their commander during the last six weeks of the war, the time when they saw most of their hard service, was Lieutenant Colonel T.A. Rothwell, a Regular Army officer. He went abroad as commander of a machine gun battalion in the 80th Division, later was transferred to the 367th infantry and finally to the 368th. Many of the officers of the latter organization had served under Colonel Rothwell as non-commissioned officers of the Regular Army. He paid them a high tribute in stating that they proved themselves excellent disciplinarians and leaders. He was also very proud of the enlisted men of the regiment.

> *"The Negroes proved themselves especially good soldiers during gas attacks,"* said Colonel Rothwell, *"which were numerous and of a very treacherous nature. During the wet weather the gas would remain close to the ground and settle, where it was comparatively harmless, but with the breaking out of the sun it would rise in clouds suddenly and play havoc with the troops."*

Green troops as they were, it is related that there was a little confusion on the occasion of their first battle, when the regiment encountered barbed wire entanglements for the first time at a place in the woods where the Germans had brought their crack gunners to keep the line. But there was no cowardice and the confusion soon subsided. They quickly got used to the wire, cut their way through and cleaned out the gunners in record time.

Every one of the enemy picked up in that section of the woods was wearing an iron cross; the equivalent of the French Croix de Guerre or the American Distinguished Service Cross. It showed that they belonged to the flower of the Kaiser's forces. But they were no match for the "Black Devils," a favorite name of the Germans for all Negro troops, and applied by them with particular emphasis to these troops and others of the 92nd Division.

On October 10th, the regiment went to Metz and took part in all the operations leading up to that campaign and the close of the war. In the Argonne, before Metz and elsewhere, they were subjected constantly to gas warfare. They behaved remarkably well under those attacks.

Major Benjamin P. Morris, who commanded the Third Battalion, has stated that in the drive which started September 26th, he lost nearly 25 per cent of his men through wounding or gassing. The battalion won eight Distinguished Service Crosses in that attack and the Major was recommended for one of the coveted decorations.

The regiment lost forty-four men killed in action, thirteen died from wounds and eight were missing in action. The list of wounded and gassed ran over three hundred.

Individual exploits were quite numerous and were valiant in the extreme. Here is an instance:

It became necessary to send a runner with a message to the left flank of the American firing line. The way was across an open field offering no covering or protection of any kind, and swept by heavy enemy machine gun fire.

Volunteers were called for. A volunteer under such circumstances must be absolutely fearless. The slightest streak of timidity or cowardice would keep a man from offering his services. Private Edward Saunders of Company I, responded for the duty. Before he had gone far a shell cut him down. As he fell he cried to his comrades:

"Someone come and get this message. I am wounded."

Lieutenant Robert L. Campbell, a Negro officer of the same company sprang to the rescue. He dashed across the shell-swept space, picked up the wounded private, and, with the Germans fairly hailing bullets around him, carried his man back to the lines. There was the case of an officer who considered it more important to save the life of a heroic, valuable soldier than to speed a message. Besides the wounded man could proceed no farther and there were other ways of getting the message through and it was sent.

Wounded negro soldiers convalescing in base hospital. In the picture are two colored women ambulance drivers.

Sample of identity card carried by soldiers of the American expeditionary forces. Each identification was printed in English and French and included a photograph of the owner. The number on the card corresponding with a metal tag on the man's arm.

Negro officers of 366th Infantry who achieved distinction in France. Left to right. Lieut c.l. Abbott, Capt. Jos. L. Lowe, Lieut. A.R. Fisher, Capt. E. White.

Distinguished officers of the 6th Illinois (370th Infantry). First Row, Left to Right, Capt. D.J. Warner, A.H. Jones. Lieut. E.G. White, Lieut. J.D. Rainey, Lieut. Bernard Mcgwin. Second Row—Lieut. Luther J. Harris, Lieut. Alvin M. Jordan, Lieut. E.L. Goodlett, Lieut. J.T. Baker. Third Row, Lieut. F.J. Johnson, Lieut. Jerome L. Hubert.

Distinguished Officers of 8th Illinois (370th Infantry). Left to Right, Lieut. Lawson Price, Lieut. O.A. Browning, Lieut. W. Stearles, Capt. Lewis E. Johnson, Lieut. Edmond G. White, Lieut. F.W. Bates, Lieut. E.F.E. Williams, Lieut. Binga Dismond.

Colonel Charles Young, ranking negro officer of the regular army. One of three who have been commissioned from the United States Military Academy at West point. A veteran officer of the Spanish-American war and western campaigns. Detailed to active service, Camp Grant, Rockford, Illinois. During the World War.

Two Noted Partisans of the Allies in the Great World War: Mrs. J.H.H. Sengstacke, and her famous son, Robert Sengstacke Abbott, editor and publisher of the Chicago Defender. It was Mrs. Sengstacke who, when the Defender had reached the one hundred thousand mark of its circulation, started the press that ran off the edition, flaming with cheer an inspiration for "Our Boys" in the trenches "Over There."

Reunited and happy. Lieut. Colonel Otis B. Duncan of 8th Illinois (370th Infantry), who came out of the war the ranking negro in the American expeditionary forces; his father and mother.

Miss Vivian Harsh, member Chicago chapter of canteen workers, passing out smokes to returned soldiers of 8th Illinois (370th Infantry).

Officers of 8th Illinois (370th Infantry). Decorated by French for gallantry in action. Left to right. Lieut. Thomas A. Painter, Capt. Stewart Alexander, Lieut. Frank Robinson.

For the valor shown both were cited for the Distinguished Service Cross. Lieutenant Campbell's superiors also took the view that in that particular instance the life of a brave soldier was of more importance than the dispatch of a message, for as a result, he was recommended for a captaincy.

Another single detail taken from the same Company I:

John Baker, having volunteered, was taking a message through heavy shell fire to another part of the line. A shell struck his hand, tearing away part of it, but the Negro unfalteringly went through with the message.

He was asked why he did not seek aid for his wounds before completing the journey. His reply was:

"I thought that the message might contain information that would save lives."

Has anything more heroic and unselfish than that ever been recorded? Nature may have, in the opinions of some, been unkind to that man when she gave him a dark skin, but he bore within it a soul, than which there are none whiter; reflecting the spirit of his Creator, that should prove a beacon light to all men on earth, and which will shine forever as a "gem of purest ray serene" in the Unmeasurable and great Beyond.

Under the same Lieut. Robert Campbell, a few colored soldiers armed only with their rifles, trench knives, and hand grenades, picked up from shell holes along the way, were moving over a road in the Chateau Thierry sector. Suddenly their course was crossed by the firing of a German machine gun. They tried to locate it by the sound and direction of the bullets, but could not. To their right a little ahead, lay a space covered with thick underbrush; just back of it was an open field. Lieutenant Campbell who knew by the direction of the bullets that his party had not been seen by the Germans, ordered one of his men with a rope which they happened to have, to crawl to the thick underbrush and tie the rope to several stems of the brush; then to withdraw as fast as possible and pull the rope making the brush shake as though men were crawling through it. The purpose was to draw direct fire from the machine gun, and by watching, locate its position.

The ruse worked. Lieutenant Campbell then ordered three of his men to steal out and flank the machine gun on one side, while he and two others moved up and flanked it on the other side.

The brush was shaken more violently by the concealed rope. The Germans, their eyes focused on the brush, poured a hail of bullets into it. Lieutenant Campbell gave the signal and the flanking party dashed up; with their hand grenades they killed four of the Boches and captured the remaining three—also the machine gun. There was an officer who could think and plan in an emergency, and evolve strategy like a Napoleon.

First Lieutenant Edward Jones, of the Medical Corps of the regiment, was cited for heroism at Binarville. On September 27th Lieutenant Jones went into an open area subjected to direct machine gun fire to care for a wounded soldier who was being carried by another officer. While dressing the wounded man, a machine gun bullet passed between his arms and body and a man was killed within a few yards of him.

In a General Order issued by the commander of the division, General Martin, Second Lieutenant Nathan O. Goodloe, one of the Negro officers of the regimental Machine Gun Company, was commended for excellent work and meritorious conduct. During the operations in the Argonne forest, Lieutenant Goodloe was attached to the Third Battalion. In the course of action it became necessary to reorganize the battalion and withdraw part of it to a secondary position. He carried out the movement under a continual machine gun fire from the enemy. General Martin said: "Lieutenant Goodloe's calm courage set an example that inspired confidence in his men."

General Martin also cited for meritorious conduct near Vienne le Chateau, Tom Brown, a wagoner, who as driver of an ammunition wagon, displayed remarkable courage, coolness and devotion to duty under fire. Brown's horses had been hurled into a ditch by shells and he was injured. In spite of his painful wounds he worked until he had extricated his horses from the ditch, refusing to quit until he had completed the work even though covered with blood from his hurts.

Private Joseph James of the 368th, received the Distinguished Service Cross for extraordinary heroism in action, September 27th, in the Argonne forest.

A regiment of the 92nd Division which gained distinction, received its share of decorations and was mentioned several times in General Orders from the high officers, was the 367th Infantry, "Moss's Buffaloes." This title was attached to them while they were undergoing training at Yaphank, N.Y., under Colonel James A. Moss of the Regular Army. It stuck to the outfit all through the war and became a proud title, a synonym of courage and fighting strength.

The 367th went to France in June 1918 and spent two months training back of the lines. It was sent to supporting trenches August 20th and finally to the front line at St. Die, near Lorraine border. It remained there until September 21st and was then transferred to the St. Mihiel salient where Pershing delivered his famous blow, the one that is said to have broken the German heart. It was at any rate, a blow that demonstrated the effectiveness of the American fighting forces. In a few days the overseas commander of the Yankee troops conquered a salient which the enemy had held for three years and which was one of the most menacing positions of the entire line.

On October 9th, the regiment was sent to the left bank of the Moselle, where it remained until the signing of the armistice.

Colonel Moss was taken from combatant duty early in October to become an instructor at the training school at Gondrecourt, the regiment passing under the command of Colonel W.J. Doane.

Composed of selectives mostly from the state of New York, the regiment was trained with a view to developing good assault and shock troops, which they were.

Casualties of all descriptions in the 367th, amounted to about ten per cent of the regimental strength. A number of decorations for personal bravery were bestowed, and the regiment as a whole was cited and praised by General Pershing in his review of the 92nd Division at Le Mans.

The entire First Battalion of the 367th, was cited for bravery and awarded the Croix de Guerre by the French. The citation was made by the French Commission because of the splendid service and bravery shown by the regiment in the last engagement of the war, Sunday and Monday, November 10th and 11th in the drive to Metz. The men went into action through the bloody valley commanded by the heavy guns of Metz, and held the Germans at bay until the 56th regiment could retreat, but not until it had suffered a heavy loss. The First Battalion was commanded by Major Charles L. Appleton of New York, with company commanders and lieutenants, Negroes.

Another distinguished component of the 92nd Division was the 365th Infantry made up of selectives principally from Chicago and other parts of Illinois. This regiment saw about the same service as the 367th, perhaps a little more severe, as the casualties were greater. In the action at Bois Frehaut in the drive on Metz, the 365th lost forty-three men killed in action and dead from wounds. In addition there were thirty-two missing in action, most of whom were killed or succumbed to wounds. About 200 were wounded or gassed.

In General Orders, issued by the commander of the division, a number of Negro officers, non-commissioned officers and privates of the 365th were commended for meritorious conduct in the actions of November 10th and 11th. Those named were; Captain John H. Allen, First Lieutenants Leon F. Stewart, Frank L. Drye, Walter Lyons, David W. Harris, and Benjamin F. Ford; Second Lieutenants George L. Games and Russell C. Atkins; Sergeants Richard W. White John Simpson, Robert Townsend, Solomon D. Colson, Ransom Elliott and Charles Jackson; Corporals Thomas B. Coleman, Albert Taylor, Charles Reed and James Conley, and Privates Earl Swanson, Jesse Cole, James Hill, Charles White and George Chaney.

Captain Allen of the Machine Gun Company of the 365th, died in France of pneumonia. Only a short time before his death he had been awarded the Distinguished Service Cross by General Pershing, for exceptional gallantry before Metz.

Private Robert M. Breckenridge of Company B, 365th regiment, also gave his life in France, but had received the Distinguished Service Cross for extraordinary heroism in action at Ferme de Belwir, October 29th, 1918.

Corporal Russell Pollard of Company H received his Distinguished Service Cross shortly before his return home. He was cited for extraordinary heroism in action in the first days battle at Metz.

The remaining infantry regiment of the Division not heretofore specially mentioned, was the 366th, a highly efficient organization of selectives assembled from the mobilization and training camps of various sections of the country. Like the other regiments of the division, the greater number of these men were assembled in the autumn of 1917, trained continuously in this country until the early part of the summer of 1918, sent to France and given at least two months' intensive training there. During the training periods their instructors were mostly officers from the Regular Army or the military instruction schools of this country and France. Some English officers also assisted in the training. That they possessed the requisite intelligence for absorbing the instruction they received is evidenced by the high type of soldier into which they developed, their records in battle, and the unstinted praise which they received from their superior officers, the French commanders and others who witnessed or were familiar with their service.

The 366th went through the campaign in the Marbache sector and suffered all its rigors and perils. In the final two days of fighting they were right at the front and achieved distinction to the extent that in the review at Le Mans they also were singled out by General Pershing for special commendation. During the campaign the regiment had a loss of forty-three men killed in action or died of wounds. Seven men were missing in action. The wounded and gassed were upwards of 200.

In General Orders issued by the commander of the division, First Lieutenant John Q. Lindsey was cited for bravery displayed at Lesseux; Sergeant Isaac Hill for bravery displayed at Frapelle and Sergeant Walter L. Gross for distinguished service near Hominville. These men were all colored and all of the 366th regiment.

Wherever men were cited in General Orders or otherwise, it generally followed that they received the Distinguished Service Cross or some other coveted honor.

CHAPTER XXII

Glory That Wont Come Off

167th First Negro Artillery Brigade—"Like Veterans" Said Pershing—First Artillery to be Motorized—Record by Dates—Selected for Lorraine Campaign—Best Educated Negroes in American Forces—Always Stood by Their Guns—Chaplain's Estimate—Left Splendid Impression—Testimony of French Mayors—Christian Behavior—Soldierly Qualities

To the 92nd Division belonged the distinction of having the first artillery brigade composed entirely of Negroes, with the exception of a few commissioned officers, ever organized in this country. In fact, the regiments composing the brigade, the 349th, the 350th and 351st were the first complete artillery regiments of Negroes and the only important Negro organizations in the artillery branch of the service, ever formed in this country.

Their record was remarkable considering the brief time in which they had to distinguish themselves, and had the war continued, they would surely have gained added glory; General Pershing in the review at Le Mans complimenting them particularly, stating that when the armistice came he was planning important work for them. Following are the general's words which brought much pride to the organization:

> *"Permit me to extend to the officers and men of the 167th Field Artillery Brigade, especially the 351st regiment, my congratulations for the excellent manner in which they conducted themselves during the twelve days they were on the front. The work of the unit was so meritorious that after the accomplishments of the brigade were brought to my attention I was preparing to assign the unit to very important work in the second offensive. You men acted like veterans, never failing to reach your objective, once orders had been given you. I wish to thank you for your work."*

The unit was organized largely from men of Western Pennsylvania, the District of Columbia, Maryland and Virginia. Camp Meade, near

Washington, D.C., was their principal training point from the fall of 1917 until June, 1918, when they went abroad.

To the brigade belongs the additional distinction of being the first in the service to be motorized. Tractors hauled the big guns along the front at a rate of twelve miles an hour, much better than could have been done with horses or mules.

Brigadier General W.E. Cole commanded the unit until about the middle of September, 1918, when he was elevated to a major generalship and the command of the 167th passed to Brigadier General John H. Sherburne. In a General Order issued by the latter shortly before he left the unit, he said:

> "I will ever cherish the words of the Commander in Chief, the compliment he paid, in all sincerity to this brigade, when he watched it pass in review. I wish the brigade to understand that those words of appreciation were evoked only because each man had worked conscientiously and unflaggingly to make the organization a success. The men went into the line in a manner to win the praise of all."

The history of the brigade from the time it left Camp Meade until the end of the war may be summarized as follows:

June 27—Disembarked from ship at Brest, France.

July 2—Started for the training area, reaching there July 4.

July 5—Began a period of six weeks training at Lathus in the Montmorillion section.

August 20—Went to La Courtine and remained until September 16th, practicing at target range. Its gun squads excelled in target work and the brigade, especially the 351st regiment, won distinction there. October 4—Finished training at La Courtine and moved into a sector directly in front of Metz, where about three weeks were spent in obtaining the tractors and motor vehicles necessary for a completely motorized artillery outfit.

October 25—Preparing for action. The enemy had noted the great movement of troops in the vicinity and German planes constantly hovered over the unit dropping missiles of death upon it.

The brigade supported the infantry of the division in its attacks on Eply, Cheminot, Bouxieres, Bois Frehaut, Bois La Cote, Champey, Vandieres, Pagny and Moulin Farm. Attacks of more than mediocre importance were: Pagny, November 4 and 5; Cheminot, November 6,

Epley, November 7; Bois Frehaut, November 10; Bois La Cote and Champey, November 11.

In addition to those attacks certain machine gun nests of the enemy were destroyed and strategic points were bombarded. During the entire advance the batteries of the brigade were in front positions and very active. The attack on Bois La Cote and Champey began at 4:30 in the morning and ended just fifteen minutes before the beginning of the armistice. During the engagement the batteries kept up such a constant fire that the guns were almost white with heat.

Private Carl E. Southall of 2538 Elba street, Pittsburgh, Pa., claims to have fired the brigade's last shot. He was a member of Battery D, 351st regiment. When the watch showed the last minute of the war, he jumped forward, got to the gun ahead of his comrades and fired.

Had the war continued the artillery brigade would have taken part in the offensive which was to have begun after November 11 with twenty French and six American divisions investing Metz and pushing east through Lorraine.

The history of one regiment in the artillery outfit is practically the same as another, with the exception that the 351st seems to have had the most conspicuous service. This unit of the brigade was commanded by Colonel Wade H. Carpenter, a West Pointer.

Owing to the technical requirements, a thorough knowledge of mathematics especially being necessary before one can become a good non-commissioned or commissioned officer of artillery, this branch of the service appeals to men of schooling. It has been claimed that the 351st regiment contained the best educated group of Negroes in the American forces; most of them being college or high school men. They were praised highly by their officers, especially by Colonel Carpenter:

> *"When the regiment trained at Camp Meade,"* he said, *"the men showed the best desire, to make good soldiers. In France they outdid their own expectations and shed glory for all.*
>
> *"We didn't get into action until October 28th, but after that we kept at the Germans until the last day.*
>
> *"The men of the 351st were so anxious to get into service that before they were ordered to the front they found it difficult to restrain their impatience at being held back. However, their long training in France did them a lot of good, the experience of being taught by veteran Americans and Frenchmen proving of great value when it came to actual battle.*

> "They never flinched under fire, always stood by their guns and made the famous 155 millimeter French guns, with which we were equipped, fairly smoke.
>
> "I have been a regular army man for many years, and have always been in command of white troops. Let me say to you that never have I commanded a more capable, courageous and intelligent regiment than this. It would give me the greatest pleasure to continue my army career in command of this regiment of Negroes.
>
> "Not only was their morale splendid but they were especially ready to accept discipline. They idolized their officers and would have followed them through hell if necessary.
>
> "Fortunately, though many were wounded by shrapnel and a number made ill by gas fumes, we suffered no casualties in the slain column. About twenty-five died of sickness and accidents, but we lost none in action.
>
> "When the armistice came our hits were making such tremendous scores against the enemy that prisoners taken by the Americans declared the destruction wrought by the guns was terrific. On the last day and in the last hour of the war our guns fairly beat a rat-a-tat on the enemy positions. We let them have it while we could."

Lieutenant E.A. Wolfolk, of Washington, D.C., chaplain of the regiment, aid:

> "The morale and morals of the men were splendid. Disease of the serious type was unknown. The men were careful to keep within bounds. They gave their officers no trouble, and each man strove to keep up the high standard expected of him. From the time we reached France in June, 1918, until the time we quit that country we worked hard to maintain a clean record and we certainly succeeded."

At the Moselle river, Pont a Mousson and Madieres, the regiment first saw action. The first and second battalions went into action immediately in the vicinity of St. Genevieve and Alton. The third battalion crossed the river and went into action in the vicinity of Pont a Mousson. That was on October 31st. The balance of the regiment's service corresponds to that of the brigade, already mentioned.

As already gleaned from the reports of generals, regimental officers and the testimony of the chaplain of the 351st, the artillery boys created a good impression and left behind them a clean record everywhere. It has remained for the officers of the 349th regiment to preserve this in additional documentary form in the shape of regimental orders and letters from the mayors of French towns in which the regiment stopped or was billeted. The following are some of the bulletins and letters:

>Headquarters 349th Field Artillery, American Expeditionary Forces, France, A.P.O. 722, September 6, 1918.

The following letter having been received, is published
for the information of the regiment, and will be read at retreat
Saturday, September 7, 1918. By order of
>COLONEL MOORE.
>JOSEPH H. McNALLY, Captain and Adjutant

>FRENCH REPUBLIC
>Town Hall of Montmorillion
>(Vienne)
>Montmorillion, August 12, 1918

Dear Colonel:

At the occasion of your departure permit me to express to you my regrets and those of the whole population. From the very day of its arrival your regiment, by its behavior and its military appearance, it excited the admiration of all of us.

Of the sojourn of yourself and your colored soldiers among us we will keep the best memory and remember your regiment as a picked one.

From the beginning a real brotherhood was establishedbetween your soldiers and our people, who were glad to

Having learned to know them, the whole populationholds them in great esteem, and we all join in saying the best of them.

I hope that the white troops replacing your regiment will give us equal satisfaction; but whatever their attitude may be, they cannot surpass your 349th Field Artillery. Please accept the assurance of my best and most distinguished feelings.

>G. DE FONT-REAULX,
>Assistant Mayor.

> Headquarters 349th Field
> Artillery, American
> Expeditionary
> Forces, France,
> A.P.O. 766,
>
> January 25, 1919

The following letter having been received is published for the information of the regiment. By order of

COLONEL O'NEIL.

GEORGE B. COMPTON, Captain and Adjutant.

> MAIRIE DE DOMFRONT
>
> (Orne)
>
> Domfront, January 22, 1919
>
> The mayor of the town of Domfront has the very great pleasure to state and declare that the 349th regiment of the 167th Field Artillery Brigade, has been billeted at Domfront from the 28th of December, 1918, to the 22nd of January, 1919, and that during this period the officers as well as the men have won the esteem and sympathy of all the population.
>
> The black officers as well as the white officers have made here many friends, and go away leaving behind them the best remembrances. As to the private soldiers, their behavior during the whole time has been above all praise.
>
> It is the duty of the mayor of Domfront to bid the general, officers and men a last farewell, and to express to all his thanks and gratitude for their friendly intercourse with the civilian population.
>
> F. BERLIN, Mayor

After such testimony who can doubt the Christianlike behavior and soldierly qualities of the black man? It has been noted that the artillerymen were in education considerably above the average of the Negro force abroad, but no severe criticism has been heard concerning the conduct of any of the Negro troops in any part of France. The attitude of the French people had much to do with this. The unfailing courtesy and consideration with which they treated the Negroes awoke an answering sentiment in the natures of the latter. To be treated as Men, in the highest sense of the term, argued that they must return that treatment, and it is not of record that they failed to give adequate return. Indeed the record tends to show that they added a little for good measure, although it is hard to outdo a Frenchman in courtesy and the common amenities of life.

This showing of Negro conduct in France takes on increased merit when it is considered that the bulk of their forces over there were selectives; men of all kinds and conditions; many of them from an environment not likely to breed gentleness, self restraint or any of the finer virtues. But the leaders and the best element seem to have had no difficulty in impressing upon the others that the occasion was a sort of a trial of their race; that they were up for view and being scrutinized very carefully. They made remarkably few false steps.

CHAPTER XXIII

Nor Storied Urn, Nor Mounting Shaft

Glory Not All Spectacular—Brave Forces Behind the Lines—325th Field Signal Battalion—Composed of Young Negroes—See Real Fighting—Suffer Casualties—An Exciting Incident—Colored Signal Battalion A Success—Ralph Tyler's Stories—Burial of Negro Soldier At Sea—More Incidents of Negro Valor—A Word From Charles M. Schwab

Out of the glamor and spectacular settings of combat comes most of the glory of war. The raids, the forays, the charges; the pitting of cold steel against cold steel, the hand to hand encounters in trenches, the steadfast manning of machine guns and field pieces against deadly assault, these and kindred phases of battle are what find themselves into print. Because they lend themselves so readily to the word painter or to the artist's brush, these lurid features are played to the almost complete exclusion of others, only slightly less important.

There are brave forces behind the lines, sometimes in front of the lines, about which little is written or pictured. Of these the most efficient and indispensable is the Signal Corps. While this branch of the service was not obliged to occupy front line trenches; make raids for prisoners, or march in battle formation into big engagements, it must not be supposed that it did not have a very dangerous duty to perform.

One of the colored units that made good most decisively was the 325th Field Signal Battalion of the 92nd Division. The men of this battalion had to string the wires for telegraphic and telephonic connections at times when the enemy guns were trained upon them. Therefore, in many respects, their duty took them into situations fully as dangerous as those of the combatant units.

This battalion was composed entirely of young Negroes excepting the Lieutenant Colonel, Major and two or three white line officers. With few exceptions, they were all college or high school boys, quite a number of them experts in radio or electric engineering. Those who were not experts when the battalion was formed, became so through the training which they received.

Major Spencer, who was responsible for the formation of the battalion, the only Negro signal unit in the American Army, was firm in the belief that Negroes could make good, and he remained with it long enough to see his belief become a realization.

After arriving at Brest, June 19, 1918, the battalion proceeded to Vitrey, and from that town began a four-day hike to Bourbonne les Baines. From that point it proceeded after a few days to Visey, where the boys got their first taste of what was to be, later, their daily duties. Here the radio (wireless telegraphy) company received its quota of the latest type of French instruments, a battery plant was established and a full supply of wire and other equipment issued to Companies B and C. Here, too, the Infantry Signal platoons of the battalion joined the outfit and shared in the training.

A courage test and their first introduction into real fighting in addition to stringing wires and sending and receiving radio messages, came on the afternoon of September 27th. A party including the Colonel, Lieutenant Herbert, the latter a Negro, and some French liaison officers, advanced beyond the battalion post and soon found themselves outside the lines and directly in front of a German machine gun nest.

The colonel divided his men into small groups and advanced on the enemy's position. The sortie resulted in the Signal boys capturing eight prisoners and two machine guns, but it cost the loss of Corporal Charles E. Boykin, who did not return. Two days later during a general advance, Sergeant Henry E. Moody was mortally wounded while at his post. Boykin was killed outright, while Sergeant Moody died in the hospital, these being the first two of the Signal Battalion to make the supreme sacrifice.

On the 10th of October the 92nd Division, having taken over the Marbache sector and relieved the 167th French Division, the 325th Field Signal Battalion took over all existing lines of communication. In the days following they installed new lines and made connections between the various units of the division. This was no small duty, when it is remembered that an army sector extends over a wide area of many square miles, including in it from 50 to 100 cities and towns.

The Marbache sector was an active front and time and time again the boys went ahead repairing lines and establishing new communications under shell fire, with no heed to personal danger—inspired only by that ideal of the Signal Corps man—get communication through at any cost, but get it through.

On the morning of November 10th, when the Second Army launched its attack on the famous Hindenburg line before Metz, the 92nd Division held the line of Vandieres—St. Michel, Xon and Norry. The engagement lasted for twenty-eight hours continuously, during which time the Signal Corps functioned splendidly and as one man, keeping up communications, installing new lines and repairing those shelled out.

One of the most exciting incidents was that participated in by the First Platoon of the Signal Battalion on the first day of the Metz battle. Shortly after the lighter artillery barrage was lifted, the big guns of the enemy began shelling Pont a Mousson. The first shells hit on the edge of the city and then they began peppering the Signal Battalion's station.

Sergeant Rufus B. Atwood of the First Platoon was seated in the cellar near the switchboard; Private Edgar White was operating the switchboard, and Private Clark the buzzerphone. Several officers and men were standing in the "dugout" cellar. Suddenly a shell struck the top, passed through the ceiling and wall and exploded, making havoc of the cellar.

Officers of the 15th New York (369th Infantry), marching in parade prior to the war. Left to Right—Col. Wm. Hayward, Bert Williams. Famous Comedian and Dr. G. Mcsweeney.

After the war. One of the number of automobiles bearing wounded officers and soldiers of the 15th New York (369th Infantry). Major David L. 'Esperance (with helmet) and Major Lorrilard Spencer.

A representative group of negro officers of "Moss's Buffaloes" (167th Infantry). The little lady with the bouquet is one of their French acquaintances.

Captain John H. Patton, Regimental Adjutant, 8th Illinois Infantry. From June 26, 1916, to September 11, 1918. Commanding 2nd Battalion, 370th Infantry, from September 11, 1918, to December 25, 1918. Saint Mihiel sector from June 21, 1918, to July 3, 1918. Argonne Forest from July 6, 1916, to August 15, 1918. Battles for Mont des Signes, from September 16 to 30, 1918. Oise-Aisne offensive, from September 30, 1918. to November 11, 1918. Awarded the French Croix de Guerre for meritorious service covering period from September 11 to November 11, 1918.

W. Allison Sweeney

Emil Laurent, negro corporal of 8th Illinois (370th Infantry), a Croix de Guerre winner, engaged in field telephone service in a French wood.

Group of "Hell Fighters' (369th infantry) with their jewelry (Croix de Guerre). Front row, left to right, "Eagle Eye" Edward Williams, "Lamp Light" Herb Taylor, Leon Trainor, "Kid Hawk" Ralph Hawkins, back row, left to right, Sergt. M.D. Primus, Sergt. Daniel Storms, "Kid Woney" Joe Williams, "Kid Buck" Alfred Hanly and Corp. T.W. Taylor.

Dr. Joseph H. Ward on transport France. The only negro attaining the rank of major in the medical corps of the American Expeditionary Forces.

Captain Napoleon B. Marshall, famous Harvard athlete, who helped organize 15th New York and was one of its original negro officers. He was seriously wounded at Metz.

Brave negroes homeward bound from war. First call for dinner.

"Moss's Buffaloes" (367th infantry), reviewed by Governor Whitman after flag presentation in front of Union League Club, New York.

History of the American Negro in the Great World War

The "Buffaloes" (367th Infantry), returning to New York after valiant service in France. Their colors still flying.

Soldiers who distinguished themselves at the fortress of Metz. Group belonging to 365thInfantry arriving at Chicago station.

Homeward bound in a Pullman car. No "Jim crowing there." the negro bears on his shoulder the citation cord and emblem denoting valorous service.

Lieutenant Walker, who arrived just at this time, took hold of matters with admirable coolness and presence of mind. Sergeant Atwood tried out the switchboard and found all lines broken. He also found on trying it the buzzerphone out. Lieutenant Walker gave orders to Private White to stay on the switchboard and Corporal Adolphus Johnson to stay on the buzzerphone. The twelve-cord monocord board was nailed up by White and then began the connecting up of the lines from outside to the monocord board. All this time the shelling by the Germans was fierce and deadly. Shells struck all around the boys and one struck a nearby ammunition dump, causing the explosion of thousands of rounds of ammunition, which created a terrific shock and extinguished all the lights.

But still the men worked on and would not leave the dangerous post, a veritable target for the enemy's big guns, until the lieutenant of the Military Police arrived and ordered them out.

The 325th Field Signal Battalion was a great success. What the boys did not learn about radio, telephonic and telegraphic work would be of little advantage to anyone. It will be of great advantage to many of them in the way of making a living in times of peace.

By the time the armistice stopped the fighting the different units of the 92nd Division had taken many prisoners and gained many objectives. They finally retired to the vicinity of Pont a Mousson, where time was spent salvaging material and cleaning equipment, while the men, knowing there was to be no more fighting, anxiously awaited the time until they were ordered to an embarkation point and thence home.

The trip home in February, 1919, was about as perilous to some of them as the war had been. It was a period of unusually rough weather. The north Atlantic, never very smooth during the winter months, put on some extra touches for the returning Negro soldiers. An experience common to many on several different transports has been described by Mechanic Charles E. Bryan of Battery B, 351st Artillery upon his return to his home, 5658 Frankstown Avenue, Pittsburgh, Pa. Asked about his impressions of the war, he said that which impressed him the most was the storm at sea on the way home.

"That storm beat the war all hollow," he said. "Me and my buddies were messing when the ship turned about eighteen somersaults, and we all pitched on the floor, spilling soup and beans and things all over the ship.

> "The lights went out and somehow the automatic bell which means 'abandon ship' was rung by accident. We didn't know it was an accident, and from the way the ship pitched we thought she was on her way down to look up one Mr. Davy Jones. So we made a break for the decks, and believe me, some of those lads who had come through battles and all sorts of dangers were about to take a dive over the side if our officers had not started explaining in time."

Stories of varying degrees of interest, some thrilling, some humorous and some pathetic to the last degree, have been brought back.

Ralph Tyler, the Negro newspaper man, who was sent to France as the official representative of the Afro-American press by the Committee on Public Information, has written many of the incidents, and told others from the rostrum. He has told how the small insignificant, crowded freight cars in which the soldiers traveled looked like Pullman parlor coaches to the Negro soldiers.

"To many of our people back in the 'States,'" wrote Mr. Tyler from France, *"who saw our boys embark on fine American railroad coaches and Pullman sleepers to cover the first lap of their hoped-for pilgrimage to Berlin, the coaches they must ride in over here would arouse a mild protest. I stood at Vierzon, one of France's many quaint old towns recently, and saw a long train of freight cars roll in, en route to some point further distant. In these cars with but a limited number of boxes to sit upon, and just the floors to stand upon, were crowded some 1,000 of our own colored soldiers from the States. But a jollier crowd never rode through American cities in Pullman sleepers and diners than those 1,000 colored troopers. They accepted passage on these rude box freight cars cheerfully, for they knew they were now in war, and palace cars, downy coaches and the usual American railroad conveniences were neither available nor desirable.*

"The point I wish to convey to the people back home is that did they but know how cheerfully, even eagerly our boys over here accept war time conveniences, they would not worry quite so much about how the boys are faring. They are being wholesomely and plenteously fed; they are warmly clothed, they are cheerful and uncomplaining as they know this is war and for that reason know exactly what they must expect. To the soldier who must at times sleep with but the canopy of heaven as a covering, and the earth as a mattress, a box freight car that shields him from the rain and wind is a real luxury, and he accepts it as such.

"There need not be any worry back home as to the maintenance of our colored soldiers over here. They receive the same substantial fare the white soldier receives, and the white soldier travels from point to point in the same box freight cars as afford means of passage for colored soldiers. In short, when it comes to maintenance and equipment, and consideration for the comfort of the American soldier, to use a trite saying, 'the folks are as good as the people.' There is absolutely no discrimination, and the cheerfulness of those 1,000 boys whose freight cars became, in imagination, Pullman palace cars, was the proof to me that the colored boys in the ranks are getting a fifty-fifty break."

"Two more stories have come to me," continues Mr. Tyler, *"to prove that our colored soldiers preserve and radiate their humor even where shells and shrapnel fly thickest. A colored soldier slightly wounded in the Argonne fighting—and let me assure you there was 'some' fighting there—sat down beside the road to wait for a chance to ride to the field hospital. A comrade hastening forward to his place in the line, and anxious for the latest news of the progressing battle, asked the wounded brother if he had been in the fight; did he know all about it, and how were things going at the front. 'I*

sure does know all about it,' the wounded man replied. 'Well, what's happened to them?' quickly asked the trooper on his way to the front. 'Well, it was this way,' replied the wounded one, 'I was climbin' over some barbed wire tryin' to get to those d——n Boches, and they shot me; that's what I know about it.'

"A company water cart was following the advancing troops when a German shell burst in the ditch almost beside the cart. The horse on the shell side was killed, and the driver was wounded in the head. While the blood from his wound ran freely down his face, the driver took one look at the wreckage, then started stumbling back along the road. A white lieutenant who had seen it all stopped the driver of the cart and said:

"The dressing station is——"

"Before he could finish his sentence, the wounded driver, with the blood flowing in rivulets down his face, said: 'Dressing station hell; I'm looking for another horse to hitch to that cart and take the place of the one the shell put out of commission.'

"That was a bit of nerve, grim humor and evidence of fidelity to duty. A mere wound in the head could not stop that driver from keeping up with the troops with a needed supply of water."

Dr. Thomas Jesse Jones, who went to France under the auspices of the Y.M.C.A., sent back the following account of the burial of a Negro soldier at sea:

"A colored soldier was buried at sea today. The flags on all the ships of the fleet have been at half-mast all day. It mattered not that the soldier came from a lowly cabin. It mattered not that his skin was black. He was a soldier in the army of the United States, and was on his way to fight for Democracy and Civilization.

"The announcement of his death was signalled to every commander and every ship prepared to do honor to the colored soldier. As the sun was setting the guard of honor, including all the officers from commander down, came to attention. The body of the Negro trooper wrapped in the American flag, was tenderly carried to the stern of the ship. The chaplain read the solemn burial service. The engines of the fleet were checked. The troop ship was stopped for the only time in the long trip from America to Europe. The bugle sounded Taps and the body of the American soldier was committed to the great ocean and to God.

"The comradeship of the solemn occasion was the comradeship of real Democracy. There was neither black nor white, North nor South, rich nor

W. Allison Sweeney

poor. All united in rendering honor to the Negro soldier who died in the service of humanity."

First Lieutenant George S. Robb of the 369th Infantry was cited for "conspicuous gallantry and intrepidity above and beyond the call of duty" in action with the enemy near Sechault, September 29 and 30, 1918.

While leading his platoon in the assault at Sechault, Lieutenant Robb was severely wounded by machine gun fire, but rather than go to the rear for proper treatment, he remained with his platoon until ordered to the dressing station by his commanding officer. Returning within forty-five minutes, he remained on duty throughout the entire night, inspecting his lines and establishing outposts. Early the next morning he was again wounded, once again displaying remarkable devotion to duty by remaining in command of his platoon.

Later the same day a bursting shell added two more wounds, the same shell killing the captain and two other officers of his company. He then assumed command of the company and organized its position in the trenches. Displaying wonderful courage and tenacity at the critical times, he was the only officer of his battalion who advanced beyond the town and, by clearing machine gun and sniping posts, contributed largely to the aid of his battalion in holding its objective. His example of bravery and fortitude and his eagerness to continue with his mission despite the several wounds, set before the enlisted men of his command a most wonderful standard of morale and self-sacrifice. Lieutenant Robb lived at 308 S. 12th Street, Salina, Kansas.

Second Lieutenant Harry C. Sessions, Company I, 372nd Infantry, was cited for extraordinary heroism in action near Bussy Farm, September 29, 1918.

Although he was on duty in the rear, Lieutenant Sessions joined his battalion and was directed by his battalion commander to locate openings through the enemy's wire and attack positions. He hastened to the front and cut a large opening through the wire in the face of terrific machine gun fire. Just as his task was completed, he was so severely wounded that he had to be carried from the field. His gallant act cleared the way for the rush that captured enemy positions.

In August, 1918, back in the Champagne, a German raiding party captured a lieutenant and four privates belonging to the 369th Infantry, and was carrying them off when a lone Negro, Sergeant William Butler, a former elevator operator, made his presence known from a shell hole. He communicated with the lieutenant without the knowledge of the Germans and motioned to him to flee. The Lieutenant signalled to the four privates to make a run from the Germans. As they started Butler yelled, "Look out, you Bush Germans! Here we come," and he let go with his pistol. He killed one Boche officer and four privates, and his own men made good their escape. Later the German officer who had been in charge of this raiding party was captured and his written report was obtained. In it he said that he had been obliged to let his prisoners go because he was attacked by an "overwhelming number of blutlustige schwartzemaenner." The overwhelming number consisted of Elevator Operator Bill Butler alone.

September 30th the 3rd Battalion, of the 370th Infantry, composed of down-state Illinois boys from Springfield, Peoria, Danville and Metropolis, achieved a notable victory at Ferme de la Riviere. This battalion, under the brilliant leadership of Lieutenant Colonel Otis B. Duncan, made an advance of one kilometer against enemy machine gun nests and succeeded in silencing them, thereby allowing the line to advance. This battalion of the Illinois down-state boys succeeded in doing what, after three similar attempts by their French comrades in arms, had proven futile. During this engagement many were killed and wounded and many officers and men were cited and given decorations.

Company C, of the 370th, under the command of Captain James H. Smith, a Chicago letter-carrier, signally distinguished itself by storming and taking the town of Baume and capturing three pieces of field artillery. For this the whole company was cited and the captain was decorated with the Croix de Guerre and Palm.

Lieutenant Colonel Duncan, who has been attached to the office of State Superintendent of Public Instruction of Illinois for over twenty years, is one of the greatest heroes the Negroes of America have produced. He returned as the ranking colored officer in the American Expeditionary Forces. Instead of being merely an assistant Colonel, he was actively in command of one of the hardest fighting battalions in the regiment. He has been pronounced a man of native ability, an able tactician and of natural military genius.

Sergt. Norman Henry, 5127 Dearborn St., Chicago, attached to the 3d Machine Gun Company, 370th Infantry, won the Croix de Guerre and Distinguished Service Cross. It was in the Soissons sector September 30 in the first rush on the Hindenburg line.

All of the officers and men fell under a heavy machine gun barrage except two squads of which Sergeant Henry was left in command. They took two German dugouts and were cut off from their own line without food. They held the Germans off with one machine gun for three days. Often the gun became jammed, but they would take it apart and fix it before the enemy could get to them.

Lieut. Samuel S. Gordon, 3934 Indiana Avenue, Chicago, of the 370th Infantry, exposed himself to open machine gun fire for six hours and effected the rescue of two platoons which had been cut off by the barrage.

Company H had been badly cut up in a sudden burst of machine gun fire. Lieutenant Gordon with some men were rushed up to relieve what was left of the company, and while reconnoitering were cut off by the same fire. A stream of water four feet deep lay between them and their trenches. By standing in the stream, Lieutenant Gordon let the men crawl to the edge of the bank, where he lifted them across without their having to stand up and become targets.

Corporal Emile Laurent, 5302 So. Dearborn Street, Chicago, a member of the 370th Infantry, had a busy time dodging machine gun bullets one night near Soissons. Volunteering as a wire cutter, he crawled out with his lieutenant's automatic in one hand and the wire clippers in the other. Half a dozen machine guns were opened upon him as he sneaked along the terrain. "Never touched me," he would yell every time a chunk of steel parted his hair. He was out for three hours and cut a broad line through the charged wire. Then he crawled back without a mark on him.

Private Leroy Davis of the same regiment, won a decoration at the Aillette Canal for bringing a comrade back under machine gun fire. When he got back to his own lines he would not trust him with the ambulance outfit, but carried him three miles to the emergency dressing station and then he ran back to the canal to get even. This little stunt saved his comrade's life.

Praise for the American soldier comes from Charles M. Schwab, the eminent steel manufacturer, who was chosen by President Wilson to head the Emergency Fleet Cororation, and rendered such conspicuous service in that position. Returning in February, 1919, from a trip to Europe, Mr. Schwab said in an interview:

> *"I have come back with ten times the good opinion I had of our soldiers for the work they did. Everywhere I went I found that the American soldiers had left a good impression behind and there was nothing but the greatest praise for them.*

"During the present voyage I have been among the colored troops on board and talked with them and learned what American soldiering has done for them. They are better men than they were when they went away."

CHAPTER XXIV

Those Who Never Will Return

A Study of War—Its Compensations and Benefits—Its Ravages and Debasements—Burdens Fall Upon the Weak—Toll of Disease—Negroes Singularly Healthy—Negroes Killed in Battle—Deaths From Wounds and Other Causes—Remarkable Physical Stamina of Race—Housekeeping in Khaki—Healthiest War in History—Increased Regard for Mothers—An Ideal for Child Minds—Morale and Propaganda

It has been said that war has its compensations no less than peace. This saying must have had reference largely to the material benefits accruing to the victors—the wealth gained from sacked cities, the territorial acquisitions and the increased prestige and prosperity of the winners. There is also an indirect compensation which can hardly be measured, but which is known to exist, in the increased courage inculcated, the banishment of fear, the strengthened sense of devotion, heroism and self-sacrifice, and all those principles of manliness and unselfishness which are inspired through war and react so beneficially on the morals of a race. There are some, however, who contend that these compensations do not overbalance the pain, the heart-rending, the horrors, brutalities and debasements which come from war. Viewed in the most favorable light, with all its glories, benefits and compensations, war is still far removed from an agreeable enterprise.

Like so many of the other material compensations of life, its benefits accrue to the strong while its burdens fall upon the weak. A contemplation of the maimed, the crippled and those stricken with disease, fails to engender anything but somber reflections.

Owing to the advancement of science, the triumph of knowledge over darkness, the late war through the unusual attention given to the physical fitness of the soldiers, probably conferred a boon in sending back a greater percentage of men physically improved than the toll of destroyed or deteriorated would show. Yet with all the improvement in medical and sanitary science, the fact remains that disease claimed more lives than bullets, bayonets, shrapnel or gas.

Negro soldiers in the war were singularly free from disease. Deaths from this cause were surprisingly few, the mortality being much lower than it would have been among the same men had there been no war. This was due to the general good behavior of the troops as testified to by so many commanding officers and others. The men observed discipline, kept within bounds and listened to the advice of those competent to give it.

Out of a total of between 40,000 and 45,000 Negro soldiers who went into battle or were exposed to the enemy's attack at some time, about 500 were killed in action. Between 150 and 200 died of wounds. Deaths from disease did not exceed 200 and from accident not over fifty. Those who were wounded and gassed amounted to about 4,000.

It speaks very highly for the medical and sanitary science of the army as well as for the physical stamina of a race, when less than 200 died out of a total of 4,000 wounded and gassed. The bulk of the battle casualties were in the 93rd Division.

The figures as given do not seem very large, yet it is a fact that the battle casualties of the American Negro forces engaged in the late war were not very far short of the entire battle casualties of the Spanish-American war. In that conflict the United States lost less than 1,000 men in battle.

While battle havoc and ravages from disease were terrible enough, and brought sadness to many firesides, and while thousands of survivors are doomed to go through life maimed, suffering or weakened, there is a brighter side to the picture. Evidences are plentiful that "housekeeping in khaki" was not unsuccessful.

According to a statement issued by the War Department early in 1919, the entire overseas army was coming back 18,000 tons heavier and huskier than when it went abroad. Many of the returning soldiers found that they literally burst through the clothing which they had left at home. Compared with the records taken at time of enlistment or induction into the draft forces, it is shown that the average increase in weight was twelve pounds to a man.

Improvement of course was due to the healthful physical development aided by the seemingly ceaseless flow of wholesome food directed into the training camps and to France. Secretary Baker was very proud of the result and stated that the late war had been the healthiest in history. The test he applied was in the number of deaths from disease. The best previous record, 25 per 1,000 per year was attained by the Germans in the Franco-Prussian war. Our record in the late war was only eight per 1,000 per year. The Medical Corps did heroic service in keeping germs away, but cooks, clothing designers and other agencies contributed largely in the making of bodies too healthy to permit germ lodgments.

The hell of war brought countless soldiers to the realization that no matter how much they believed they had loved their mothers, they had never fully appreciated how much she meant to them.

"I know, mother," cried one youth broken on the field, whose mother found him in a hospital, "that I began to see over there how thoughtless, indeed, almost brutal, I had always been. Somehow, in spite of my loving you, I just couldn't talk to you. Why, when I think how I used to close up like a clam every time you asked me anything about myself——" He broke off and with fervent humility kissed the hand in his own. "Please forget it all, mother," he whispered. "It's never going to be that way again. I found out over there—I knew what it was not to have anyone to tell things to—and now, why you've got to listen to me all the rest of your life, mother."

Angelo Patri, the new York schoolmaster who has been so successful in instilling ideals into the child mind has addressed himself to the children of today, they who will be the parents of tomorrow. His words are:

> *"Man has labored through the ages that you might be born free. Man has fought that you might live in peace. He has studied that you might have learning. He has left you the heritage of the ages that you might carry on.*
>
> *"Ahead are the children of the next generation. It's on, on, you must be going. You, too, are torch-bearers of liberty. You, too, must take your place in the search for freedom, the quest for the Holy Grail. 'Twas for this you, the children of America were born, were educated. Fulfill your destiny."*

Morale and propaganda received more attention in the late war than they ever did in any previous conflict. Before the end of the struggle the subject of morale was taken up and set apart as one of the highly specialized branches of the service. The specialists were designated as morale officers. They had many problems to meet and much smoothing over to do. In the army, an Americanism very soon attached to them and they became known as "fixers."

History of the American Negro in the Great World War

With respect to the Negro, the section of the War Department presided over by Emmett J. Scott was organized and conducted largely for purposes of morale and propaganda. Much of the work was connected with good American propaganda to counteract dangerous German propaganda.

It is now a known fact that the foe tried to lure the Negro from his allegiance by lies and false promises even after he had gone into the trenches. This has been attested to publicly by Dr. Robert R. Moton, the head of Tuskegee Institute, who went abroad at the invitation of President Wilson and Secretary Baker to ascertain the spirit of the Negro soldiers there.

Dr. Moton was told of the German propaganda and the brazen attempts made on members of the 92nd Division near Metz. He gave the following as a sample:

"To the colored soldiers of the United States Army.

"Hello, boys, what are you doing over there? Fighting the Germans? Why? Have they ever done you any harm?

"Do you enjoy the same rights as the white people do in America, the land of freedom and democracy, or are you not rather treated over there as second class citizens? And how about the law? Are lynchings and the most horrible crimes connected therewith a lawful proceeding in a democratic country?

"Now, all this is entirely different in Germany, where they do like colored people; where they treat them as gentlemen and not as second class citizens. They enjoy exactly the same privileges as white men, and quite a number of colored people have fine positions in business in Berlin and other German cities.

"Why then fight the Germans? Only for the benefit of the Wall street robbers and to protect the millions they have loaned the English, French and Italians?

"You have never seen Germany, so you are fools if you allow yourselves to hate us. Come over and see for yourselves. To carry a gun in this service is not an honor but a shame. Throw it away and come over to the German lines. You will find friends who will help you along."

Negro officers of the division told Dr. Moton this propaganda had no effect. He said the Negroes, especially those from the South, were anxious to return home, most of them imbued with the ambition to become useful, law-abiding citizens. Some, however, were apprehensive that they might not be received in a spirit of co-operation and racial good will. This anxiety arose mainly from accounts of increased lynchings and persistent rumors that the Ku Klux Clan was being revived in order, so the rumor ran, "to keep the Negro soldier in his place."

After voicing his disbelief in these rumors, Dr. Moton said:

"The result of this working together in these war activities brought the whites and Negroes into a more helpful relationship. It is the earnest desire of all Negroes that these helpful cooperating relationships shall continue."

In conversation with a morale officer the writer was told that the principal problem with the Negroes, especially after the selective draft, was in classifying them fairly and properly. Some were in every way healthy but unfit for soldiers. Others were of splendid intelligence and manifestly it was unjust to condemn them to the ranks when so many had excellent qualities for non-commissioned and commissioned grades. The Service of Supply solved the problem so far as the ignorant were concerned; all could serve in that branch.

The officer stated that the trouble with the War Department and with too many other people, is the tendency to treat Negroes as a homogeneous whole, which cannot be done. Some are densely ignorant and some are highly intelligent and well educated. In this officer's opinion, there is as much difference between different types of Negroes as there is between the educated white people and the uneducated mountaineers and poor whites of the South; or between the best whites of this and other countries and the totally ignorant peasants from the most oppressed nations of Europe.

In the early stages of the war, there was a great scarcity of non-commissioned officers—sergeants and corporals, those generals in embryo, upon whom so much depends in waging successful war. It was a great mistake in the opinion of this informant, and he stated that the view was shared by many other officers, to take men from white units to act as non-commissioned officers in Negro regiments, when there were available so many intelligent, capable Negroes serving in the ranks, who understood their people and would have delighted in filling the non-commissioned grades. He also thought the same criticism applied to selections for commissioned grades.

It is agreeable to note that such views rapidly gained ground. The excellent service of the old 8th Illinois demonstrated that colored officers are capable and trustworthy. An action and expression that will go far in furthering the view is that of Colonel William Hayward of the old 15th New York, who resigned command of the regiment which he organized and led to victory, soon after his return from the war. Like the great magnanimous, fair-minded man which he is and which helped to make him such a successful officer, he said that he could not remain at the head of the organization when there were so many capable Negroes who could and were entitled to fill its personnel of officers from colonel down. Colonel Hayward has been laboring to have the organization made a permanent one composed entirely of men of the Negro race. A portion of his expression on the subject follows:

> *"I earnestly hope that the state and city will not allow this splendid organization to pass entirely out of existence, but will rebuild around the nucleus of these men and their flags from which hang the Croix de Guerre, a 15th New York to which their children and grandchildren will belong; an organization with a home of its own in a big, modern armory. This should be a social center for the colored citizens of New York, and the regiment should be an inspiration to them. It should be officered throughout by colored men, though I and every other white officer who fought with the old 15th will be glad and proud to act in an honorary or advisory capacity. Let the old 15th 'carry on' as our British comrades phrase it."*

It is to be hoped that we never have another war. Nevertheless these Negro military organizations should be kept up for their effect upon the spirit of the race. If they are ever needed again, let us hope that by that time, the confidence of the military authorities in Negro ability, will have so gained that they will coincide with Colonel Hayward's view regarding Negro officers for Negro units.

CHAPTER XXV

Quiet Heroes Of The Brawny Arm

Negro Stevedore, Pioneer and Labor Units—Swung the Axe and Turned the Wheel—They were Indispensable—Everywhere in France—Hewers of Wood, Drawers of Water—Numbers and Designations of Units—Acquired Splendid Reputation—Contests and Awards—Pride in Their Service—Measured Up to Military Standards—Lester Waltons Appreciation—Ella Wheeler Wilcox's Poetic Tribute

Some went forth to fight, to win deathless fame or the heroes' crown of death in battle. There were some who remained to be hewers of wood and drawers of water. Which performed the greater service?

For the direct uplift and advancement of his race; for the improved standing gained for it in the eyes of other races, the heroism, and steadfastness and the splendid soldierly qualities exhibited by the Negro fighting man, were of immeasurable benefit. Those were the things which the world heard about, the exemplifications of the great modern forces and factors of publicity and advertising. In the doing of their "bit" so faithfully and capably, the Negro combatant forces won just title to all the praise and renown which they have received. Their contribution to the cause of liberty and democracy, cannot be discounted; will shine through the ages, and through the ages grow brighter.

But their contribution as fighting men to the cause of Justice and Humanity was no greater, in a sense than that of their brethren: "Unwept, unhonored and unsung," who toiled back of the lines that those at the front might have subsistence and the sinews of conflict.

The most indispensable cog in the great machine which existed behind the lines, was the stevedore regiments, the butcher companies, the engineer, labor and Pioneer battalions, nearly all incorporated in that department of the army technically designated as the S.O.S. (Service of Supply). In the main these were blacks. Every Negro who served in the combatant forces could have been dispensed with. They would have been missed, truly; but there were enough white men to take their places if necessary. But how seriously handicapped would the Expeditionary forces have been without the great army of Negroes, numbering over 100,000 in France, with thousands more in this country designed for the same service; who unloaded the ships, felled the trees, built the railroad grades and laid the tracks; erected the warehouses, fed the fires which turned the wheels; cared for the horses and mules and did the million and one things, which Negro brawn and Negro willingness does so acceptably.

Theirs not to seek "the bubble reputation at the cannon's mouth," that great composed, uncomplaining body of men; content simply to wear the uniform and to know that their toil was contributing to a result just as important as the work of anyone in the army. Did they wish to fight? They did; just as ardently as any man who carried a rifle, served a machine gun or a field piece. But some must cut wood and eat of humble bread, and there came in those great qualities of patience and resignation which makes of the Negro so dependable an asset in all such emergencies.

How shall we describe their chronology or write their log? They were everywhere in France where they were needed. As one officer expressed it, at one time it looked as though they would chop down all the trees in that country. Their units and designations were changed. They were shifted from place to place so often and given such a variety of duties it would take a most active historian to follow them. In the maze of data in the War Department at Washington, it would take months to separate and give an adequate account of their operations.

Back with the heroic 15th (369th Infantry). Lieut. James Reese Europe's Famous Band Parading Up Lenox Avenue, Harlem, New York City. Lieut. Europe specially enlarged in left foreground.

Sergeant Henry Johnson (Standing with flowers), negro hero of 369th Infantry. In New York parade. He was the first soldier of any race in the American Army to receive the Croix de Guerre with palm. Needham Roberts, his fighting companion, in inset.

Returning from the war. Musicians of 365th Infantry leading parade of the regiment in Michigan Boulevard. Chicago.

Soldiers of 365th Infantry marching down Michigan Boulevard. Chicago. This regiment was part of the celebrated 92nd Division of selective draft men.

The Seven Ages of Men. Curbstone groups in New York lined up to give the heroes welcome. The scenes were typical of many in cities and towns all over the country.

Colonel Franklin A. Denison, former commander of 8th Illinois (370th Infantry), invalided home from France July 12, 1918.

First commander of the 8the Illinois Infantry, Colonel John R. Marshall, who increased the organization from a battalion to a regiment, every officer and man a negro. Under Col. Marshall the regiment saw distinguished service in the Spanish-American War.

Former Officers of 370th Infantry (Old 8th). Left, Colonel Franklin A. Denison, Commander until July, 1918; Center, Colonel T.A. Roberts (White). Succeeding Commander; Right, Lieut. Colonel Otis B. Duncan. Appointed Colonel to succeed Colonel T.A. Roberts.

Crowd on the lake front in Chicago almost smothers returning soldiers of "fighting 8th" (370th Infantry).

It is known that a contingent of them accompanied the very first forces that went abroad from this country. In fact, it may be said, that the feet of American Negroes were among the first in our forces to touch the soil of France. It is known that they numbered at least 136 different companies, battalions and regiments in France. If there were more, the records at Washington had not sufficiently catalogued them up to the early part of 1919 to say who they were.

In the desire to get soldiers abroad in 1918, the policy of the administration and the Department seems to have been to make details and bookkeeping a secondary consideration. The names of all, their organizations and officers were faithfully kept, but distinctions between whites and blacks were very obscure. Until the complete historical records of the Government are compiled, it will be impossible to separate them with accuracy.

Negro non-combatant forces in France at the end of the war included the 301st, 302nd and 303rd Stevedore Regiments and the 701st and 702nd Stevedore Battalions; the 322nd and 363rd Butchery Companies; Engineer Service battalions numbered from 505 to 550, inclusive; Labor battalions numbered from 304 to 348, inclusive, also Labor battalion 357; Labor companies numbered from 301 to 324, inclusive; Pioneer Infantry regiments numbered 801, 809, 811, 813, 815 and 816, inclusive. These organizations known as Pioneers, had some of the functions of infantry, some of those of engineers and some of those of labor units. They were prepared to exercise all three, but in France they were called upon to act principally as modified engineering and labor outfits. They also furnished replacement troops for some of the combatant units.

Service was of the dull routine void of the spectacular, and has never been sufficiently appreciated. In our enthusiasm over their fighting brothers we should not overlook nor underestimate these. There were many thousands of white engineers and Service of Supply men in general, but their operations were mostly removed from the base ports.

Necessity for the work was imperative. Owing to the requirements of the British army, the Americans could not use the English Channel ports. They were obliged to land on the west and south coasts of France, where dock facilities were pitifully inadequate. Railway facilities from the ports to the interior were also inadequate. The American Expeditionary Forces not only enlarged every dock and increased the facilities of every harbor, but they built railways and equipped them with American locomotives and cars and manned them with American crews.

Great warehouses were built as well as barracks, cantonments and hospitals. Without these facilities the army would have been utterly useless. Negroes did the bulk of the work. They were an indispensable wheel in the machinery, without which all would have been chaos or inaction.

Headquarters of the Service of Supply was at Tours. It was the great assembling and distributing point. At that point and at the base ports of Brest, Bordeaux, St. Nazaire and La Pallice most of the Negro Service of Supply organizations were located. The French railroads and the specially constructed American lines ran from the base ports and centered at Tours.

This great industrial army was under strict military regulations. Every man was a soldier, wore the uniform and was under commissioned and non-commissioned officers the same as any combatant branch of the service.

The Negro Service of Supply men acquired a great reputation in the various activities to which they were assigned, especially for efficiency and celerity in unloading ships and handling the vast cargoes of materials and supplies of every sort at the base ports. They were a marvel to the French and astonished not a few of the officers of our own army. They sang and joked at their work. The military authorities had bands to entertain them and stimulate them to greater efforts when some particularly urgent task was to be done. Contests and friendly rivalries were also introduced to speed up the work.

The contests were grouped under the general heading of "A Race to Berlin" and were conducted principally among the stevedores. Prizes, decorations and banners were offered as an incentive to effort in the contests. The name, however, was more productive of results than anything else. The men felt that it really was a race to Berlin and that they were the runners up of the boys at the front.

Ceremonies accompanying the awards were quite elaborate and impressive. The victors were feasted and serenaded. Many a stevedore is wearing a medal won in one of these conquests of which he is as proud, and justly so, as though it were a Croix de Guerre or a Distinguished Service Cross. Many a unit is as proud of its banner as though it were won in battle.

Thousands of Service of Supply men remained with the American Army of Occupation after the war; that is, they occupied the same relative position as during hostilities—behind the lines. The Army of Occupation required food and supplies, and the duty of getting them into Germany devolved largely upon the American Negro.

Large numbers of them were stationed at Toul, Verdun, Epernay, St. Mihiel, Fismes and the Argonne, where millions of dollars worth of stores of all kinds were salvaged and guarded by them. So many were left behind and so important was their work, that the Negro Y.M.C.A. sent fifteen additional canteen workers to France weeks after the signing of the armistice, as the stay of the Service of Supply men was to be indefinitely prolonged.

The Rev. D.L. Ferguson, of Louisville, Ky., who for more than a year was stationed at St. Nazaire as a Y.M.C.A. worker, and became a great favorite with the men, says that during the war they took great pride in their companies, their camps, and all that belonged to the army; that because their work was always emphasized by the officers as being essential to the boys in the trenches, the term "stevedore" became one of dignity as representing part of a great American Army.

How splendidly the stevedores and others measured up to military standards and the great affection with which their officers regarded them, Rev. Dr. Ferguson makes apparent by quoting Colonel C.E. Goodwin, who for over a year was in charge of the largest camp of Negro Service of Supply men in France. In a letter to Rev. Dr. Ferguson he said:

> "It is with many keen thrusts of sorrow that I am obliged to leave this camp and the men who have made up this organization. The men for whose uplift you are working have not only gained, but have truly earned a large place in my heart, and I will always cherish a loving memory of the men of this wonderful organization which I have had the honor and privilege to command."

Lester A. Walton, who went abroad as a correspondent for the New York Age, thus commented on the stevedores and others of the same service:

> "I had the pleasure and honor to shake hands with hundreds of colored stevedores and engineers while in France. The majority were from the South, where there is a friendly, warm sun many months of the year. When I talked with them no sun of any kind had greeted them for weeks. It was the rainy season when a clear sky is a rarity and a downpour of rain is a daily occurrence. Yet, there was not one word of complaint heard, for they were 'doing their bit' as expected of real soldiers. Naturally they expressed a desire to get home soon, but this was a wish I often heard made by a doughboy.
>
> "Members of the 'S.O.S.' will not came back to America wearing the Distinguished Service Cross or the Croix de Guerre for exceptional gallantry under fire, but the history of the great world war would be incomplete and lacking in authenticity if writers failed to tell of the blood-

History of the American Negro in the Great World War

less deeds of heroism performed by non-combatant members of the American Expeditionary Forces."

During the summer of 1918, Ella Wheeler Wilcox, the poetess, went to France to write and also to help entertain the soldiers with talks and recitations. While at one of the large camps in Southern France, the important work of the colored stevedore came to her notice and she was moved to write a poem which follows:

```
THE STEVEDORES

We are the Army Stevedores, lusty and virile and strong.
We are given the hardest work of the war, and the hours
                                                 are long.
We handle the heavy boxes and shovel the dirty coal;
While soldiers and sailors work in the light, we burrow
                                        below like a mole.
But somebody has to do this work or the soldiers could
                                                not fight!
And whatever work is given a man is good if he does it
                                                   right.
We are the Army Stevedores, and we are volunteers.
We did not wait for the draft to come, and put aside our
                                                   fears.
We flung them away to the winds of fate at the very first
                                        call of our land.
And each of us offered a willing heart, and the strength
                                         of a brawny hand.

We are the Army Stevedores, and work we must and may,
The cross of honor will never be ours to proudly wear and
                                                    sway.
But the men at the front could not be there, and the
                                     battles could not be won.
If the stevedores stopped in their dull routine and left
                                       their work undone.
Somebody has to do this work; be glad that it isn't you.

We are the Army Stevedores—give us our due.
```

CHAPTER XXVI

Unselfish Workers in the Vineyard

Mitigated the Horrors of War—At The Front, Behind the Lines, At Home—Circle for Negro War Relief—Addressed and Praised By Roosevelt—A Notable Gathering—Colored Y.M.C.A. Work—Unsullied Record of Achievement—How The "Y" Conducted Business—Secretaries All Specialists—Negro Women in "Y" Work—Valor of a Non-Combatant

Negroes in America are justly proud of their contributions to war relief agencies and to the financial and moral side of the war. The millions of dollars worth of Liberty Bonds and War Savings stamps which they purchased were not only a great aid to the government in prosecuting the war, but have been of distinct benefit to the race in the establishing of savings funds among many who never were thrifty before. Thousands have been started on the road to prosperity by the business ideas inculcated in that manner. Their donations to the Red Cross, the Y.M.C.A. and kindred groups were exceptionally generous.

An organization which did an immense amount of good and which was conducted almost entirely by Negro patriots, although they had a number of white people as officers and advisers, was the "Circle for Negro War Relief," which had its headquarters in New York City.

At a great meeting at Carnegie Hall, November 2, 1918, the Circle was addressed by the late Theodore Roosevelt. On the platform also as speakers were Emmett J. Scott, Irvin Cobb, Marcel Knecht, French High Commissioner to the United States; Dr. George E. Haynes, Director of Negro Economics, Department of Labor; Mrs. Adah B. Thorns, Superintendent of Nurses at Lincoln hospital, and Dr. W.E.B. Du Bois, who presided.

Mr. Roosevelt reminded his hearers that when he divided the Nobel Peace Prize money among the war charities he had awarded to the Circle for Negro War Relief a sum equal to those assigned to the Y.M.C.A., the Knights of Columbus, and like organizations.

History of the American Negro in the Great World War

"I wish to congratulate you," Mr. Roosevelt said, *"upon the dignity and self-restraint with which the Circle has stated its case in its circulars. It is put better than I could express it when your officers say: 'They, (the Negroes) like the boys at the front and in the camps to know that there is a distinctly colored organization working for them. They also like the people at home to know that such an organization, although started and maintained with a friendly cooperation from white friends, is intended to prove to the world that colored people themselves can manage war relief in an efficient, honest and dignified way, and so bring honor to their race.*

"The greatest work the colored man can do to help his race upward," continued Mr. Roosevelt, *"is through his or her own person to show the true dignity of service. I see in the list of your vice-presidents and also of your directors the name of Colonel Charles Young, and that reminds me that if I had been permitted to raise a brigade of troops and go to the other side, I should have raised for that brigade two colored regiments, one of which would have had all colored officers. And the colonel of that regiment was to have been Colonel Charles Young.*

"One of the officers of the other regiment was to have been 'Ham' Fish. He is now an officer of the 15th, the regiment of Negroes which Mr. Cobb so justly has praised, and when 'Ham' Fish was offered a chance for promotion with a transfer to another command, I am glad to say he declined with thanks, remarking that he 'guessed he's stay with the sunburned Yankees.'"

A guest of honor at the meeting was Needham Roberts, who won his Croix de Guerre in conjunction with Henry Johnson. The cheering of the audience stopped proceedings for a long time when Mr. Roosevelt arrived and shook hands with Roberts.

"Many nice things were said at the meeting," commented the New York Age, *"but the nicest of all was the statement that after the war the Negro over here will get more than a sip from the cup of democracy."*

One of the splendid activities of the Circle was in the providing of an emergency relief fund for men who were discharged or sent back, as in the case of Needham Roberts, on account of sickness or injuries. Many a soldier who was destitute on account of his back pay having been held up was temporarily relieved, provided with work or sent to his home through the agency of the Circle.

While the war was in progress the Circle attended to a variety of legal questions for the soldiers, distributed literature, candy and smokes to the men going to the war and those at the front; visited and ministered to those in hospitals, looked after their correspondence and did the myriad helpful things which other agencies were doing for white soldiers, including relief in the way of garments, food, medicine and money for the fami- families and dependents of soldiers.

The organization had over three score units in different parts of the country. They engaged in the same activities which white women were following in aid to their race. Here is a sample clipped from one of the bulletins of the Circle:

> "On the semi-tropical island of St. Helena, S.C., the native islanders have, in times past, been content to busy themselves in their beautiful cotton fields or in their own little palmetto-shaded houses, but the war has brought to them as to the rest of the world broader vision, and now, despite their very limited resources, 71 of them have formed Unit No. 29 of the Circle. They not only do war work, but they give whatever service is needed in the community. The members knit for the soldiers and write letters to St. Helena boys for their relatives. During the influenza epidemic the unit formed itself into a health committee in cooperation with the Red Cross and did most effective work in preventing the spread of the disease."

Similar and enlarged activities were characteristic of the units all over the nation. They made manifest to the world the Negro's generosity and his willingness in so far as lies in his power, to bear his part of the burden of helping his own race.

After the war the units of the Circle did not grow weary. Their inspiration to concentrate was for the relief of physical suffering and need; to assist existing organizations in all sorts of welfare work. As they had helped soldiers and soldiers' families, they proposed to extend a helping hand to working girls, children, invalids and all Negroes deserving aid.

To the lasting glory of the race and the efficient self-sacrificing spirit of the men engaged, was the wonderful work of the Negro Young Men's Christian Association among the soldiers of this country and overseas. Some day a book will be written dealing adequately with this phase of war activity.

The best writers of the race will find in it a theme well worthy of their finest talents. The subject can be touched upon only briefly here.

To the untiring efforts and great ability of Dr. J.E. Moorland, senior secretary of the Negro Men's Department of the International Committee, with his corps of capable assistants at Washington, belongs the great credit of having organized and directed the work throughout the war.

History of the American Negro in the Great World War

Not a serious complaint has come from any quarter about the work of the Y.M.C.A. workers; not a penny of money was wrongfully diverted and literally not a thing has occurred to mar the record of the organization. Nothing but praise has come to it for the noble spirit of duty, good will and aid which at all times characterized its operations. The workers sacrificed their pursuits and pleasures, their personal affairs and frequently their remuneration; times innumerable they risked their lives to minister to the comfort and well being of the soldiers. Some deeds of heroism stand forth that rank along with those of the combatants.

The splendid record achieved is all the more remarkable and gratifying when the extensive and varied personnel of the service is taken into consideration. No less than fifty-five Y.M.C.A. centers were conducted in cantonments in America, presided over by 300 Negro secretaries. Fourteen additional secretaries served with Student Army Training Corps units in our colleges. Sixty secretaries served overseas, making a grand total of 374 Y.M.C.A. secretaries doing war work.

Excellent buildings were erected in the cantonments here and the camps overseas, which served as centers for uplifting influences, meeting the deepest needs of the soldier's life. In the battle zones were the temporary huts where the workers resided, placed as near the front lines as the military authorities could permit. Many times the workers went into the most advanced trenches with the soldiers, serving them tobacco, coffee, chocolate, etc., and doing their utmost to keep up spirits and fighting morale. Much of the uniform good discipline and behavior attributed to the Negro troops undoubtedly was due to the beneficial influence of the "Y" men and women.

As an example of the way the work was conducted it is well to describe a staff organization in one of the buildings.

It was composed of a building secretary, who was the executive; a religious work secretary, who had charge of the religious activities, including personal work among the soldiers, Bible class and religious meetings; an educational secretary, who promoted lectures, educational classes and used whatever means he had at hand to encourage intellectual development, and a physical secretary, who had charge of athletics and various activities for the physical welfare of the soldiers. He worked in closest relationship with the military officers and often was made responsible for all the sports and physical activities of the camp. Then there was a social secretary, who promoted all the social diversions, including entertainments, stunts and motion pictures, and a business secretary, who looked after the sales of stamps, post cards and such supplies as were handled, and who was made responsible for the proper accounting of finances.

The secretaries were either specialists in their lines or were trained until they became such. Some idea of their tasks and problems, and of the tact and ability they had to use in meeting them, may be gained by a contemplation of the classes with which they had to deal. The selective draft assembled the most remarkable army the world has ever seen. Men of all grades from the most illiterate to the highly trained university graduate messed together and drilled side by side daily. There were men who had grown up under the best of influences and others whose environment had been 370TH or vicious, all thrown together in a common cause, wearing the same uniform and obeying the same orders.

The social diversions brought out some splendid talent. A great feature was the singing. It was essential that the secretary should be a leader in this and possessed of a good voice. These were not difficult to find, as the race is naturally musical and most of them sing well. Noted singers were sent to sing for the boys, but it is said that frequently the plan of the entertainment was reversed, as they requested the privilege of listening to the boys sing.

A wonderful work was done by "Y" secretaries among the illiterates. Its fruits are already apparent and will continue to multiply. They found men who hardly knew their right hand from their left. Others who could not write their names are said to have wept with joy when taught to master the simple accomplishment. Many a poor illiterate was given the rudiments of an education and started on the way to higher attainments.

Headquarters of the overseas work was at Paris, France, and was in charge of E.C. Carter, formerly Senior Student secretary in America, and when war was declared, held the position of National Secretary of India. Much of the credit for the splendid performance of the "Y" workers abroad belonged to him and to his able aid, Dr. John Hope, president of Morehouse college, Atlanta, Ga. The latter went over in August, 1918, as a special overseer of the Negro Y.M.C.A.

Three distinguished Negro women were sent over as "Y" hostesses, with a secretarial rating, during the war. Their work was so successful that twenty additional women to serve in the same capacities were sent over after the close of hostilities. They were to serve as hostesses, social secretaries and general welfare workers among the thousands of Negro soldiers who had been retained there with the Army of Occupation and the Service of Supply.

The first Negro woman to go abroad in the Y.M.C.A. service was Mrs. Helen Curtis of 208 134th Street, New York, in May, 1918. For a number of years she had been a member of the committee of management of the Colored Women's Branch of the Y.M.C.A., and had assisted at the Camp Upton hostess house. Her late husband, James L. Curtis, was minister resident and consul general for the United States to Liberia. Mrs. Curtis lived in Monrovia, Liberia, until her husband's death there. She had also lived in France, where she studied domestic art for two years. Being a fluent speaker of the French language, her appointment was highly appropriate.

So successful was the appointment of Mrs. Curtis that another Negro secretary in the person of Mrs. Addie Hunton of 575 Greene Avenue, Brooklyn, N.Y., followed the next month. Her husband was for many years senior secretary of the International Committee of the Y.M.C.A. Negro Men's Department, and her own work had always been with the organization.

A short time later Miss Catherine Johnson of Greenville, Ohio, followed in the wake of Mrs. Curtis and Mrs. Hunton. She is a sister of Dr. Johnson of Columbus, Ohio, appointed early in 1919 minister to Liberia.

No less successful at home than abroad was the work of the Y.M.C.A. among the Negroes in cantonments and training camps. It is known that the services rendered by the Association to the officers' training camp at Fort Des Moines had much to do with making that institution such a remarkable success. From that time on comment was frequent that the best work being done by the Association in many of the camps was done by Negro secretaries.

The heroic exploit of Professor Cook, the "Y" secretary, which secured him a recommendation for the Distinguished Service Cross, is mentioned elsewhere. It was only equalled by the valiant performance of A.T. Banks of Dayton, Ohio, a Negro "Y" secretary who went over the top with the 368th Infantry. Secretary Banks, during the action, tarried to give aid to a wounded soldier. The two were forced to remain all night in a shell hole. During the hours before darkness and early the following morning they were targets for a German sniper. The secretary succeeded in getting the wounded man back to the lines, where he then proceeded to organize a party to go after the sniper. They not only silenced him, but rendered him unfit for any further action on earth. Mr. Banks returned to

America with the sniper's rifle as a souvenir. His work was additionally courageous when it is considered that he was a non-combatant and not supposed to engage in hostilities. Had he been taken by the Germans he would not have been accorded the treatment of a prisoner of war, but undoubtedly would have been put to death.

Were the records sufficiently complete at the present time to divulge them, scores of examples of valorous conduct on the part of the "Y" workers, Red Cross and other non-combatants who ministered to Negro soldiers could be recounted. The work of all was of a noble character. It was accompanied by a heroic spirit and in many cases by great personal bravery and sacrifice.

CHAPTER XXVII

Negro in Army Personnel

His Mechanical Ability Required—Skilled at Special Trades—Victory Depends Upon Technical Workers—Vast Range of Occupations—Negro Makes Good Showing—Percentages of White and Black—Figures for General Service

In 1917 and 1918 our cause demanded speed. Every day that could be saved from the period of training meant a day gained in putting troops at the front.

Half of the men in the Army must be skilled at special trades in order to perform their military duties. To form the units quickly and at the same time supply them with the technical ability required, the Army had to avail itself of the trade knowledge and experience which the recruit brought with him from civil life. To discover this talent and assign it to those organizations where it was needed was the task of the Army Personnel organization.

The army could hardly have turned the tide of victory if it had been forced to train from the beginning any large proportion of the technical workers it needed. Every combat division required 64 mechanical draughtsmen, 63 electricians, 142 linemen, 10 cable splicers, 156 radio operators, 29 switchboard operators, 167 telegraphers, 360 telephone repairmen, 52 leather and canvas workers, 78 surveyors, 40 transitmen, 62 topographers, 132 auto mechanics, 128 machinists, 167 utility mechanics, 67 blacksmiths, 151 carpenters, 691 chauffeurs (auto and truck), 128 tractor operators and 122 truckmasters.

Besides these specialists each division required among its enlisted men those familiar with 68 other trades. Among the latter were dock builders, structural steel workers, bricklayers, teamsters, hostlers, wagoners, axemen, cooks, bakers, musicians, saddlers, crane operators, welders, rigging and cordage workers, stevedores and longshoremen. Add to these the specialists required in the technical units of engineers, ordnance, air service, signal corps, tanks, motor corps and all the services of supply, and the impossibility of increasing an army of 190,000 in March 1917, to an army of 3,665,000 in November, 1918, becomes apparent unless every skilled man was used where skill was demanded. To furnish tables showing the number of Negroes which the selective draft produced for the various occupations mentioned was at the compilement of this work not practicable. In many cases the figures for white and black had not been separated. The Army Personnel organization did not get into the full swing of its work until well along in 1918.

A good general idea of the percentages of white and black can be gained from the late drafts of that year. Figures for white drafts were not available with the exception of that of September 3rd. But a very fair comparison may be made from the following table showing some occupations to which both whites and blacks were called. Take any of the three general service drafts made upon Negro selectives and it makes a splendid showing alongside the whites. Out of 100,000 men used as a basis for computation, it shows that among the Negro selectives an average of slightly over 25 percent were available for technical requirements, compared with slightly over 36 percent among the whites. It reveals a high number of mechanics and craftsmen among a race which in the minds of many has been regarded as made up almost entirely of unskilled laborers:

Supply per 100,000 in late Negro drafts for general service, compared with supply of white men in same occupations for the September 3rd draft.

		Misc. Figures Sept. 3		
Occupation—	Sept. 1 Draft	Sept 25 Draft	Upon 59,826 Men	Draft White
Mechanical engineer	7	30	8	25
Blacksmith	393	334	331	733
Dock builder	...	...	15	...
Carpenter	862	571	670	2,157
Stockkeeper	161	176	140	562
Structural steel worker	463	326	351	334
Chauffeur	3,561	4,003	3,300	7,191
Chauffeur, heavy truck	1,304	1,356	987	2,061
Bricklayer	189	99	132	223
Hostler	3,351	1,433	2,062	3,559
Teamster or wagoner	8,678	12,660	9,534	13,691
Transit and levelman	...	4	2	47
Axeman logger	1,192	1,759	1,423	1,827
Clerical worker	603	395	324	4,159
Baker and cook	4,129	3,157	2,974	1,077
Musician	105	17	115	160
Alto horn	56	47	38	46
Baritone	21	21	15	16
Bass horn	35	21	18	16
Clarinet	21	64	25	66

```
Cornet                           98         56       67      132
Flute                            21        ...        5       29
Saxaphone                         7         13       10       23
Trap drum                       217        197      100       46
Trombone                         42         69       40       67
Bugler                           14         13       12       24
Saddler                         ...         26        3       12
Crane operator, hoistman         21         39       42       44
Crane operator, pile driver     ...         13       12        7
Crane operator, shovel          ...         13        5       30
Oxy-acetylene welder            ...         21        8       44
Rigger and cordage worker        49         77       57       40
Stevedore, cargo handler        161         34       68       10
Longshoreman                    652        664      651       15
                               ----       ----     ----     ----
                             26,413     27,708   23,544   38,473
```

Figures are for general service drafts and do not include the enlarged list of occupations for which both whites and Negroes were selected.

Five sea tugs pushing transport "France" into dock. Ship laden with members of New York's "fighting 15th" (369th Infantry) and Chicago's "Fighting 8th" (370th Infantry) negro heroes from battlefields of Europe.

CHAPTER XXVIII

The Knockout Blow

Woodrow Wilson, an Estimate—His Place in History—Last of Great Trio—
Washington, Lincoln, Wilson—Upholds Decency, Humanity, Liberty—
Recapitulation of Year 1918—Closing Incidents of War

When sufficient years have elapsed for the forming of a correct perspective, when the dissolving elements of time have swept away misunderstandings and the influences engendered by party belief and politically former opinions, Woodrow Wilson is destined to occupy a place in the Temple of Fame that all Americans may well be proud of. Let us analyze this and let us be fair about it, whatever may be our beliefs or affiliations.

Washington gave us our freedom as a nation and started the first great wave of democracy. Probably, had some of us lived in Washington's time, we would have been opposed to him politically. Today he is our national hero and is revered by all free people of the earth, even by the nation which he defeated at arms. Lincoln preserved and cemented, albeit he was compelled to do it in blood, the democracy which Washington founded. He did infinitely more; he struck the shackles from four million human beings and gave the Negro of America his first opportunity to take a legitimate place in the world. Lincoln's service in abolishing slavery was not alone to the Negro. He elevated the souls of all men, for he ended the most degrading institution that Satan ever devised—more degrading to the master who followed it, than to the poor subject he practiced it upon. Unitedly, we revere Lincoln, yet there were those who were opposed to him and in every way hampered and sneered at his sublime consecration to the service of his country. It takes time to obtain the proper estimate of men.

Enough light has already been cast on President Wilson and his life work to indicate his character and what the finished portrait of him will be.

History of the American Negro in the Great World War

We see him at the beginning of the European conflict, before any of us could separate the tangled threads of rumor, of propaganda, of misrepresentation, to determine what it was all about; before even he could comprehend it, a solitary and monitory figure, calling upon us to be neutral, to form no hasty judgments. We see him later in the role of peacemaker, upholding the principles of decency and honor. Eventually as the record of atrocities and crimes against innocents enlarges, we see him pleading with the guilty to return to the instincts of humanity. Finally as the ultimate aim of the Hun is revealed as an assault upon the freedom of the world; after the most painstaking and patient efforts to avoid conflict, during which he was subjected to humiliation and insult, we see him grasp the sword, calling a united nation to arms in clarion tones, like some Crusader of old; his shibboleth: DECENCY, HUMANITY, LIBERTY.

What followed? His action swept autocracy from its last great stronghold and made permanent the work which Washington began and upon which Lincoln builded so nobly. This of Woodrow Wilson; an estimate—there can be no other thought, that will endure throughout history.

In the earlier chapters are sketched the main events of the great war up to the end of the year 1917, when the history of the Negro in the conflict became the theme. It remains to give an outline review of battles and happenings from the beginning of 1917 until the end of hostilities; culminating in the most remarkable armistice on record; a complete capitulation of the Teutonic forces and their allies, and a complete surrender by them of all implements and agencies for waging war. The terms of the armistice, drastic in the extreme, were largely the work of Marshal Ferdinand Foch, commander-in-chief of the Allied armies.

Early in 1918 it became evident that England, France and Italy were rapidly approaching the limit of their man power. It became necessary for America to hasten to the rescue.

Training of men and officers in the various cantonments of America was intensified and as rapidly as they could be brought into condition they were shipped to France. The troop movement was a wonderful one and before the final closing of hostilities in November there were more than 2,000,000 American troops in Europe. The navy was largely augmented, especially in the matter of destroyers, submarine chasers and lighter craft.

W. Allison Sweeney

Our troops saw little actual warfare during the first three months of the year. Americans took over a comparatively quiet sector of the French front near Toul, January 21. Engagements of slight importance took place on January 30 and February 4, the latter on a Lorraine sector which Americans were holding. On March 1, they repulsed a heavy German raid in the Toul sector, killing many. On March 6, the Americans were holding an eight mile front alone.

On March 21 the great German offensive between the Oise and the Scarpe, a distance of fifty miles, began. General Haig's British forces were driven back about twenty miles. The French also lost much ground including a number of important towns. The Germans drove towards Amiens in an effort to separate the British and French armies. They had some successes in Flanders and on the French front, but were finally stopped. Their greatest advance measured thirty-five miles and resulted in the retaking of most of the territory lost in the Hindenburg retreat of the previous year. The Allies lost heavily in killed, wounded and prisoners, but the Germans being the aggressors, lost more.

While the great battle was at its height, March 28, the Allies reached an agreement to place all their forces from the Arctic Ocean to the Mediterranean, under one supreme command, the man chosen for the position being General Foch of the French. On March 29, General Pershing placed all the American forces at the disposal of General Foch.

The Germans began a new offensive against the British front April 8 and won a number of victories in the La Basse canal region and elsewhere. The battle of Seicheprey, April 20, was the Americans' first serious engagement with the Germans. The Germans captured the place but the Americans by a counter attack recovered it.

Another great offensive was started by the Germans, May 27, resulting in the taking of the Chemin des Dames from the French and crossing the river Aisne. On the following day they crossed the Vesle river at Fismes. Here the Americans won their first notable victory by capturing the village of Cantigny and taking 200 prisoners. They held this position against many subsequent counter-attacks. By the 31st the Germans had reached Chateau Thierry and other points on the Marne, where they were halted by the French. They made a few gains during the first days of June. On June 6, American marines made a gallant attack, gaining two miles on a front two and one-half miles long near Veuilly la Poterie. On the following day they assisted the French in important victories. In the second battle northwest of Chateau Thierry, the Americans advanced nearly two and one-half miles on a six mile front, taking 300 prisoners. It was in these engagements that the Americans established themselves as fighters equal to any.

On June 9, the Germans began their fourth offensive, attacking between Montdidier and the river Oise. They advanced about four miles, taking several villages. In the operations of the following day which gained them several villages, they claimed to have captured 8,000 French. This day the American marines took the greater portion of Belleau wood and completed the capture of it June 11. The French at the same time defeated the Germans between Robescourt and St. Maur. There were other battles on the 12th and 13th, but on the 14th it became evident that the German offensive was a costly failure.

The fighting from this time until the end of June was of a less serious nature, although the Americans in the Belleau and Vaux regions gave the Germans no rest, attacking them continually and taking prisoners. The Americans at this time were also engaged in an offensive in Italy. July 2, President Wilson announced there were 1,019,115 American soldiers in France.

The Fourth of July was celebrated in England, France and Italy as well as in the United States. On that day Americans assisted the Australians in taking the town of Hamel and many prisoners. On the 8th and 9th the French advanced in the region of Longpont and northwest of Compiegne. On the 12th they took Castel and other strong points near the west bank of the Avre river. July 14, the French national holiday was observed in America, and by the American soldiers in France.

The fifth and last phase of the great offensive which the Germans had started in March, began July 15, in an attack from Chateau Thierry to Massignes, along a sixty-five mile front and crossing the Marne at several places. At Chateau Thierry the Americans put up a strong resistance but the enemy by persistent efforts finally succeeded in getting a footing on the south bank. The battle continued east and west of Rheims with the Allies holding strongly and the Germans meeting heavy losses.

While the Germans were trying to force their way regardless of cost, in the direction of Chalons and Epernay, General Foch was preparing a surprise in the Villers-Cotterets forest on the German right flank. In the large force collected for the surprise were some of the best French regiments together with the famed Foreign Legion, the Moroccan regiment and other crack troops including Americans. On the morning of July 18, a heavy blow was launched at the Germans all along the line from Chateau Thierry on the Marne to the Aisne northwest of Soissons.

The foe was taken completely by surprise and town after town fell with very little resistance. Later the resistance stiffened but the Allies continued to advance. Cavalrymen assisted the infantry and tanks in large numbers, helped to clean out the machine gun nests. The Americans who fought side by side with the French won the unbounded admiration of their comrades. Thousands of prisoners were taken with large numbers of heavy cannon, great quantities of ammunition and thousands of machine guns. By the 20th Soissons was threatened. The Germans finding themselves caught in a dangerous salient and attacked fiercely on both flanks, retreated hurriedly to the north bank of the Marne and still farther.

Meanwhile things were going badly for the Austrians. After its retreat in 1917 to the line of the Piave river, the Italian army had been reorganized and strengthened under General Diaz, who had succeeded General Cadorna in command. French and British regiments had been sent to assist in holding the line, and later some American forces.

The Austrians began an offensive June 15 along a 100-mile front, crossing the Piave in several places. For three days they made violent attacks on the Montello plateau, and along the Piave from St. Andrea to San Dona and at Capo Sile, twenty miles from Venice. Then the Italians, British, French and Americans counter-attacked and within three days had turned the great Austrian offensive into a rout, killing thousands, taking thousands of prisoners, and capturing an immense amount of war material including the Austrian's heavy caliber guns. The whole Austrian scheme to advance into the fertile Italian plains where they hoped to find food for their hungry soldiers, failed completely. It was practically the end of Austria and the beginning of the end for Germany. Bulgaria gave up September 26, due to heavy operations by the French, Italians and Serbians during July, August and September, in Albania, Macedonia and along the Vardar river to the boundaries of Bulgaria. They signed an armistice September 29 and the king of Bulgaria abdicated October 3. Turkey being in a hopeless position through the surrender of Bulgaria, and the success of the British forces under General Allenby, kept up a feeble resistance until the end of October when she too surrendered. The collapse of Austria-Hungary followed closely on that of Turkey. They kept up a show of resistance and suffered a number of disastrous defeats until the end of October when they raised the white flag. An armistice was signed by the Austrian representatives and General Diaz for the Italians, November 3.

History of the American Negro in the Great World War

On the anniversary of Britain's entry into the war, August 4, Field Marshall Haig, commander-in-chief of the British forces issued a special order of the day, the opening paragraph of which was:

> *"The conclusion of the fourth year of the war marks the passing of the period of crisis. We can now with added confidence, look forward to the future."*

On August 4, General Pershing reported:

> *"The full fruits of victory in the counter offensive begun so gloriously by Franco-American troops on July 18, were reaped today, when the enemy who met his second great defeat on the Marne, was driven in confusion beyond the line of the Vesle. The enemy, in spite of suffering the severest losses, has proved incapable of stemming the onslaught of our troops, fighting for liberty side by side with French, British and Italian veterans. In the course of the operations, 8,400 prisoners and 133 guns have been captured by our men alone. Our troops have taken Fismes by assault and hold the south bank of the Vesle in this section."*

On August 8, the British and French launched an offensive in Picardy, pressed forward about seven miles on a front of 20 miles, astride the river Somme and captured several towns and 10,000 prisoners. It was in this engagement that the hard fighting at Chipilly Ridge occurred, in which the Americans so ably assisted, notably former National Guardsmen from Chicago and vicinity. Montdidier was taken by the French August 10. The British also continued to advance and by the 11th the Allies had captured 36,000 prisoners and more than 500 guns. A French attack August 19-20 on the Oise-Aisne front, netted 8,000 prisoners and liberated many towns. On the 21st Lassigny was taken by the French. This was the cornerstone of the German position south of the Avre river. On August 29 the Americans won the important battle of Guvigny. By September 2 the Germans were retreating on a front of 130 miles, from Ypres south to Noyon. By the 9th the Germans had been driven back to the original Hindenburg line, where their resistance began to strengthen.

On September 12 the American army, led by General Pershing, won a great battle in the attack on and wiping out of the famous St. Mihiel salient. This victory forced the enemy back upon the Wotan-Hindenburg line, with the French paralleling him from Verdun to the Moselle. Pershing's forces continued fighting steadily, wearing out the Germans by steady pressure. On September 26 the Americans began another offensive along a front of 20 miles from the Meuse river westward through the Argonne forest. This developed into one of the bloodiest battles of the war for the Americans. On September 29 American and British troops smashed through the Hindenburg line at its strongest point between Cambrai and St. Quentin. British troops entered the suburbs of Cambrai and outflanked St. Quentin. Twenty-two thousand prisoners and more than 300 guns were captured. Meanwhile the Belgians tore a great hole in the German line, ten miles from the North sea, running from Dixmude southward.

On October 3 the French launched three drives, one north of St. Quentin, another north of Rheims, and a third to the east in Champagne. All were successful, resulting in the freeing of much territory and the capture of many prisoners. On October 4 the Americans resumed the attack west of the Meuse. In the face of heavy artillery and machine gun fire, troops from Illinois, Wisconsin, Pennsylvania, Virginia, and West Virginia, forced the Germans back to the so-called Kriemhilde line. In the Champagne, American and French troops were moving successfully. On the 6th the Americans captured St. Etienne; on the 9th they reached the southern outskirts of Xivry and entered Chaune wood. On the same day the armies of Field Marshall Haig made a clean break through the Hindenburg system on the west. Through a twenty-mile gap, they advanced from nine to twelve miles, penetrating almost to the Le Selle and Sambre rivers.

On October 12 the British General Rawlinson, with whom an American division had been operating, sent a telegram of congratulation to the commander of the division, which comprised troops from Tennessee, in which he highly praised the gallantry of all the American troops. French troops on October 13 captured the fortress of La Fere, the strongest point on the south end of the old Hindenburg line. They also entered Laon and occupied the forest of St. Gobain. On October 15 the Americans took and passed St. Juvin after desperate fighting. On October 16 they occupied the town of Grandpre, a place of great strategic importance, being the junction of railways feeding a large part of the German armies. The Germans now began a retreat on an enormous scale in Belgium. So fast did they move that the British, French and Belgians could not keep in touch with them. The North sea ports of Belgium were speedily evacuated. Northwest of Grandpre the Americans captured Talma farm October 23, after a stiff machine gun resistance. Victories continued to be announced from day to day from all portions of the front.

On November 1 the Americans participated in a heavy battle, taking Champaigneulle and Landres et St. George, which enabled them to threaten the enemy's most important line of communication. On November 4 the Americans reached Stenay and on the 6th they crossed the Meuse. By the 7th they had entered Sedan, the place made famous by the downfall of Napoleon III in the war of 1870. On other parts of the American front the enemy retreated so fast that the infantry had to resort to motor cars to keep in touch with him. It was the same on other fronts. The Germans put up a resistance at the strong fortress of Metz, which the Americans were attacking November 10 and 11.

Armistice negotiations had been started as early as October, 5, and were concluded November 11th. This date saw the complete collapse of the German military machine and will be one of the most momentous days in history, as it marked the passing of an old order and the inauguration of a new era for the world. In the armistice terms every point which the Americans and Allies stipulated was agreed to by the Germans. The last shot in the war is thus described in an Associated Press dispatch of November 11:

> *"Thousands of American heavy guns fired the parting shot to the Germans at exactly 11 o'clock this morning. The line reached by the American forces was staked out this afternoon. The Germans hurled a few shells into Verdun just before 11 o'clock.*
>
> *"On the entire American front from the Moselle to the region of Sedan, there was artillery activity in the morning, all the batteries preparing for the final salvos.*
>
> *"At many batteries the artillerists joined hands, forming a long line as the lanyard of the final shot. There were a few seconds of silence as the shells shot through the heavy mist. Then the gunners cheered. American flags were raised by the soldiers over their dugouts and guns and at the various headquarters. Soon afterward the boys were preparing for luncheon. All were hungry as they had breakfasted early in anticipation of what they considered the greatest day in American history."*

The celebration, which occurred November 11, upon announcement of the news, has never been equalled in America. It spontaneously became a holiday and business suspended voluntarily. Self-restraint was thrown to the winds for nearly twenty-four hours in every city, town and hamlet in the country. There was more enthusiasm, noise and processions than ever marked any occasion in this country and probably eclipsed anything in the history of the world.

Return of the 15th New York, 369th infantry. Shown swinging up Lenox Avenue. New York City where they received a royal welcome.

CHAPTER XXIX

Homecoming Heroes

New York Greets her Own—Ecstatic Day for Old 15th—Whites and Blacks do Honors—A Monster Demonstration—Many Dignitaries Review Troops—Parade of Martial Pomp—Cheers, Music, Flowers and Feasting—"Hayward's Scrapping Babies"—Officers Share Glory—Then Came Henry Johnson—Similar Scenes Elsewhere

No band of heroes returning from war ever were accorded such a welcome as that tendered to the homecoming 369th by the residents of New York, Manhattan Island and vicinity, irrespective of race. Being one of the picturesque incidents of the war, the like of which probably will not be repeated for many generations, if ever, it well deserves commemoration within the pages of this book.

Inasmuch as no more graphic, detailed and colorful account of the day's doings has been printed anywhere, we cannot do better than quote in its entirety the story which appeared in the great newspaper, The World of New York, on February 18, 1919. The parade and reception, during which the Negro troops practically owned the city, occurred the preceeding day. The World account follows:

> *"The town that's always ready to take off its hat and give a whoop for a man who's done something—'no matter who or what he was before,' as the old Tommy Atkins song has it—turned itself loose yesterday in welcoming home a regiment of its own fighting sons that not only did something, but did a whole lot in winning democracy's war.*
>
> *"In official records, and in the histories that youngsters will study in generations to come, this regiment will probably always be known as the 369th Infantry, U.S.A.*
>
> *"But in the hearts of a quarter million or more who lined the streets yesterday to greet it, it was no such thing. It was the old 15th New York.*

And so it will be in this city's memory, archives and in the folk lore of the descendants of the men who made up its straight, smartly stepping ranks.

"New York is not race-proud nor race-prejudiced. That this 369th Regiment, with the exception of its eighty-nine white officers, was composed entirely of Negroes, made no difference in the shouts and flagwaving and handshakes that were bestowed upon it. New York gave its Old 15th the fullest welcome of its heart.

"Through scores of thousands of cheering white citizens, and then through a greater multitude of its own color, the regiment, the first actual fighting unit to parade as a unit here, marched in midday up Fifth Avenue and through Harlem, there to be almost assailed by the colored folks left behind when it went away to glory.

"Later it was feasted and entertained, and this time very nearly smothered with hugs and kisses by kin and friends, at the 71st Regiment Armory. Still later, perfectly behaved and perfectly ecstatic over its reception, the regiment returned to Camp Upton to await its mustering out.

"You knew these dark lads a year and a half ago, maybe, as persons to be slipped a dime as a tip and scarcely glanced it. They were your elevator boys, your waiters, the Pullman porters who made up your berths (though of course you'd never dare to slip a Pullman porter a dime). But, if you were like many a prosperous white citizen yesterday you were mighty proud to grasp Jim or Henry or Sam by the hand and then boast among your friends that you possessed his acquaintance.

"When a regiment has the medal honors of France upon its flags and it has put the fear of God into Germany time after time, and its members wear two gold stripes, signifying a year's fighting service, on one arm, and other stripes, signifying wounds, on the other, it's a whole lot different outfit from what it was when it went away. And that's the old 15th N.Y. And the men are different—and that's Jim and Henry and Sam.

"Col. William Hayward, the distinguished white lawyer and one time Public Service Commissioner, who is proud to head these fighters, was watching them line up for their departure shortly after 6 o'clock last evening, when someone asked him what he thought of the day.

"'It has been wonderful!' he said, and he gazed with unconcealed tenderness at his men. 'It's been far beyond my expectations. But these boys deserve it. There's only one thing missing. I wish some of Gen. Gouraud's French boys, whom we fought beside, could be here to see it.'

"The Colonel slapped his hand affectionately upon the shoulder of his dark-skinned orderly.

"'How about that, Hamilton, old boy?' he inquired.

"'That's right, Colonel, sir; Gen. Gonraud's boys sure would have enjoyed this day!' the orderly responded as he looked proudly at the Colonel.

"There's that sort of paternal feeling of the white officers toward their men, and that filial devotion of the men to their officers, such as exists in the French Army.

"Much as the white population of the town demonstrated their welcome to the Regiment, it was, after all, those of their own color to whom the occasion belonged. And they did themselves proud In making it an occasion to recall for years in Harlem, San Juan Hill and Brooklyn, where most of the fighters were recruited.

"At the official reviewing stand at 60th street, the kinsfolk and admirers of the regimental lads began to arrive as beforehandedly as 9 o'clock. They had tickets, and their seats were reserved for them. The official committee had seen to that—and nine-tenths of the yellow wooden benches were properly held for those good Americans of New York whom birth by chance had made dark-skinned instead of fair. BUT this was their Day of Days, and they had determined (using their own accentuation) to BE there and to be there EARLY.

"The first-comers plodded across 59th Street from the San Juan Hill district, and it was fine to see them. There seemed to be a little military swank even to the youngsters, as platoons of them stepped along with faces that had been scrubbed until they shone. Had a woman a bit of fur, she wore it. Had a man a top hat—origin or vintage-date immaterial—he displayed that. All heads were up, high; eyes alight. Beaming smiles everywhere. No not quite everywhere. Occasionally there was to be seen on a left sleeve a black band with a gold star, which told the world that one of the Old 15th would never see the region west of Columbus Circle, because he had closed his eyes in France. And the faces of the wearers of these were unlaughing, but they held themselves just as proudly as the rest.

"Few of the welcomers went flagless. No matter whether a man or woman wore a jewel or a pair of patent leather boots as a sign of "class," or tramped afoot to the stand or arrived in a limousine, nearly every dark hand held the nation's emblem.

"*Nearly every one wore white badges bearing the letters: "Welcome, Fighting 15th,"* or had pennants upon which stood out the regimental insignia—a coiled rattlesnake of white on a black field.*

"*Those colored folk who could afford it journeyed to the stand in closed automobiles. Gorgeously gowned women alighted with great dignity beneath the admiring gaze of their humbler brethren. Taxies brought up those whose fortunes, perhaps, were not of such amplitude. Hansoms and hacks conveyed still others, and one party came in a plumber's wagon, its women members all bundled up in shawls and blankets against the cold, but grinning delightedly as the whole stand applauded.*

"*Children by the thousands lined the east side of the avenue—Boy Scouts and uniformed kids and little girls with their school books under their arms, and they sang to the great delight of the crowd.*

"*Just why it was that when Governor Smith and former Governor Whitman and Acting Mayor Moran and the other reviewers appeared behind a cavalcade of mounted policemen, the youngsters struck up that army classic, "Oh, How I Hate to Get Up in the Morning," no one could tell, but it gave the reviewers and the crowd a laugh.*

"*With the state and city officials were the members of the Board of Aldermen, the Board of Estimate, Major Gen. Thomas J. Barry, Vice Admiral Albert Gleaves, Secretary of State, Francis Hugo; Rodman Wannamaker and—in a green hat and big fur coat—William Randolph Hearst. Secretary Baker of the War Department was unable to attend, but he did the next best thing and sent his colored assistant, Emmett J. Scott.*

"*The reviewers arrived at 11:30 and had a good long wait, for at that time the paraders had not yet left 23rd Street. But what with the singing, and the general atmosphere of joyousness about the stand, there was enough to occupy everyone's time.*

"*There was one feature which took the eye pleasingly—the number of babies which proud mothers held aloft, fat pickaninnies, mostly in white, and surrounded by adoring relatives. These were to see (and be seen by) their daddies for the first time. Laughingly, the other day, Col. Bill Hayward spoke of 'our boys' posthumous children,' and said he thought there were quite a few of them.*

"'*Some of our boys had to go away pretty quickly,' he reminisced. 'Some of them were only married about twenty minutes or so.'*

"'*O Colonel!' said the modest Major Little on that occasion.*

"'Well, maybe it was a trifle longer than twenty minutes,' admitted Bill. But anyhow, there was the regiment's posthumous children in the stand.

"It was 11:26 when the old 15th stepped away from 23rd Street and Fifth Avenue. They looked the part of the fighting men they were. At an exact angle over their right shoulders were their long-bayonetted rifles. Around their waists were belts of cartridges. On their heads were their 'tin hats,' the steel helmets that saved many a life, as was attested by the dents and scars in some of them. Their eyes were straight forward and their chins, held high naturally, seemed higher than ever because of the leather straps that circled them. The fighters wore spiral puttees and their heavy hobbed hiking shoes, which caused a metallic clash as they scraped over the asphalt.

"At the head of the line rode four platoons of mounted police, twelve abreast, and then, afoot and alone, Col. Hayward, who organized the 15th, drilled them when they had nothing but broomsticks to drill with, fathered them and loved them, and turned them into the fightingest military organization any man's army could want.

"The French called them 'Hell Fighters.' The Germans after a few mix-ups named them 'Blutlustige Schwartzmanner' (blood-thirsty black men.) But Col. Bill, when he speaks of them uses the words 'those scrapping babies of mine,' and they like that best of all. Incidentally (when out of his hearing) they refer tenderly to him as 'Old Bill, that fightin' white man.' So it's fifty-fifty.

"The Colonel had broken a leg in the war, so there were those who looked for him to limp as he strode out to face the hedge of spectators that must have numbered a quarter of a million. But nary a limp. With his full six feet drawn up erectly and his strong face smiling under his tin hat, he looked every bit the fighting man as he marched up the centre of the avenue, hailed every few feet by enthusiasts who knew him socially or in the law courts or in the business of the Public Service Commission.

"'Didn't your leg hurt you, Bill?' his friends asked him later.

"'Sure it hurt me; he said, 'but I wasn't going to peg along on the proudest day of my life!' Which this day was.

"Behind the Colonel marched his staff, Lieut. Col. W.A. Pickering, Capt. Adjutant Robert Ferguson, Major E.A. Whittemore, Regimental Sergt. Majors C.A. Connick and B.W. Cheeseman, Regimental Sergts. L.S. Payne, H.W. Dickerson and W.W. Chisum, and Sergts. R.C. Craig, D.E. Norman and Kenneth Bellups.

W. Allison Sweeney

"*The Police Band was at the front of the line of march, but it was a more famous band that provided the music to which the Black Buddies stepped northward and under the Arch of Victory—the wonderful jazz organization of Lieut. Jimmie Europe, the one colored commissioned officer of the regiment. But it wasn't jazz that started them off. It was the historic Marche du Regiment de Sambre et Meuse, which has been France's most popular parade piece since Napoleon's day. As rendered now it had all the crash of bugle fanfares which is its dominant feature, but an additional undercurrent of saxaphones and basses that put a new and more peppery tang into it.*

"*One hundred strong, and the proudest band of blowers and pounders that ever reeled off marching melody—Lieut. Jimmie's boys lived fully up to their reputation. Their music was as sparkling as the sun that tempered the chill day.*

"*Four of their drums were instruments which they had captured from the enemy in Alsace, and ma-an, what a beating was imposed upon those sheepskins! 'I'd very much admire to have them bush Germans a-watchin' me today!' said the drummer before the march started. The Old 15th doesn't say 'Boche' when it refers to the foe it beat. 'Bush' is the word it uses, and it throws in 'German' for good measure.*

"*Twenty abreast the heroes marched through a din that never ceased. They were as soldierly a lot as this town, now used to soldierly outfits, has ever seen. They had that peculiar sort of half careless, yet wholly perfect, step that the French display. Their lines were straight, their rifles at an even angle, and they moved along with the jaunty ease and lack of stiffness which comes only to men who have hiked far and frequently.*

"*The colored folks on the official stand cut loose with a wild, swelling shriek of joy as the Police Band fell out at 60th Street and remained there to play the lads along when necessary and when—now entirely itself—the khaki-clad regiment filling the street from curb to curb, stepped by.*

"*Colonel Hayward, with his hand at salute, turned and smiled happily as he saw his best friend, former Governor Whitman, standing with his other good friend, Governor Al Smith, with their silk tiles raised high over their heads. It was the Governor's first review in New York and the first time he and Mr. Whitman had got together since Inauguration Day. They were of different parties, but they were united in greeting Colonel Bill and his Babies.*

"*From the stand, from the Knickerbocker Club across the street, from the nearby residences and from the curbing sounded shouts of individual greet-*

ings for the commander and his staff. But these were quickly drowned as a roar went up for Lieutenant Europe's band, with its commander at the head—not swinging a baton like a common ordinary drum-major, but walking along with the uniform and side-arms of an officer.

"'The Salute to the 85th,' which they learned from their comrade regiment of the French Army of General Gouraud, was what they were playing, a stirring thing full of bugle calls and drum rolls, which Europe says is the best march he ever heard.

"So swiftly did the platoons sweep by that it took a quick eye to recognize a brother or a son or a lover or a husband; but the eyes in the stand were quick, and there were shouts of 'Oh, Bill!' 'Hey, boy, here's your mammy!' 'Oliver, look at your baby!' (It wasn't learned whether this referred to a feminine person or one of those posthumous children Colonel Hayward spoke about.) 'Hallelujah, Sam! There you are, back home again!'

"Half way down the ranks of the 2,992 paraders appeared the colors, and all hats came off with double reverence, for the Stars and Stripes and the blue regimental standard that two husky ebony lads held proudly aloft had been carried from here to France, from France to Germany and back again, and each bore the bronze token with its green and red ribbon that is called the Croix de Guerre. Keen eyes could see these little medals swinging from the silk of the flags, high toward the top of the poles.

"At the end of the lines which filled the avenue came a single automobile, first, with a round-faced smiling white officer sitting in it and gazing happily from side to side. This was Major Lorillard Spencer, who was so badly wounded that he came back in advance of the outfit some weeks ago. There was a special racket of cheers for him, and then another for Major David L. 'Esperance, also wounded and riding.

"Then a far different figure, but one of the most famous of the whole war. Henry Johnson! That Henry, once a mild-mannered chauffeur, who to protect his comrade, Needham Roberts, waded into a whole patrol of 'bush Germans' with a lot of hand grenades, his rifle and his trusty 'steel' in the shape of a bolo knife, and waded into them so energetically that when the casualties were counted there were four dead foemen in front of him, thirty-four others done up so badly they couldn't even crawl away, and heaven knows how many more had been put to flight.

"And now Henry, in commemoration of this exploit, was riding alone in an open machine. In his left hand he held his tin hat. In his right he held

high over his head a bunch of red and white lilies which some admirer had pressed upon him. And from side to side Henry—about as black as any man in the outfit if not a trifle blacker—bowed from the waist down with all the grace of a French dancing master. Yes, he bowed, and he grinned from ear to ear and he waved his lilies, and he didn't overlook a bet in the way of taking (and liking) all the tributes that were offered to him.

"A fleet of motor ambulances, back of Henry, carried the wounded men who were unable to walk, nearly 200 of them. But though they couldn't walk, they could laugh and wave and shout thanks for the cheers, all of which they did.

"Almost before the happy colored folk could realize at the official stand that here were their lads back home again, the last of the parade rolled along and it was over. With that formation and the step that was inspired by Lieutenant Europe's band—and by the Police Band which stood at 60th Street and kept playing after the music of the other died away—it required only seventeen minutes for the regiment to pass.

"From this point north the welcome heightened in intensity. Along the park wall the colored people were banked deeply, everyone giving them the first ranks nearest the curb. Wives, sweethearts and mothers began to dash into the ranks and press flowers upon their men and march alongside with them, arm-in-arm. But this couldn't be, and Colonel Hayward had to stop the procession for a time and order the police to put the relatives back on the sidewalks. But that couldn't stop their noise.

"The residents of the avenue paid fine tribute to the dusky marchers. It seemed inspiring, at 65th Street, to see Mrs. Vincent Astor standing in a window of her home, a great flag about her shoulders and a smaller one in her left hand, waving salutes. And Henry Frick, at an open window of his home at 73d Street, waving a flag and cheering at the top of his voice.

"At the corner of 86th street was a wounded colored soldier wearing the Croix de Guerre and the Victoria Cross as well. Colonel Hayward pressed to his side with a hearty handshake, exclaiming: 'Why, I thought you were dead!' It was one of his boys long ago invalided home.

"No, sir, Colonel, not me. I ain't dead by a long ways yet, Colonel, sir,' said the lad.

"'How's it going, Colonel?' asked a spectator.

"'Fine,' said the Commander. 'All I'm worrying about is whether my boys are keeping step.' He needn't have worried.

"The real height of the enthusiasm was reached when, after passing through 110th street and northward along Lenox Avenue, the heroes arrived in the real Black Belt of Harlem. This was the Home, Sweet Home for hundreds of them, the neighborhood they'd been born in and had grown up in, and from 129th Street north the windows and roofs and fireescapes of the five and six story apartment houses were filled to overflowing with their nearest and dearest.

"The noise drowned the melody of Lieut. Europe's band. Flowers fell in showers from above. Men, women and children from the sidewalks overran the police and threw their arms about the paraders. There was a swirling maelstrom of dark humanity in the avenue. In the midst of all the racket there could be caught the personal salutations: 'Oh, honey!' 'Oh, Jim!' 'Oh, you Charlie!' 'There's my boy!' 'There's daddie!' 'How soon you coming home, son?' It took all the ability of scores of reserve policemen between 129th Street and 135th Street, where the uptown reviewing stand was, to pry those colored enthusiasts away from their soldiermen.

"There was one particular cry which was taken up for blocks along this district: 'O-oh, you wick-ed Hen-ery Johnson! You wick-ed ma-an!' and Henry the Boche Killer still bowed and grinned more widely than ever, if possible.

"'Looks like a funeral, Henry, them lilies!' called one admirer.

"'Funeral for them bush Germans, boy! Sure a funeral for them bushes.' shouted Henry.

"The official reviewing party, after the parade had passed 60th street, had hurried uptown, and so had the Police Band, and so there were some doings as the old 15th breezed past 135th Street. But no one up there cared for Governors or ex-Governors or dignitaries. Every eye was on the Black Buddies and every throat was opened wide for them.

"At 145th Street the halt was called. Again there was a tremendous rush of men and women with outstretched arms; the military discipline had to prevail, and the soldiers were not allowed to break ranks, nor were the civilians (save the quickest of them) able to give the hugs and kisses they were overflowing with.

"As rapidly as possible the fighters were sent down into the subway station and loaded aboard trains which took them down to the 71st Regiment Armory at 34th Street and Fourth Avenue. Here the galleries were filled with as many dusky citizens as could find places (maybe 2,500 or 3,000) and so great was the crowd in the neighborhood that the police had to block off 34th Street almost to Fifth Avenue on the west and Third on the east.

"As each company came up from the subway the friends and relatives were allowed to go through the lines, and, while the boys stood still in ranks, but at ease, their kinsfolk were allowed to take them in their arms and tell them really and truly, in close-up fashion, what they thought about having them back.

"When the entire regiment was in the Armory, the civilians in the gallery broke all bounds. They weren't going to stay up there while their heroes were down below on the drill-floor! Not they! They swarmed past the police and depot battalion and so jammed the floor that it was impossible for the tired Black Buddy even to sit down. Most of the boys had to take their chicken dinner—served by colored girls, and the chow, incidentally, from Delmonico's—standing up with arms about them and kisses punctuating assaults upon the plates.

"'Some chow, hey Buddy?' would be heard.

"'Pretty bon.' You'd get the answer. 'I'd like to have beaucoup more of this chicken.' There was noticeable a sprinkling of French words in the conversation of the Old 15th, and, indeed, some of them spoke it fluently.

"'Sam told me,' one girl was heard to say, 'that he killed nineteen of them Germans all his own self, but nobody saw him and so he didn't get that Cross doo Gare.'"

Mustering out commenced at Camp Upton the following day. Thus ended the service of the 369th. Their deeds are emblazoned on the roll of honor. Sons and grandsons of slaves, welcomed by the plaudits of the second largest city in the world. What a record of progress in a trifle over half a century of freedom. What an augury of promise for the future of the colored race, and what an augury for the world freedom which they helped to create, and, overshadowing all else, WHAT an object lesson it should be to our country at large: east, west, north, south, that, "One touch of nature makes 'all men' kin." That in her opinion and treatment of her faithful, loyal black citizens; niggardly, parsimonious, grudging and half-heartedly, how shameful she has been, how great has been her sin; forgetting; or uncaring, even as Pharoh of old, that: "God omnipotent liveth," and that "He is a JUST and a vengeful God!"

New York's welcome to her returning Negro boys was fairly typical of similar scenes all over the country. Chicago gave a tremendous ovation to the heroes of the old 8th Infantry. In Washington, Cleveland, and many other cities were great parades and receptions when theirs came home. In hundreds of smaller towns and hamlets the demonstrations were repeated in miniature.

CHAPTER XXX

Reconstruction and the Negro

By Julius Rosenwald, President Sears, Roebuck & Co, and Trustee of Tuskegee Institute—A Plea for Industrial Opportunity for the Negro—Tribute to Negro as Soldier and Civilian—Duty of Whites Pointed Out—Business Leader and Philanthropist Sounds Keynote

Although American sacrifices in the European War have been great, we find compensation for them in many directions. Not the least of these is the vastly increased number of opportunities the reconstruction period will offer to many of our citizens.

Today the United States is the leading nation of the world in virtually every line of activity. We have been thrust into a new world leadership by the war. It behooves us to make the most of our new opportunities. To equip ourselves creditably we must utilize the best there is in the manhood and womanhood of our nation, drawing upon the intellect and ability of every person who has either to give.

Approximately ten percent of our present population is colored. Every man, woman and child of this ten percent should be given the opportunity to utilize whatever ability he has in the struggle for the maintenance of world leadership which we now face. Just insofar as we refuse to give this part of our population an opportunity to lend its strength to helping us set a pace for the rest of the world, as best it can, so do we weaken the total strength of our nation. In other words, we can either give our colored population the right and the opportunity to do the best work of which it is capable and increase our efficiency, or we can deny them their rights and opportunities, as we have done in many instances, and decrease our efficiency proportionately.

Of course, the question naturally arises as to how efficient the colored man and the colored woman are when given the opportunity to demonstrate their ability. No better answer can be found than that given by the splendid work of the majority of our colored people during the war. On the firing line, in the camps behind the line, and in civil life our colored population has done well indeed. Four hundred thousand Negroes offered their lives for their country. Many more made noble sacrifices in civilian life.

It was my privilege not only to observe the work done in civil life by colored persons in this country during the war, but to visit colored troops in France during hostilities.

There is no question that the Negro has given a splendid account of himself both as an exceptionally fearless fighting man and as a member of non-combatant troops. I made diligent effort to ascertain the manner in which the Negro troops conducted themselves behind the lines. It is much easier for a man to become lax in his conduct there than in actual fighting. Without exception every officer I questioned stated he could not ask for more obedient, willing, harder working or more patriotic troops than the Negro regiments had proven themselves to be. Every account I have read regarding the engagement of colored men in fighting units and every case in which I had the opportunity to inquire personally regarding the bravery of colored troops has led me to believe our colored men were as good soldiers as could be found in either our own army or the armies of our allies, regardless of color.

One needs only to scan the records of the War Department and the official reports of General Pershing to find positive proof of the valor, endurance and patriotism of the colored troops who battled for liberty and democracy for all the world. The entire nation notes with pride the splendid service of the 365th to the 372nd Infantry units, inclusive. When historians tell the story of the sanguinary conflicts at Chateau Thierry, in the Forest of Argonne, in the Champagne sector, Belleau Wood and at Metz, the record will give reason to believe that the victories achieved on those memorable fields might have shown a different result had it not been for the remarkable staying and fighting abilities of the colored troops. French, English and American commanding officers unite in singing the praises of these gallant warriors and agree that in the entire Allied Army no element contributed more signally than did they to the final downfall of the German Military Machine in proportion to their numbers.

Not only did the combatant units of the colored troops win laurels across the sea, but the 301st Stevedore Regiment was cited for exceptionally efficient work, having broken all records by unloading and coaling the giant steamer "Leviathan" in fifty-six hours, competing successfully with the best stevedore detachments on the western front of

France. Everywhere, behind the lines as well as when facing shot, shell and gas, the colored soldiers have given a most creditable account of themselves and are entitled to the product of their patriotism and loyalty.

Those who remained at home during the war realize fully that the patriotic service rendered by colored persons in civil life, both in doing war work and in the purchase of Liberty Bonds and War Savings Stamps is to be commended.

Surely after the many demonstrations of patriotism both on the battlefield and at home the white people of this country will be willing to accord the colored people a square deal by at least giving them a fair opportunity to earn a livelihood in accordance with their ability.

We have been asking the impossible of the colored man and the colored woman. We have demanded that they be honest, self-respecting citizens, and at the same time we have forced them into surroundings which almost make this result impossible. In many places they are deprived of a fair opportunity to obtain education or amusement in a decent environment. Only the most menial positions are offered them. An educated girl particularly has practically no opportunity to earn a livelihood in the manner for which her education fits her.

We whites of America must begin to realize that Booker T. Washington was right when he said it was impossible to hold a man in the gutter without staying there with him, because "if you get up, he will get up." We do not want to remain in the gutter. We, therefore, must help the *Negro to rise*.

If we are to obtain the best results from colored labor, unions should admit it to their membership. It is not the universal practice to admit colored persons to unions. The result, of course, is that even if a colored man has the opportunity to learn a trade, knowing he will not be permitted to enjoy the benefits of a union, he does not have the highest incentive for learning it. The north is especially neglectful in not providing openings for the colored men in trades. In the south it is not unusual to see a colored brick-mason working alongside a white brick-mason. But in the north the best a colored man can hope for on a building job now is a position as a hod-carrier or mortar-mixer.

When the alien arrives in this country, he is given opportunity for virtually every kind of employment. But the colored man who is born in the United States, and, therefore, *should share in its opportunities*, is not given as fair a chance as the alien worker.

Naturally, we cannot hope that these conditions will be remedied in a day or a month nor can the colored man expect that the millennium will come to him through the action of white people alone. He can improve his chances of securing greater rights and opportunities in the United States, if he will make the most of the limited opportunities now afforded him. He who does the best he can with the tools he has at hand is bound in time to demand by his good work better tools for the performance of more important and profitable duties. The conviction is general that "He that is faithful in that which is least is faithful also in much."

The late Colonel Theodore Roosevelt, who was a good friend of the black man as well as the white, struck the right note in his introduction to the biography of Booker T. Washington when he said:

"If there is any lesson more essential than any other for this country to learn, it is the lesson that the enjoyment of rights should be made conditional upon the performance of duty."

There exist certain rights which every colored man and woman may enjoy regardless of laws and prejudice. For instance, nothing can prevent a colored person from practicing industry, honesty, saving and decency, if he or she desires to practice them.

The helpfulness of the colored race to the Government need not be confined to fighting in the army nor to service in the manifold domestic callings. It is the duty of the colored citizens, as it is their right, to have a part in the substantial development of the nation and to assist in financing its operations for war or peace. The colored people, as a rule, are industrious and thrifty and have come to appreciate their importance as a factor in the economic and financial world, as indicated by their prosperous business enterprises, their large holdings in real estate, their management of banks, and their scrupulous handling of the millions of deposits entrusted to their care. This capital, saved through sacrifice, has been placed in a most generous manner at the disposal of the Government throughout its period of need, and the list of corporations, fraternities and individuals who have aided in bringing success to American arms by the purchase of Liberty Bonds and War Savings Stamps and by contributions to other war relief agencies, is indeed a long one.

Opportunities of the colored people to make safe investment of their savings never were so great as they are today. The financial program the Government has entered upon and is continuing to carry out to meet the expense of the war gives a chance to save in sums as small as twenty-five cents and makes an investment upon which return of both principal and interest is absolutely guaranteed. Too often colored people have entrusted their savings to wholly irresponsible persons, lost them through the dishonesty of these persons, and in discouragement abandoned all attempts at saving. Today, however, there is no excuse for any man not saving a certain amount of his earnings no matter how small it may be. It is a poor person, indeed, who cannot invest twenty-five cents at stated intervals in a Thrift Stamp. Many are able also to buy small Liberty Bonds. It is a duty and a privilege for colored persons to help the Government finance the war, which was for both whites and blacks.

It is the particular duty of white persons, in cooperation with the most influential members of their own race, to explain these Government financial plans to the colored men and women that they may make safe investments, acquire a competence, and thus become better citizens.

It is my belief that the Negro soldier returning from France will be a better citizen than when he left. He will be benefited mentally and physically by his military training and experience. He will have a broader vision. He will appreciate American citizenship. He will know, I believe, that freedom, for which he risked his life and all, is not license. He will find his brothers at home who did not go overseas better for their war sacrifices. Both the soldier and the civilian have proved their devoted loyalty. Justice demands that they now be rewarded with an equal chance with the white man to climb as high in the industrial and professional world as their individual capacity warrants.

Homecoming heroes of 8th Illinois (370th Infantry). Famous negro fighters marching in Michigan Boulevard, Chicago.

CHAPTER XXXI

The Other Fellow's Burden

An Emancipation Day Appeal for Justice

By W. Allison Sweeney

Publisher's Note: At our request, Mr. Sweeney consented to the reproduction of this poem, which with the accompanying letter from the late Dr. Booker T. Washington, and the comment by the Chicago Daily News, appeared in that newspaper just prior to New Years Day, 1914. We regard it as a powerful argument, affecting the Negro's past condition and his interests.

"President Lincoln signed the emancipation proclamation Sept. 22, 1862. It went into effect at the beginning of January, 1863. New Year's day has thus become 'Emancipation day' to the colored people of the United States and to all members of the white race who realize the great significance of Lincoln's act of striking off the shackles of an enslaved race. Services on that day combine honor to Lincoln with appeals to the people of Lincoln's nation to grant justice to the Negro. A remarkable appeal of this sort is embodied in the poem here presented.

"W. Allison Sweeney, author of "The Other Fellow's Burden" is well known among his people as writer, editor and lecturer. His poem, which sketches with powerful strokes the lamentable history of the colored race in America and tells of their worthy achievements in the face of discouragements, deserves a thoughtful reading by all persons. Of this poem and its author Dr. Booker T. Washington writes as follows:

"TUSKEGEE INSTITUTE, ALA., Dec. 24, 1913.—To the Editor of the Chicago Daily News: I have read with sincere interest and appreciation W. Allison Sweeney's poem, 'The Other Fellow's Burden.' All through Mr. Sweeney's poem there is an invitation put in rather a delicate and persuasive way, but nevertheless it is there, for the white man to

W. Allison Sweeney

put himself in the negro's place and then to lay his hand upon his heart and ask how he would like for the other fellow to treat him. If every man who reads this poem will try sincerely to answer this question I believe that Mr. Sweeney's poem will go a long way toward bringing about better and more helpful conditions.

"Mr. Sweeney is, of course, a member of the Negro race and writes from what might be called the inside. He knows of Negro aspirations, of Negro strivings and of Negro accomplishments. He has had an experience of many years as writer and lecturer for and to Negroes and he knows probably as well as anyone wherein the Negro feels that 'the shoe is made to pinch.' The poem, it seems to me, possesses intrinsic merit and I feel quite sure that Mr. Sweeney's appeal to the great American people, for fair play will not fall upon deaf ears. Booker T. Washington."

The "white man's burden" has been
  told the world,
But what of the other fellow's—
The "lion's whelp"?
Lest you forget,
May he not lisp his?
Not in arrogance,
Not in resentment,
But that truth
May stand foursquare?
This then,
Is the Other Fellow's Burden.

    *   *   *   *   *

Brought into existence
Through the enforced connivance
Of a helpless motherhood
Misused through generations—
America's darkest sin!—
There courses through his veins
In calm insistence—incriminating irony
Of the secrecy of blighting lust!
The best and the vilest blood
Of the South's variegated strain;
Her statesmen and her loafers,
Her chivalry and her ruffians.
Thus bred,

His impulses twisted
At the starting point
By brutality and sensuous savagery,
Should he be crucified?
Is it a cause for wonder
If beneath his skin of many hues—
Black, brown, yellow, white—
Flows the sullen flood
Of resentment for prenatal wrong
And forced humility?
Should it be a wonder
That the muddy life current
Eddying through his arteries,
Crossed with the good and the bad,
Poisoned with conflicting emotions,
Proclaims at times,
Through no fault of his,
That for a surety the sins of fathers
Become the heritage of sons
Even to the fourth generation?
Or that murdered chastity,
That ravished motherhood—
So pitiful, so helpless,
Before the white hot,
Lust-fever of the "master"—
Has borne its sure fruit?
You mutter, "There should be no wonder."
Well, somehow, Sir Caucasian,
Perhaps southern gentleman,
I, marked a "whelp," am moved
To prize that muttered admission.

*　　*　　*　　*　　*

But listen, please:
The wonder is—the greater one—

W. Allison Sweeney

That from Lexington to San Juan hill
Disloyalty never smirched
His garments, nor civic wrangle
Nor revolutionary ebullition
Marked him its follower.
A "striker"? Yes!
But he struck the insurgent
And raised the flag.
An ingrate?
Treacherous?
A violator?
When—oh, spectacle that moved the world!
For five bloody years
Of fratricidal strife—
Red days when brothers warred—
He fed the babe,
Shielded the mother.
Guarded the doorsill
Of a million southern homes?
Penniless when freedom came? Most true;
But his accumulations of fifty years
Could finance a group of principalities.
Homeless? Yes; but the cabin and the hut
Of Lincoln's day—uncover at that name!—
Are memories; the mansion of today,
Dowered with culture and refinement,
Sweetened by clean lives,
Is a fact.
Unlettered? Yes;
But the alumni of his schools,
Triumphant over the handicap
Of "previous condition,"
Are to be found the world over
In every assemblage inspired

By the democracy of letters.
In the casting up what appears?
The progeny of lust and helplessness,
He inherited a mottled soul—
"Damned spots" that biased the looker on.
Clothed a freeman,
Turned loose in the land
Creditless, without experience,
He often stumbled, the way being strange,
Sometimes fell.
Mocked, sneered at from every angle,
spurned, hindered in every section,
North, south, east, west,
Refused the most primitive rights,
His slightest mistakes
Made mountains of,
Hunted, burned, hanged,
The death rattle in his throat
Drowned by shouts and laughter
And—think of it!—
The glee of little children.
Still he pressed on, wrought,
Sowed, reaped, builded.
His smile ever ready,
His perplexed soul lighted
With the radiance
Of an unquenchable optimism,
God's presence visualized,
He has risen, step by step.
To the majesty of the home builder,
Useful citizen,
Student, teacher,
Unwavering patriot.
This of the Other Fellow.

W. Allison Sweeney

What of you, his judges and his patrons?
If it has been your wont
In your treatment of him
Not to reflect,
Or to stand by in idle unconcern
While, panting on his belly,
Ambushed by booted ruffianism,
He lapped in sublime resignation
The bitter waters
Of unreasoning intolerance,
Has not the hour of his deliverance,
Of your escape from your "other selves"
Struck?
If you have erred,
Will you refuse to know it?
Has not the time arrived
To discriminate between
Those who lower
Those who raise him?
You are shamed by your abortions,
Your moral half growths
Who flee God's eye
And stain his green earth,
But you are not judged by yours;
Should he be judged by his?
In his special case—if so, why?
Is manhood a myth,
Womanhood a toy,
Integrity unbelievable,
Honor a chimera?
Should not his boys and girls,
Mastering the curriculum of the schools,
Pricked on to attainment by the lure
Of honorable achievement,

Be given bread and not a stone
When seeking employment
In the labor mart,
At the factory gate
Or the office door?
Broadened by the spirit of the golden rule,
Will you not grant these children of Hagar
An even break?
Is the day not here, O judges,
When the Other Fellow
May be measured in fairness,
Just fairness?

* * * * *

It is written men may rise
"On their dead selves to higher things;"
But can it be that this clear note of cheer
To sodden men and smitten races
Was meant for all save him?
Chants an immortal:
"He prayeth best who loveth best
All things both great and small;
For the dear God who loveth us,
He made and loveth all."

CHAPTER XXXII

An Interpolation

Held by Distinguished Thinkers and Writers, That the Negro Soldier Should Be Given a Chance For Promotion as Well as a Chance to Die—Why White Officers Over Negro Soldiers?

Ever since the conclusion of the conflict of '61-'65, in which Negro troops numbered by thousands, took an active part upon behalf of the Union, there has been a growing and insistent wonder in the minds of many, why, given a chance to die in the military service of the nation, they should not also at the same time be given a chance for promotion.

Subsequent affairs engaged in by the government requiring the intervention of its military arm, the Spanish-American war, the Philippines investiture incident thereto, the Mexican disagreement, the whole crowned by the stupendous World War; its frightful devastation and din yet fresh to our sight, still filling our ears, as it will for years; in all of which they have contributed their share of loyalty and blood—of LIVES!—have but added to, strengthened the wonder mentioned.

Up to the beginning of the European muddle it was discussed if at all, not so much as a condition demanding uncensored condemnation, as one to continue to be patient with, trusting to time and an awakened sense of fair play upon the part of the nation at large to note the custom complained of, and banish the irritation by abolishing the cause.

However, there has not been lacking those who have spoken out, who have raised their voices in protest against what they deemed an injustice to the loyal "fighting men" of their race, and so feeling, have not hesitated to make their plea to those above empowered to listen, regardless of the mood in which they did so.

As long ago as the summer of 1915, or to be exact, August 26th of that year, Capt. R.P. Roots of Seattle, Washington, addressed a letter to the Hon. Lindley M. Garrison at Washington, at the time Secretary of

War, directing his attention to the discrepancy of assignment complained of, accompanied with certain suggestions; having to do with a condition that the government must eventually face; that will not down, and must sooner or later be abrogated. Captain Roots' communication to the Secretary of War, also one addressed to the Hon. Joseph Tumulty, private secretary to President Wilson, follows:

"Seattle, Wash., August 26, 1915

"Hon. Lindley M. Garrison, Secretary of War,

Dear Sir: As an ex-officer of the Spanish-American war, having served as Captain of Company "E" of the Eighth Illinois Volunteers, I am taking the liberty to ask that, if you should recommend any increase in the Army you give the Negro a chance in the manner, and for reasons I shall further explain

You will notice by my service with the 8th Illinois that I am a colored man, and as such am offering these suggestions, which, in the main, are just.

If the increase is sufficient, we should have:

TWO COAST ARTILLERY COMPANIES.

ONE REGIMENT OF FIELD ARTILLERY (In these branches we are not represented at all).

ONE REGIMENT OF CAVALRY.

The above to be embodied in the Regular Army and to be officered as you think fit. But my main object is: Three Regiments of Infantry officered from COLONEL DOWN WITH COLORED MEN. I should not have these Infantry Regiments of the regular service for the reason that to appoint officers to the rank of Colonel, Majors, etc., would not be fair to the regular service officers, and would interfere with the promotion of the same, but I would have them rank as volunteers. Give them the name of "IMMUNES," "FOREIGN SERVICE REGIMENTS," or any other name that you choose.

My further reasons are as to officering these regiments, that there would be many misfits in such organizations and I would leave it so that you or the President could remove them without prejudice from the service, but to fill by OTHER

COLORED MEN the vacancies that might occur. I should officer these regiments with Spanish War veterans, non-commissioned officers of the retired and regulars, but should appoint all 2d Lieutenants from the schools of the country giving military training.

The 2d Lieutenants upon passing the regular army examination could be placed in the eligible list of the regular army, but NOT until at least two years' service with these regiments. You could set a time limit on these regiments if you so desire, say ten or twelve years duration; either mustered out or in the regular service.

"Now Mr. Secretary, I have striven to meet any objections which might be made by the Army on account of social prejudice, etc. With this thought I should send these regiments to some foreign post to serve where there are dark races; to the Philippines, Mexico, or Haiti. The object lesson would be marked politically, both at home and abroad.

"The 48th and 49th Regiments organized in 1899 and sent to Philippines were unsatisfactory because of there being three social lines of separation in those organizations—THE FIELD AND STAFF of these regiments WERE WHITE, and the LINE OFFICERS WERE COLORED. In a social way the line officers WERE ENTIRELY IGNORED, and even officially were treated very little better than enlisted men or with no more courtesy, to such an extent as to cause comment by both soldiers and natives.

"Now as to the colored citizen of this country coming to its defense there is no question, as he has always done so But, to use a late phrase, he is beginning to want HIS "PLACE IN THE SUN"—he wants a chance to rise on his merits AND TO KNOW WHEN HE SHOULDERS A GUN, THAT IF HE IS DESERVING OF IT, HE WILL HAVE A CHANCE TO RISE. He can fight and will, but will fight better with an incentive than without one. He is a, citizen regardless of all laws to the contrary; also he is the NEW Negro, and NOT of the "Uncle Tom" class, the passing of whom so many white citizens regret.

"He reads your literature, attends your theaters, goes to your schools, observes you in his capacity as a waiter or porter, and is absorbing the best you have in the ways of civilization, and in fact, in every walk of life, he is a factor;

and when he is asked to defend his country should he not be given THE SAME CHANCE AS THE WHITE MAN?

"You will say that he should go to West Point. Well and good; but who is to send him? Next, who will defend him while there against the "Unwritten Law" of the white students not to allow him to matriculate?   "The first officers of such regiments could be easily picked, made from Spanish War veterans and non-commissioned officers of the regular army, and second lieutenants from graduates from colleges giving military training. Such an organization officered in this manner would be ideal, speaking from my experience as a veteran of the Spanish War.

"One thing you may have overlooked: We are twelve million in this country, WITH AN ESTIMATE OF A MILLION MEN FIT FOR SERVICE.

"Suppose at such a crisis as is now transpiring in Europe, this country, with its millions of foreign citizens, should suddenly find itself face to face with a revolution. The presence and loyalty of these MILLION NEGROES might mean much for the stability of this government.

"I have spoken plainly because I am a citizen; this is my country. I was born here, and shall at all times be found with the flag; hence I ask, that in your recommendations, looking to the betterment and enlargement of the army, you give THE BLACK PATRIOT such consideration, as I cannot but feel is due him, the thousands of young colored men who have passed through colleges and schools in an effort to prepare themselves for filling a place in the world.

"I am opposed to segregation, but as it seems, under the present conditions of the races socially to be the ONLY way to a square deal, I accept it. There are Irish regiments, German regiments, etc., let us then have Negro regiments. The coming generations will look after the rest. I am, very respectfully,

R.P. ROOTS

400 26th Ave., North, Late Capt. 8th Ill. Vol. Infantry"

W. Allison Sweeney

"Seattle, Wash., Nov. 9, 1915

"Hon Joseph Tumulty, Secretary to the President, Washington, D.C.

Dear Sir:—I am enclosing a copy of a letter sent to the Secretary of War, which I would be very much pleased to have you call the President's attention to, and ask if he can approve of it.

"I was not fully informed as to the President's policy in regard to Haiti at the time of writing, and am not now, except through such information as received by the daily press. Taking that, in the main as authentic, I wish to add that I think a Brigade of Colored Troops, such as recommended in my letter to the Secretary for foreign service, would be the proper thing for Haiti.

"It being a Negro Republic, the racial feeling as to the Negro's treatment in this country, which I need not mention, has been enlarged upon and not understood by the Negroes of other parts of the world, so that as it seems to me, to organize a constabulary officered by white Americans, would be inviting murder; for agitators from other governments, if they so desired, would soon cause a rebellion, and then you would have it all to do over again.

"Colored troops from this country, I mean officers as well, would tend to cause a good feeling among the natives, not at first but later on as each became used to the other. THE WHITE MAN THINKS HE IS SUPERIOR TO ANY NEGRO, AND WOULD SHOW IT EVEN THOUGH HE TRIED NOT TO, and the Haitian would be going around with a chip on his shoulder looking for someone to knock it off.

"You have three men in the regular army who could supervise the organization of these troops, and one who is already a Colonel of the Eighth Illinois National Guard, also several others if you wished to consider them.

"Hoping that you will see the advisability of such an organization for diplomatic reasons and for JUSTICE TO THE AMERICAN NEGRO—who has been loyal—and served from Bunker Hill until now, I am,

Very respectfully,

R.P. ROOTS,

History of the American Negro in the Great World War

400 26th St. N. Seattle, Wash., Late Capt. Eighth Illinois Volunteer Infantry during Spanish War."

As touching upon the above, Editor E.S. Abbott of THE CHICAGO DEFENDER, made the following comment:

"There may be reasons deemed good and sufficient upon the part of President Wilson and Secretary Garrison for not having replied to the very courteous and finely conceived letters of appeal and suggestion, having to do with a new deal—with justice and fair play in the future towards the Negro soldiery of our country, written them some weeks ago by CAPT. R.P. ROOTS of Seattle.

"It is not always meet, especially in times like these, of war and stress, of worries and apprehension, reaching across the world, for our rulers and servants facing great responsibilities and perplexing situations, to respond to every query and satisfy all curiosities. Much reticence must be permitted them. Much accepted, as a matter of course, without pursuing curiosity to the limit.

"There may be ideas conveyed by Captain Roots to the president, through his communications to Secretaries Garrison and Tumulty that some people may not agree with, but there can be no disagreement over the proposition that the lot of colored soldiers in the armies of the United States—in the past, and at the present, is much different than that accorded to white soldiers; very little to really be proud of; very, very much to be ashamed of—much that is humiliating and depressing.

"Because the present administration may be powerless in the matter, afraid to touch it, fearing a live wire or something of that kind, should OUR duty in the premises, TOWARD OUR OWN, be influenced thereby?

"I wonder—is the time not NOW—right now, to commence an attack upon this intrenched scandal—this dirty, HUMILIATING AMERICANISM?

"No other nation on earth, Christian or pagan, treats its defenders, its soldiery, so meanly, so shabbily, as does this, her black defenders; but whether the nation is more to blame, than we, who so long have submitted without a murmur, is a question. 'The trouble' shouted Cassius to Brutus, 'is not in our stars, that we are Underlings, BUT IN OURSELVES.'

"Shall we, responding to the initiative furnished by CAPTAIN ROOTS, commence an organized assault upon this national vice against the soldiers of our race? Is this the time, readers of The Defender? Is this the time, brothers and editors of the contemporary press?

R.S. ABBOTT."

Following in the footsteps of Captain Roots; apparently obsessed by the same vision and spirit, Mr. Willis O. Tyler, eminent Los Angeles race representative, attorney and Harvard graduate, also makes a plea for justice for Negro troops in the regular army, also for Negro officers, and proposes reforms and legislation for utilizing the present force of Negro officers, and creating enlarged opportunities for others. Says Mr. Tyler:

> "*Officers in the regular army for the most part, are graduates of West Point. They are commissioned second lieutenants at graduation. No Negro has graduated from West Point in the past twenty-nine years, and none has entered there in 32 years. Col. Charles Young graduated in 1889, twenty-nine years ago,—he entered in 1884. Henry W. Holloway entered in 1886, but attended only that year. In all, only twelve Negroes have ever attended West Point and only three have graduated. Of the three graduates, the first, Henry O. Flipper (1877) was afterwards discharged.*
>
> "*The second, John H. Alexander (1887) died in 1894. The third and last graduate, Charles Young (1889) has but recently been returned to active duty. We understand he has attained the rank of Colonel. The Negroes of the United States, to the number of twelve millions, have only one West Point graduate in the regular army. There are however four regiments of Colored troops, two of infantry, and two of cavalry, and these have been maintained for 52 years, (since 1866), and more than two hundred officers find places in the four Colored regiments. These two hundred officers, with about three exceptions are white officers. In all, only twelve Negroes have held commissions in the regular army. Of this number seven were Chaplains and two were paymasters.*
>
> "*In 1917 there were two first lieutenants; and (then) Major Charles Young in the regular army. Hence only two officers of the line and only one of the staff (other than Chaplains), out of more than two hundred who found places with the four colored regiments.*

"*We need not stop for the reasons why Negroes have not been attending West Point, nor even admitted there for the past 32 years. Certain it is they have not been attending the nation's great military school, and certain it is that in law, good conscience and right, one cadet at West Point in every twelve should be a Negro.*

"*The future lies before us. The four regiments of Colored Troops have vindicated their right to be maintained as such by having made for the army some of its finest traditions. Why not have the four colored regiments officered by colored men from the Colonel down to the second lieutenants?*

"*The United States is just making an end to a glorious participation in the great world's war. In this war the Negro soldiers played well their part. They laughed in the face of death on the firing line; they have been awarded the 'Ribbon' and the Croix de Guerre—with palms. Who were their officers?*

"*From the officers training camp at Fort Des Moines, Iowa, 639 colored men were commissioned. Since then 267 more have been commissioned, not counting those in Medical Reserve Corps, nor the 41 Chaplains. Colored Captains and Lieutenants led colored soldiers "Over the Top" and commanded them on march and in trench. Many officers were given but three months in the officer's Training camp; many of them had served as non-commissioned officers in one of the four colored regiments. But not one word of criticism or complaint of them has reached us. Their adaptability to their new duties is beyond cavil. Their efficiency, bravery—leadership, are all unquestioned and permanently established.*

"*The future lies before us. What will our country do? Surely it will not retire all of these fine young colored officers, who responded so nobly to the call of their country, to private life and continue the discrimination which in the past deprived them of admission to West Point and of commissions in the regular army. I do not believe it. I believe that the sense of justice and fair play is deeply rooted in the American people. I believe that our four colored regiments in the regular army will in the future be officered by colored men. That the doors of West Point will be opened in accordance with justice and fair play to a proper number and proportion of colored Cadets. But this is not all nor is it enough.*

"*We believe that at present the nation owes the Colored people certain legislation and that the nation being solvent and loud in its protestations of kindness toward the Colored people for their loyal and patriotic participation in the war both at home and on the battlefield, should now pay its debt toward the colored people and reward them to the extent that the best* of the nearly one thousand officers now serving in the National Army be transferred to the Regular army, and assigned to duty in the four Colored regiments, and that these be from colonel down to second lieutenants. We also believe that in the future West Point and Annapolis should 'lend a little colour' to their graduation exercises in the presence of Colored graduates.

"No doubt legislation will be needed to this end. At present commissions are granted first to the graduates of West Point, and even a fair and more liberal policy in this regard in the future will not meet present needs. What is needed now is legislation providing for the transfer (or at least the opportunity to enter) into the regular army of a sufficient number of our Colored Officers now with commissions to officer in toto the four Colored regiments we now have.

"Commissions are also granted at present to a limited number of enlisted men who are recommended for these examinations, and who succeed in passing. The candidates must be under 27 years of age and unmarried. They must have had a certain amount of secondary school, or college education which few privates or non com's (colored) have had. This is the case because few young Colored men with the necessary growth 'single blessedness,' and college training, feel, or have heretofore felt that the door of 'equal opportunity' announced by Mr. Roosevelt stands open to them in the regular army. To trust the officering of four Colored Regiments to this second mode of selecting and commissioning officers, would prove fatal to our hopes and fail of accomplishment.

"The third method of selecting officers at present is by examinations of civilians, certain college presidents and other civilians being permitted to recommend certain civilians, (students and others) for examination for second lieutenants.

"In this regard Negroes have met the same difficulties that they have encountered in the past 32 years in their efforts to gain admission to West Point. At best only a small percent of each year's graduating class from West Point can get commissions in this manner. Those selected have been white men, what we are after now is a present day, practical way of utilizing the best material we now have, holding commissions and making secure the opportunity for other Colored men to enter the army as second lieutenants and by dint of industry, close application, obedience, brains and time gain their promotion step by step, just as white men have been doing and can do now. This is the American—democratic, fair play, reward and justice we seek for the twelve million Negro citizens of our great republic. Congress could if it would, provide for the present by an appropriate measure *giving the right and opportunity to our returning officers to stand examination for commissions in the Regular army; Military experience and knowledge, and general and special educational qualifications to determine the rank or grade received.*

"In this way our four colored regiments could be officered by colored men. Otherwise, the fine talents and desire for service to the country held by the one thousand intelligent and courageous young Negroes who are officers, will be lost and rejected by the country, and the 12 million Negroes in the United States will continue, notwithstanding their patriotism and devotion, to be denied of their just representation in commissions in the regular army.

"We believe that once this is done the sense of fairness and justice that, after all is said and done is so firmly imbedded in the American people, will see to it that our proper and proportionate number of young Colored men are admitted to West Point and Annapolis annually and that the other avenues for gaining admission in the army and navy will not be blocked, closed and denied Negroes by the unreasonable race prejudice which has heretofore done so.

"Our country is either a country of 'equal opportunity' or it is not. It is either a democracy or it is not.

"Certainly the Negroes have failed to realize this 'equal opportunity' in the matter of training at West Point and Annapolis, and is gaining commissions in the Regular army.

"The great war in Europe is closed or soon will be. We have again shown our country that 'our hearts are on the right side.' What will our country do for us? We ask only that the door of 'equal opportunity' be unbarred—that we may enter."

CHAPTER XXXIII

The New Negro and the New America

"THE OLD ORDER

Changeth, yielding place to new."
THROUGH THE
Arbitrament of war, behold a new and better America!
a new and girded Negro!
"The watches
Of the night have PASSED!

"The watches
Of the day BEGIN!"

Out of war's crucible new nations emerge. New ideas seize mankind and if the conflict has been a just one, waged for exalted ideals and imperishable principles and not alone for mere national security and integrity, a new character, a broader national vision is formed.

Such was the result of the early wars for democracy. The seeds of universal freedom once sown, finally ripened not alone to the unshackling of a race, but to the fecundity and birth of a spirit that moved all nations and peoples to seek an enlarged liberty. The finger of disintegration and change is never still; is always on the move; always the old order is passing; always the new, although unseen of man, is coming on. And so it is, that nations are still in the throes of reconstruction after the great war. That it was the greatest and most terrible of all wars, increases the difficulties incident to the establishment of the new order, precedent to a restoration of tranquil conditions.

So radical were some of the results of the conflict, such as the overthrow of despotism in Russia, and a swinging completely to the other extreme of the pendulum; similar happenings in Germany and Austria transpiring, that subject peoples in general, finding themselves in possession of a liberty which they did not expect and were not prepared for, are in a sense bewildered; put to it, as to just what steps to take; the wisest course to pursue.

At home we have a nearer view and can begin to see emerging a new America. The men who fought abroad will be the dominant factor in national affairs for many years. These men have returned, and will return with a broadened vision and with new and enlarged ideas regarding themselves and, quite to be expected, of progress and human rights.

With the leaven of thought which has been working at home, added to the new and illuminating; more liberal viewpoint regarding the Negro attained by the American whites who served with him in France, will come; is already born, a new national judgment and charity of opinion and treatment, that will not abate; will grow and flourish through the coming years, a belated sense of justice and restitution due the Negro; a most wholesome sign of shame and repentance upon the part of the nation. The old order based on slavery and environment; the handicap of "previous condition" has passed. Will never return! THAT, or the "Fatherhood of God and Brotherhood of Man" is, and always was, an iridescent dream; a barren ideality!

The new America owes much of its life to the Negro; guaranteed through centuries of a devotion, than which, there has been nothing like it; you seek in vain for a counterpart; a patriotism and suffering and shed blood; the splendor and unselfishness of which will germinate and flower through the ages; as long as history shall be read; to the last moment of recorded time.

In days to come, now on the way, men will say, one to another: "How could it have been that those faithful Blacks; those loyal citizens; whose toil enriched; whose blood guaranteed the perpetuity of our institutions; were discriminated against—WRONGED?"

In a country based and governed on the principle that all men are free and equal, discrimination or special privilege will eat at the heart of national life. Capital must not have special advantages over labor; neither labor over capital. Jew and Gentile, protestant and catholic, Negro and White men, must be equal; not alone in the spirit of the law but in the application of it. Not alone in the spirit of industrialism, commerce and ordinary affairs of life, but in their interpretation and application as well.

Social discriminations and distinctions may prevail with no great danger to the body politic, so long as people do not take them too seriously—do not mistake the shadow for the substance, and regard them the paramount things of life.

Obviously the Negro no less than the Caucasian, has a right, and no government may challenge it, to say who his associates shall be, who he shall invite into his house, but such rights are misconstrued and exceeded when carried to the point of proscribing, oppressing or hampering the development of other men, regardless of the nationality of their competitors.

The logical growth of achievement for the Negro is first within the lines of his own race, but, all things being equal; genius being the handmaiden of no particular race or clime, he is not to be hindered by the law of the land, the prejudice of sections or individuals, from seeking to climb to any height.

The bugbear and slander, raised and kept alive by that section of the land south of the imaginary line, to wit: that the Negro was ambitious for "racial equality," only is entitled to reference in these pages for the purpose of according it the contempt due it. That the whites of the country have not a complete monopoly of those unpleasing creatures known as "tuft hunters" and "social climbers," is no doubt true, but that the Negro, as represented by intelligence and race pride, ever worries over it; cares a rap for it, is not true.

Humanity's great benefit coming from the war, which cannot be changed or abridged, will consist of a newer, broader sense of manhood; a demand for the inherent opportunities and rights belonging to it; for all men of all colors, of all climes; and beyond that; of more significance; as marking the dawn indeed of a NEW AND BETTER DAY, will be a larger, juster sense; springing up in the nation's heart; watered by her tears, of repentance of past wrongs inflicted on the Negro. The Negro will become the architect of his own growth and development. The South will not be permitted; through the force of national opinion, to continue to oppress him.

The talk of the revival of KuKlux societies to intimidate the Negro; "to keep him in his place," is the graveyard yawp of a dying monster. Are the thousands of Negroes who faced bullets in the most disastrous war of history, and several hundred thousand more who were ready and willing to undergo the same perils, likely to be frightened by such a threat, such an antiquated, silly, short-sighted piece of injustice and terrorism?

Men's necessities force a resort to common sense. Racial prejudice and ignorant, contemptible intolerance, must disappear under, and before the presence of the renewal of business activity in the South, and the necessity for Negro labor. Each soldier returning from Europe is a more enlightened man than when he went away. He has had the broadening effect of travel, the chance to mingle with other races and acquire the views born of a greater degree of equality and more generous treatment.

These men desire to remain in their southern homes. Climatically they are suited and the country offers them employment to which they are accustomed; but more than all, it is home, and they are bound to it by ties of association and affection.

With a mutual desire of whites and blacks to achieve an end, common sense will find a basis of agreement. The Negro will get better pay and better treatment. His status accordingly will be improved. His employer will get better service, he also will be broadened and improved by a new spirit of tolerance and charity.

Cooperation among the white and black races received a decided impetus during the war. A movement so strongly started is sure to gather force until it attains the objects more desirious of accomplishment. Some of these objects undoubtedly are far in the distance, but will be achieved in time. When they are, the Negro will be far advanced on the road of racial development. The day has dawned and the start has been made. Before the noontime, America will be prouder of her Negro citizens and will be a happier, a more inspired and inspiring nation; a better home for all her people.

One of the results of the war will be an improvement in the government and condition of Negroes in Africa. Exploitation of the race for European aggrandisement is sure to be lessened. No such misgoverned colonies as those of Germany will be tolerated under the new rule and the new spirit actuating the victorious Allies. Evils in other sections of that continent will disappear or receive positive amelioration.

The most hopeful sign in America is the tendency in some sections where trouble has been prevalent in the past, to meet and discuss grievances. In some sections of the South, men of prominence are exhibiting a willingness to meet and talk over matters with representatives of the race. Such a spirit of tolerance will grow and eventually lead to a better understanding; perhaps a general reconciling of differences.

Many concessions will be required before complete justice prevails and the Negro comes into his own; before the soil can be prepared for the complete flowering of his spirit.

Primarily, before attaining to the full growth and usefulness of the citizen under the rights guaranteed to him by the Constitution, the Negro, especially in the South, will require better educational facilities. If he is to become a better citizen, he must have the education and training necessary to know the full duties of citizenship. He pays his share of the school taxes and it is manifestly unjust to deny him the accruing benefits.

He is ambitious too, and should be encouraged to own land, and to that end should have the assistance without prejudice or discrimination, of national and state farm loan bureaus.

Unjust suffrage restrictions must and shall be removed, giving to the Negro the full rights of other citizens in this respect. With better educational facilities and the ownership of real estate, he will vote more intelligently, and there will be no danger that his vote will be against the interests of the country at large or the section in which he resides.

The withering taint of "Jim Crow"-ism, must be obliterated; wiped out—will be. Railroads will be compelled to extend the same accommodations to white and colored passengers. The traveller; whatever his color, who pays the price for a ticket, must and shall in this land of Equality and Justice, be accorded the same accommodations.

Peonage, so-called, will end. It cannot endure under an awakened, enlightened public opinion. Negroes, all other things equal, will be admitted to labor unions, or labor unions will lose the potentiality and force they should wield in labor and industrial affairs.

The Negro's contribution to the recent war and to previous conflicts, has earned him beyond question or challenge, a right to just consideration in the military and naval establishment of the nation. America, grudging as she has been in the past to enlarge his rights, or even to guarantee those which she has granted, has grown too great indeed. Her discipline has been too real to deny him this fair consideration. There will be more Negro units in the Regular Army and National Guard organizations; untrammelled facilities for training, in government, state and college institutions.

Selective draft figures having revealed the Negro as a better; if not the best, physical risk, will make it easier for him to secure life insurance, which; after all is a plain business proposition. Insurance companies are after business and are not concerned with racial distinctions where the risk is good. The draft has furnished figures regarding the Negro's health and longevity which hitherto were not available to insurance actuaries.

Now that they have them, no reason exists for denying insurance facilities to the race.

With a growing, every minute, of a better understanding between the races; with the Negro learning thrift through Liberty Bonds, Savings Stamps and the lessons of the war; with an encouragement to own property and take out insurance; being vastly enlightened through his military service, and with improved industrial conditions about to appear, he is started on a better road, to end only when he shall have reached the full attainment belonging to the majesty of AMERICAN CITIZENSHIP.

With this start, lynchings, the law's delays, the denial of full educational advantages; segregation, insanitary conditions, unjust treatment in reform and penal institutions, will vanish from before him; will be conditions that were, but are no more.

There is a predominance of Anglo-Saxon heritage in the white blood of America. The Anglo-Saxon was the first to establish fair play and make it his shibboleth. Should he deny it to the Negro; his proudest and most vaunted principle would prove to be a doddering lie; a shimmering evanescence.

HE WILL NOT DENY IT!

The Peace Treaty

The treaty of peace was drawn by the allied and associated powers at Versailles, and was there delivered to the German Government's delegation on May 5, 1919—the fourth anniversary of the Lusitania sinking.

It stipulates in the preamble that war will have ceased when all powers have signed and the treaty shall have come into force by ratification of the signatures.

It names as party of the one part the United States, The British Empire, France, Italy, Japan, described as the five allied and associated powers, and Belgium, Bolivia, Brazil, China, Cuba, Equador, Greece, Guatemala, Haiti, the Hedjaz, Honduras, Liberia, Nicaragua, Panama, Peru, Portugal, Roumania, Serbia, Siam, Czecho-Slovakia and Uruguay; and on the other side Germany.

The treaty contains agreements in substance as follows:

Section 1. *The League of Nations*—The league of nations may question Germany at any time for a violation of the neutralized zone east of the Rhine as a threat against the world's peace. It will work out the mandatory system to be applied to the former German colonies and act as a final court in the Belgian-German frontier and in disputes as to the Kiel canal, and decide certain economic and financial problems.

Membership—The members of the league will be the signatories of the covenant, and other states invited to accede. A state may withdraw upon giving two years' notice, if it has fulfilled all its international obligations.

Section 2. A permanent secretariat will be established at Geneva. The league will meet at stated intervals. Each state will have one vote and not more than three representatives.

The council will consist of representatives of the five great allied powers, with representatives of four members selected by the assembly from time to time. It will meet at least once a year. Voting will be by states. Each state will have one vote and not more than one representative.

The council will formulate plans for a reduction of armaments for consideration and adoption. These plans will be revised every ten years.

Preventing War—Upon any war, or threat of war, the council will meet to consider what common action shall be taken. Members are pledged to submit matters of dispute to arbitration or inquiry and not to resort to war until three months after the award. If a member fails to carry out the award, the council will propose the necessary measures. The council will establish a permanent court of international justice to determine international disputes or to give advisory opinions. If agreement cannot be secured, the members reserve the right to take such action as may be necessary for the maintenance of right and justice. Members resorting to war in disregard of the covenant will immediately be debarred from all intercourse with other members. The council will in such cases consider what military or naval action can be taken by the league collectively.

The covenant abrogates all obligations between members inconsistent with its terms, but nothing in it shall affect the validity of international engagements such as treaties of arbitration or regional understandings like the Monroe doctrine, for securing the maintenance of peace.

The Mandatory System—Nations not yet able to stand by themselves will be intrusted to advanced nations who are best fitted to guide them. In every case the mandatory will render an annual report, and the degree of its authority will be defined.

International Provisions—The members of the league will in general, through the international organization established by the labor convention to secure and maintain fair conditions of labor for men, women and children in their own countries, and undertake to secure just treatment of the native inhabitants of territories under their control; they will intrust the league with general supervision over the execution of agreements for the suppression of traffic in women and children, etc.; and the control of the trade in arms and ammunition with countries in which control is necessary; they will make provision for freedom of communications and transit and equitable treatment for commerce of all members of the league, with special reference to the necessities of regions devastated during the war; and they will endeavor to take steps for international prevention and control of disease.

Boundaries of Germany—Germany cedes to France Alsace-Lorraine 5,600 square miles to the southwest, and to Belgium two small districts between Luxemburg and Holland, totaling 989 square miles. She also cedes to Poland the southeastern tip of Silesia, beyond and including Oppeln, most of Posen and West Prussia, 27,686 square miles, East Prussia being isolated from the main body by a part of Poland. She loses sovereignty over the northeastern tip of East Prussia, forty square miles north of the River Memel, and the internationalized areas about Danzig, 729 square miles, and the basin of the Saar, 738 square miles, between the western border of the Rhenish Palatinate of Bavaria and the southeast corner of Luxemburg; and Schleswig, 2,767 square miles.

Section 3. *Belgium*—Germany consents to the abrogation of the treaties of 1839 by which Belgium was established as a neutral state, and agrees to any convention with which the allied and associated powers may determine to replace them.

Luxemburg—Germany renounces her various treaties and conventions with the grand duchy of Luxemburg, and recognizes that it ceased to be a part of the German zolverein from January 1, 1919, and renounces all right of exploitation of the railroads.

Left Bank of the Rhine—Germany will not maintain any fortifications or armed forces less than fifty kilometers to the east of the Rhine, hold any maneuvers, nor within that limit maintain any works to facilitate mobilization. In case of violation she shall be regarded as committing a hostile act against the powers who sign the present treaty and as intending to disturb the peace of the world.

Alsace and Lorraine—The territories ceded to Germany by the treaty of Frankfort are restored to France with their frontiers as before 1871, to date from the signing of the armistice, and to be free of all public debts.

All public property and private property of German ex-sovereigns passes to France without payment or credit. France is substituted for Germany as regards ownership of the railroads and rights over concessions of tramways. The Rhine bridges pass to France, with the obligation for the upkeep.

Political condemnations during the war are null and void and the obligation to repay war fines is established as in other parts of allied territory.

The Saar—In compensation for the destruction of coal mines in northern France and as payment on account of reparation, Germany cedes to France full ownership of the coal mines of the Saar basin with the subsidiaries, accessories and facilities.

After fifteen years a plebiscite will be held by communes to ascertain the desires of the population as to continuance of the existing regime under the league of nations, union with France or union with Germany. The right to vote will belong to all inhabitants of over 20 years resident therein at the time of the signature.

Section 4. *German Austria*—Germany recognizes the total independence of German Austria in the boundaries traced.

Germany recognizes the entire independence of the Czecho-Slovak state. The five allied and associated powers will draw up regulations assuring East Prussia full and equitable access to and use of the Vistula.

Danzig—Danzig and the district immediately about it is to be constituted into the free city of Danzig under the guaranty of the league of nations.

Denmark—The frontier between Germany and Denmark will be fixed by the self-determination of the population.

The fortifications, military establishments and harbors of the islands of Helgoland and Dune are to be destroyed under the supervision of the allies by German labor and at Germany's expense. They may not be reconstructed, nor any similar fortifications built in the future.

Russia—Germany agrees to respect as permanent and inalienable the independence of all territories which were part of the former Russian empire, to accept abrogation of the Brest-Litovsk and other treaties entered into with the Maximalist government of Russia, to recognize the full force of all treaties entered into by the allied and associated powers with states which were a part of the former Russian empire, and to recognize the frontiers as determined therein. The allied and associated powers formally reserve the right of Russia to obtain restitution and reparation of the principles of the present treaty.

SECTION 5. *German Rights Outside of Europe*—Outside Europe, Germany renounces all rights, title and privileges as to her own or her allied territories, to all the allied and associated powers.

German Colonies—Germany renounces in favor of the allied and associated powers her overseas possessions with all rights and titles therein. All movable and immovable property belonging to the German empire or to any German state shall pass to the government exercising authority therein. Germany undertakes to pay reparation for damage suffered by French nationals in the Kameruns or its frontier zone through the acts of German civil and military authorities and of individual Germans from January 1, 1900, to August 1, 1914.

China—Germany renounces in favor of China all privileges and indemnities resulting from the Boxer protocol of 1901, and all buildings, wharves, barracks, forts, munitions or warships, wireless plants, and other property (except diplomatic) in the German concessions of Tientsin and Hankow and in other Chinese territory except Kiaochow, and agrees to return to China at her own expense all the astronomical instruments seized in 1901. Germany accepts the abrogation of the concessions of Hankow and Tientsin, China agreeing to open them to international use.

Siam—Germany recognizes that all agreements between herself and Siam, including the right of extra territory, ceased July 22, 1917. All German public property except consular and diplomatic premises passes, without compensation, to Siam.

Liberia—Germany renounces all rights under the international arrangements of 1911 and 1912 regarding Liberia.

Morocco—Germany renounces all her rights, titles and privileges under the act of Algeciras and the Franco-German agreements of 1909 and 1911 and under all treaties and arrangements with the sheriffian empire. All movable and immovable German property may be sold at public auction, the proceeds to be paid to the sheriffian government and deducted from the reparation account.

Egypt—Germany recognizes the British protectorate over Egypt declared on December 19, 1914, and transfers to Great Britain the powers given to the late sultan of Turkey for securing the free navigation of the Suez canal.

Turkey and Bulgaria—Germany accepts all arrangements which the allied and associated powers make with Turkey and Bulgaria with reference to any right, privileges or interests claimed in those countries by Germany or her nationals and not dealt with elsewhere.

Shantung—Germany cedes to Japan all rights, titles and privileges acquired by her treaty with China of March 6, 1897, and other agreements, as to Shantung. All German state property in Kiaochow is acquired by Japan free of all charges.

SECTION 6. The demobilization of the German army must take place within two months. Its strength may not exceed 100,000, including 4,000 officers, with not over seven divisions of infantry, also three of cavalry, and to be devoted exclusively to maintenance of internal order and control of frontiers. The German general staff is abolished. The army administrative service, consisting of civilian personnel, not included in the number of effectives, is reduced to one-tenth the total in the 1913 budget. Employes of the German states, such as customs officers, first guards and coast guards, may not exceed the number in 1913. Gendarmes and local police may be increased only in accordance with the growth of population. None of these may be assembled for military training.

Armaments—All establishments for the manufacturing, preparation or storage of arms and munitions of war, must be closed, and their personnel dismissed. The manufacture or importation of poisonous gases is forbidden as well as the importation of arms, munitions and war material.

Conscription—Conscription is abolished in Germany. The personnel must be maintained by voluntary enlistment for terms of twelve consecutive years, the number of discharges before the expiration of that term not in any year to exceed 5 per cent of the total effectives. Officers remaining in the service must agree to serve to the age of 45 years and newly appointed officers must agree to serve actively for twenty-five years.

No military schools except those absolutely indispensable for the units allowed shall exist in Germany. All measures of mobilization are forbidden.

All fortified and field works within fifty kilometers (thirty miles) east of the Rhine will be dismantled. The construction of any new fortifications there is forbidden.

Control—Interallied commissions of control will see to the execution of the provisions, for which a time limit is set, the maximum named being three months. Germany must give them complete facilities, and pay for the labor and material necessary in demolition, destruction or surrender of war equipment.

Naval—The German navy must be demobilized within a period of two months. All German vessels of war in foreign ports, and the German high sea fleet interned at Scapa Flow will be surrendered, the final disposition of these ships to be decided upon by the allied and associated powers. Germany must surrender forty-five modern destroyers, fifty modern torpedo boats, and all submarines, with their salvage vessels; all war vessels under construction, including submarines, must be broken up.

Germany is required to sweep up the mines in the North sea and the Baltic. German fortifications in the Baltic must be demolished.

During a period of three months after the peace, German high power wireless stations at Nauen, Hanover and Berlin, will not be permitted to send any messages except for commercial purposes.

Air—The armed forces of Germany must not include any military or naval air forces except one hundred unarmed seaplanes. No aviation grounds or dirigible sheds are to be allowed within 150 kilometers of the Rhine or the eastern or southern frontiers. The manufacture of aircraft and parts of aircraft is forbidden. All military and aeronautical material must be surrendered.

The repatriation of German prisoners and interned civilians is to be carried out without delay and at Germany's expense.

Both parties will respect and maintain the graves of soldiers and sailors buried on their territories.

Responsibility and Reparation—The allied and associated powers will publicly arraign William II of Hohenzollern, formerly German emperor, before a special tribunal composed of one judge from each of the five great powers, with full right of defense.

Persons accused of having committed acts in violation of the laws and customs of war are to be tried and punished by military tribunals under military law.

SECTION 7. *Reparation*—Germany accepts responsibility for all loss and damages to which civilians of the allies have been subjected by the war, and agrees to compensate them. Germany binds herself to repay all sums borrowed by Belgium from the Allies. Germany irrevocably recognizes the authority of a reparation commission named by the Allies to enforce and supervise these payments. She further agrees to restore to the Allies cash and certain articles which can be identified. As an immediate step toward restoration, Germany shall pay within two years $5,000,000,000 in either gold, goods, ships or other specific forms of payment.

The measures which the allied and associated powers shall have the right to take, in case of voluntary default by Germany, and which Germany agrees not to regard as acts of war, may include economic and financial prohibitions and reprisals and in general such other measures as the respective governments may determine to be necessary in the circumstances.

The commission may require Germany to give from time to time, by way of guaranty, issues of bonds or other obligations to cover such claims as are not otherwise satisfied.

The German government recognizes the right of the Allies to the replacement, ton for ton and class for class, of all merchant ships and fishing boats lost or damaged owing to the war, and agrees to cede to the Allies all German merchant ships of sixteen hundred tons gross and upward.

The German government further agrees to build merchant ships for the account of the Allies to the amount of not exceeding 200,000 tons' gross annually during the next five years.

SECTION 8. *Devastated Areas*—Germany undertakes to devote her economic resources directly to the physical restoration of the invaded areas.

Coal—Germany is to deliver annually for ten years to France coal equivalent to the difference between annual pre-war output of Nord and Pas de Calais mines and annual production during above ten year period. Germany further gives options over ten years for delivery of 7,000,000 tons coal per year to France, in addition to the above, of 8,000,000 tons to Belgium, and of an amount rising from 4,500,000 tons in 1919 to 1920 to 8,500,000 tons in 1923 to 1924 to Italy, at prices to be fixed as prescribed. Coke may be taken in place of coal in ratio of three tons to four.

Dyestuffs and Drugs—Germany accords option to the commission on dyestuffs and chemical drugs, including quinine, up to 50 per cent of total stock to Germany at the time the treaty comes into force, and similar option during each six months to end of 1924 up to 25 per cent of previous six months' output.

Cables—Germany renounces all title to specific cables, value of such as were privately owned being credited to her against reparation indebtedness.

Restitution—As reparation for the destruction of the library of Louvain, Germany is to hand over manuscripts, early printed books, prints, etc., to the equivalent of those destroyed, and all works of art taken from Belgium and France.

SECTION 9. *Finances*—Germany is required to pay the total cost of the armies of occupation from the date of the armistice as long as they are maintained in German territory.

Germany is to deliver all sums deposited in Germany by Turkey and Austria-Hungary in connection with the financial support extended by her to them during the war and to transfer to the Allies all claims against Austria-Hungary, Bulgaria or Turkey in connection with agreements made during the war.

Germany guarantees to repay to Brazil the fund arising from the sale of Sao Paulo coffee which she refused to allow Brazil to withdraw from Germany.

Contracts—Pre-war contracts between allied and associated nations, excepting the United States, Japan and Brazil, and German nationals, are canceled except for debts for accounts already performed.

Opium—The contracting powers agree, whether or not they have signed and ratified the opium convention of January 23, 1912, or signed the special protocol opened at The Hague in accordance with resolutions adopted by the third opium conference in 1914, to bring the said convention into force by enacting within twelve months of the time of peace the necessary legislation.

Missions—The allied and associated powers agree that the properties of religious missions in territories belonging or ceded to them shall continue in their work under the control of the powers, Germany renouncing all claims in their behalf.

SECTION 11. *Air Navigation*—Aircraft of the allied and associated powers shall have full liberty of passage and landing over and in German territory; equal treatment with German planes as to use of German airdromes, and with most favored nation planes as to internal commercial traffic in Germany.

SECTION 13.—*Freedom of Transit*—Germany must grant freedom of transit through her territories by rail or water to persons, goods, ships, carriages and mail from or to any of the allied or associated powers, without customs or transit duties, undue delays, restrictions and discriminations based on nationality, means of transport or place of entry or departure. Goods in transit shall be assured all possible speed of journey, especially perishable goods.

(The remainder of Section 12 concerns the use of European waterways and railroads.)

SECTION 13. *International Labor Organizations*—Members of the league of nations agree to establish a permanent organization to promote international adjustment of labor conditions, to consist of an annual international labor conference and an international labor office.

The former is composed of four representatives of each state, two from the government and one each from the employers and the employed; each of them may vote individually. It will be a deliberative legislative body, its measures taking the form of draft conventions or recommendations for legislation, which if passed by two-thirds vote must be submitted to the lawmaking authority in every state participating. Each government may either enact the terms into law; approve the principles, but modify them to local needs; leave the actual legislation in case of a federal state to local legislatures; or reject the convention altogether without further obligation.

The international labor office is established at the seat of the league of nations as part of its organization. It is to collect and distribute information on labor through the world and prepare agents for the conference. It will publish a periodical in French and English and possibly other languages. Each state agrees to make to it, for presentation to the conference, an annual report of measures taken to execute accepted conventions. The governing body is its executive. It consists of twenty-four members, twelve representing the government, six the employers and six the employes, to serve for three years.

On complaint that any government has failed to carry out a convention to which it is a party the governing body may make inquiries directly to that government and in case the reply is unsatisfactory may publish the complaint with comment. A complaint by one government against another may be referred by the governing body to a commission of inquiry nominated by the secretary-general of the league. If the commission report fails to bring satisfactory action, the matter may be taken to a permanent court of international justice for final decision. The chief reliance for securing enforcement of the law will be publicity with a possibility of economic action in the background.

The first meeting of the conference will take place in October, 1919, at Washington, to discuss the eight-hour day or forty-eight hour week; prevention of unemployment; extension and application of the international conventions adopted at Bern in 1906 prohibiting night work for women and the use of white phosphorus in the manufacture of matches; and employment of women and children at night or in unhealthful work, of women before and after childbirth, including maternity benefit, and of children as regards minimum age.

Nine principles of labor conditions are recognized on the ground that the well-being, physical and moral, of the industrial wage earners is of supreme international importance. With exceptions necessitated by differences of climate, habits and economic developments, they include: The guiding principle that labor should not be regarded merely as a commodity or article of commerce; right of association of employers and employes is granted; and a wage adequate to maintain a reasonable standard of life; the eight-hour day or forty-eight hour week; a weekly rest of at least twenty-four hours, which should include Sunday wherever practicable; abolition of child labor and assurance of the continuation of the education and proper physical development of children; equal pay for equal work as between men and women;

equitable treatment of all workers lawfully resident therein, including foreigners, and a system of inspection in which women shall take part.

SECTION 14. *Guaranties*—As a guaranty for the execution of the treaty, German territory west of the Rhine, together with bridgeheads, will be occupied by allied and associated troops for fifteen years. If before the expiration of the fifteen years Germany complies with all the treaty undertakings, the occupying forces will be withdrawn.

Eastern Europe—All German troops at present in territories to the east of the new frontier shall return as soon as the allied and associated governments deem wise.

SECTION 15. Germany agrees to recognize the full validity of the treaties of peace and additional conventions to be concluded by the allied and associated powers with the powers allied with Germany; to agree to the decisions to be taken as to the territories of Austria-Hungary, Bulgaria and Turkey, and to recognize the new states in the frontiers to be fixed for them.

Germany agrees not to put forward any pecuniary claim against any allied or associated power signing the present treaty, based on events previous to the coming into force of the treaty.

Germany accepts all decrees as to German ships and goods made by any allied or associated prize court. The Allies reserve the right to examine all decisions of German prize courts.

The treaty is to become effective in all respects for each power on the date of deposition of its ratification.

Also from Benediction Books ...
Wandering Between Two Worlds: Essays on Faith and Art
Anita Mathias
Benediction Books, 2007
152 pages
ISBN: 0955373700

Available from www.amazon.com, www.amazon.co.uk

In these wide-ranging lyrical essays, Anita Mathias writes, in lush, lovely prose, of her naughty Catholic childhood in Jamshedpur, India; her large, eccentric family in Mangalore, a sea-coast town converted by the Portuguese in the sixteenth century; her rebellion and atheism as a teenager in her Himalayan boarding school, run by German missionary nuns, St. Mary's Convent, Nainital; and her abrupt religious conversion after which she entered Mother Teresa's convent in Calcutta as a novice. Later rich, elegant essays explore the dualities of her life as a writer, mother, and Christian in the United States-- Domesticity and Art, Writing and Prayer, and the experience of being "an alien and stranger" as an immigrant in America, sensing the need for roots.

About the Author

Anita Mathias is the author of *Wandering Between Two Worlds: Essays on Faith and Art.* She has a B.A. and M.A. in English from Somerville College, Oxford University, and an M.A. in Creative Writing from the Ohio State University, USA. Anita won a National Endowment of the Arts fellowship in Creative Nonfiction in 1997. She lives in Oxford, England with her husband, Roy, and her daughters, Zoe and Irene.

Visit Anita at http://www.anitamathias.com, and on http://theoxfordchristian.blogspot.com, her Christian blog; http://wanderingbetweentwoworlds.blogspot.com/, her personal blog, and http://thegoodbooksblog.blogspot.com, her literary and writing blog.

The Church Thad Had Too Much
Anita Mathias
Benediction Books, 2010
52 pages
ISBN: 9781849026567

Available from www.amazon.com, www.amazon.co.uk

The Church That Had Too Much was very well-intentioned. She wanted to love God, she wanted to love people, but she was both hampered by her muchness and the abundance of her possessions, and beset by ambition, power struggles and snobbery. Read about the surprising way The Church That Had Too Much began to resolve her problems in this deceptively simple and enchanting fable.

About the Author

Anita Mathias is the author of *Wandering Between Two Worlds: Essays on Faith and Art*. She has a B.A. and M.A. in English from Somerville College, Oxford University, and an M.A. in Creative Writing from the Ohio State University, USA. Anita won a National Endowment of the Arts fellowship in Creative Nonfiction in 1997. She lives in Oxford, England with her husband, Roy, and her daughters, Zoe and Irene.

Visit Anita at http://www.anitamathias.com, and on http://theoxfordchristian.blogspot.com, her Christian blog; http://wanderingbetweentwoworlds.blogspot.com/, her personal blog, and http://thegoodbooksblog.blogspot.com, her literary and writing blog.

www.ingramcontent.com/pod-product-compliance
Lightning Source LLC
LaVergne TN
LVHW041247080426
835510LV00009B/621